JUSTICE DELAYED

JUSTICE DELAYED

NAZI WAR CRIMINALS IN CANADA

By David Matas
with Susan Charendoff

Summerhill Press Ltd.
Toronto

Published by:
Summerhill Press Ltd.
Five Clarence Square
Toronto, Ontario M5V 1H1

Canadian Cataloguing in Publication Data

Matas, David.
    Justice Delayed

Includes bibliographical references.
ISBN 0-920197-42-6

1. War Criminals – Canada. 2. Canada. Commission of Inquiry on War Criminals. 3. Governmental investigations – Canada. I. Charendoff, Susan, 1955– II. Title.

D803.M37 1987   364.1'38'0971   C97–094410–X

Typesetting by: The Copy Network, Toronto

Printed and bound in Canada by T.H. Best Co.

To the survivors and victims of the Holocaust

CONTENTS

"The wrongs which we seek to condemn and punish have been so calculated, so malignant and so devastating that civilization cannot tolerate their being ignored because it cannot survive their being repeated."
> — Justice Robert H. Jackson, Chief American Prosecutor, Trial of the Major Nazi War Criminals before the International Military Tribunal, Nuremberg, 1946

"When we neither punish nor reproach evildoers, we are not simply protecting their trivial old age, we are thereby ripping the foundations of justice from beneath new generations."
> — Alexander Solzhenitsyn, *The Gulag Archipelago*, Volume 1

"And so the matter of war criminals quietly disappeared from the scene; and whether by coincidence or design, in the third of a century which followed, Canada devoted not the slightest energy to the search and prosecution of war criminals."
> — Honourable Jules Deschênes, Commissioner, Commission of Inquiry on War Criminals, December 30, 1986

Introduction by the Author

There are Nazi war criminals in Canada. Some have been here since the Second World War. How did they gain entry into our country? Once they arrived, how did they manage to remain and live out their lives in virtual anonymity? Why, for more than forty years, have successive Canadian governments done nothing about Nazi war criminals in our midst? Why should Canada now take action, and what specifically should be done? These are the questions this book attempts to answer.

This book is a work of advocacy. It urges that Nazi war criminals be brought to justice. The analysis presented is not intended to be a neutral examination of whether action ought to be taken—it is steadfastly partisan in its call for action. And while the arguments in support of a "do-nothing" approach do appear, they are presented only to show the ease with which they can be rebutted.

This book is also a work of law. The story of how Nazi war criminals slipped into Canada and were able to find a safe haven here is primarily a story about this country's system of justice and law. And the question of what is to be done about Nazi war criminals is also essentially a legal issue.

But, although the book explores a good many legal issues, it is not directed towards lawyers. It is directed to the public at large. In the final analysis, justice is a matter that depends on the public will. Unless the public believes that justice will be accomplished by bringing Nazi war criminals in Canada to trial, nothing will happen.

This book is also a personal story. I have been involved in war crimes justice advocacy for years, initially through my work with the Canadian Jewish Congress, and more recently in my activities as senior counsel with the League for Human Rights of B'nai Brith Canada. I represented the League as counsel before the Commission of Inquiry on War Criminals. While the book focuses principally on the issues rather than on my own experiences, certain parts of the story can only be told from a personal perspective—by setting out what I did, or what the League did.

Much of the text was first written, in another form, in the heat of political or legal battle. The book sets out positions that I have been advocating for years as part of the overall effort to obtain a commitment from the Canadian government on bringing Nazi war criminals in Canada to justice. That commitment was finally made with the government's response to the report of Mr. Justice Deschênes at the conclusion of the Commission of Inquiry on War Criminals. I believe it is historically valuable to have on record the events leading up to this commitment and the reasons behind it.

What this book is not, is a book of names. Now that the Canadian government has finally pledged itself to action, the names of suspected Nazi war criminals still living in this country will eventually be made public as trials are launched. Even if it were legally possible, it would be most unfair to jeopardize the outcome of those trials by presenting the names of suspects and the evidence against them in book form at this time. Therefore, the names of any individuals that do appear in this book are already on the public record in one form or another, and any information about these individuals also forms part of the public record.

If the main theme of this book deals with bringing Nazi war criminals to justice, a subsidiary theme is the relationship between the Jewish and Ukrainian communities in Canada. The issue of Nazi war criminals has riveted attention on age-old tensions between the two communities. The book tells this story the same way it approaches the main theme: by examining the issues that have been raised as a result of contacts between the two groups and advocating a position, rather than by presenting a comprehensive historical account of Ukrainian-Jewish relations.

I owe thanks to a number of people. First of all, I owe thanks to Susan Charendoff. She assisted me as junior counsel to the League for Human Rights at the Commission of Inquiry on War Criminals. Susan also edited this book and wrote the most of the first three chapters and portions of other chapters. Without her help neither the book nor my effort at the Commission would have been possible.

Marvin Kurz was also junior counsel to the League for Human Rights at the Deschênes Commission. When I acted for the League for Human Rights in the Federal Court of Canada to obtain an order for the release by the Commission of reports prepared by a working group of experts, Marvin assisted me. He was also a constant source of friendly advice.

Ellen Kachuck, director of public affairs for B'nai Brith Canada, was the staff person responsible for the war criminals issue. She was always available, providing a policy perspective and making logistic arrangements.

Susan, Marvin and Ellen were all involved in the war criminals issue through B'nai Brith. The B'nai Brith as an organization deserves commendation. Its leadership, specifically Harry Bick, then president, and Frank Dimant, executive vice-president, and membership made the entire endeavour possible.

Irwin Cotler, when he was president of the Canadian Jewish Congress, appointed me as head of that organization's committee on war crimes in March 1981. He represented the Congress at the Commission of Inquiry on War Criminals. Throughout the inquiry we were in contact. He was a constant support and reinforcement, and his articulate rhetoric was an inspiration.

Ken Narvey works as a researcher for the Canadian Jewish Students Network. For years he has acted as a one-man, full-time activist on the issue of Nazi war criminals. As a legal researcher, his unflagging efforts and ingenious suggestions were greatly appreciated.

May Birnboim is the secretary at the B'nai Brith office in Winnipeg. She typed and re-typed earlier versions of much that is in this book, starting from my virtually illegible handwriting. The work was always done promptly, accurately and with good cheer.

There are many others besides. Howard Spunt, who made a skillful effort in obtaining standing on behalf of the League for Human Rights before the Deschênes Commission; Yuri Boshyk and Lubomyr Luciuk, for the ever-instructive conversations I had with them; Jack Silverstone, who assisted Irwin Cotler as the Congress representative at the Commission. I thank them all.

David Matas
Winnipeg, August 1987

Chapter One

The Deschênes Commission of Inquiry

Shortly after the Second World War, renowned Nazi hunter Simon Wiesenthal learned that a huge cache of Jewish Prayer books had been discovered in the cellar of a sixteenth-century castle in Austria. He went to investigate, and found thousands upon thousands of books that had come from Jewish homes and synagogues throughout Europe. The Nazis had planned to distribute these religious volumes among libraries, universities and scientific institutes as historical curiosities, relics of a race that had been wiped out. A young Jew who had lost his entire family in the Holocaust accompanied Wiesenthal. He picked up one book after another from the countless heaps. Finally, in one of the books—in his own sister's handwriting—he found inscribed on the first page: "They've just come into our town. In a few minutes, they will be in our house. If someone finds this prayer book, please notify my dear brother. Do not forget us! Do not forget our murderers!"[1]

On July 13, 1948, three years after the end of World War II, the Government of the United Kingdom sent a secret telegram from its Commonwealth Relations office to all Commonwealth governments, including Canada, proposing to end the Nazi war crimes trials in the British zone of occupied Germany. The communiqué explained that for reasons of political expediency the time had come to discontinue prosecutions of guilty individuals and "dispose of the past as soon as possible." Even in the wake of the Holocaust, as the survivors sat in displaced persons camps, Britain determined it was more important to bury the past than to punish war criminals. In response to the United Kingdom's invitation for reaction to the new policy proposal,

Canada replied in a secret message of its own: "The Canadian Government has no comment to make."

But if Canada had nothing to say in 1948, its actions since the Second World War until the present day have revealed a tacit and wholehearted concurrence with the view expressed by Britain. For too long, the Canadian government simply avoided the issue of Nazi war criminals and ignored their presence in this country.

It was not until 1985—with the appointment of the Deschênes Commission of Inquiry on War Criminals—that Canada began systematically to examine the presence of Nazi war criminals in this country, and to take the very first steps to redress forty years of inaction. Except for the 1982 extradition proceedings against Albert Helmut Rauca, alleged Nazi war criminals in Canada have enjoyed a virtual safe haven from prosecution.

• • •

Toronto. April 24, 1985. It was a grey and unusually muggy day for early spring. The Commission of Inquiry on War Criminals had been set down for 10:00 a.m. in Court One of the Federal Court of Canada. Inside the small packed courtroom on University Avenue, the air was close. Under the glare of television cameras a barrage of lawyers reviewed their briefs at counsel tables, observers in the crammed visitors' gallery carried on animated discussions, and news reporters placed themselves strategically around the room, as uniformed security guards watched the entrance. The courtroom was filled to capacity, and people were turned away at the door.

A quick survey of the room revealed that the elderly in attendance, men and women whose memories reached back to the Second World War, outnumbered the young. Reflected in the faces of those present during the two days of Toronto hearings was the ethnic mosaic of Eastern Europe: Ukrainians, Serbians, Estonians, Latvians, Croatians—and Jews, a number of Holocaust survivors among them. Side by side they packed the benches; despite their diverse backgrounds, all were there for the same reason. Forty years of official silence on the issue of war criminals in Canada was about to be broken.

The courtroom came to order as Mr. Justice Jules Deschênes entered and took his place on the bench. His Honour Deschênes, former chief justice of Quebec, announced the Commission's mandate. The purpose of the hearings was to determine whether there were any war criminals currently living in Canada, to find out how they entered, and to ascertain what legal remedies were available to deal with them. He carefully explained the need to maintain the delicate balance between the public interest of seeing justice done and the private interest of protecting individual reputations. As a result, there would be two types of hearings throughout the course of the Commission: public and private, or *in camera*. Deschênes warned that during the public portions of the inquiry no names were to be mentioned. Any allegations against suspected Nazi war criminals had to be brought to the Commission's attention

After setting out the rules of procedure, Mr. Justice Deschênes invited submissions from interested parties. What followed was an onslaught of requests for legal standing before the Commission. This official status to be represented by counsel and to examine witnesses throughout the inquiry was a privilege granted only to those considered to have a direct interest in the proceedings.

Two weeks earlier, in the very first round of public hearings in Ottawa, the Commission had granted standing to one group—The League for Human Rights of B'nai Brith Canada, a national Jewish service organization for which I was acting as counsel, along with lawyers Susan Charendoff and Marvin Kurz. In contrast to the Toronto media event, those initial Ottawa hearings had been relatively low-key, with moderate news coverage and a minimum of observers. Only two requests for standing had been made; that of the North American Jewish Students' Network, Canada, had been rejected. There was nothing about the hearings in Ottawa hinting at the level of electricity that would be generated in Toronto. But the grant of standing to the League for Human Rights had been a front-page news item across Canada, and had acted as a catalyst for applications from several other Jewish groups, a number of Ukrainian organizations, and associations representing Baltic peoples, Croatians and Serbs. Why these Eastern European groups were interested in legal standing was puzzling at first. When the reasons became evident, they provided the fuel for contention on many issues.

• • •

The emotionally charged atmosphere in the courtroom foretold the difficulties to come over the next two years. The Deschênes Commission became a politically explosive inquiry, the subject of heated debates across the country. One by one, speakers rose to seek recognition by the Commission and to make submissions on behalf of their organizations.

Of the five Ukrainian organizations represented, three of them—the Canadian League for the Liberation of the Ukraine, the Ukrainian National Federation of Canada, and the Ukrainian Youth Association of Canada—agreed at the request of Deschênes to be subsumed under the umbrella of the Ukrainian Canadian Committee, a broad-based national body. The Ukrainians expressed their desire to see justice done, but at the same time, fears were expressed concerning the slander of the entire Ukrainian community as a result of the probe and about the potential examination of evidence in the Soviet Union. In later submissions, similar representations about the "smearing" of ethnic groups were made by the Canadian Serbian National Committee, the Estonian Central Council in Canada, the Latvian National Federation of Canada and the Croatian Committee for Human Rights. The Commission was also urged to consider extending its mandate from the question of Nazi war criminals to all war criminals, including those responsible for Soviet repression in their homelands.

The Brotherhood of Veterans of the 1st Division of the Ukrainian National Army in Canada—previously known as the Galicia Division—also sought standing. The Galicia Division, made up of Ukrainian volunteers who had enlisted in the German forces in 1943, was part of the Waffen SS (the armed SS). The Waffen SS was later declared a criminal organization by the International Military Tribunal in Nuremberg. On behalf of its members, Toronto criminal lawyer Clay Powell argued that since their arrival in Canada after the war, the Galicia Division had been the subject of war crimes allegations. As a result, the six hundred members of the Galicia Division living in Canada would undoubtedly be among those under investigation.

A number of Jewish organizations came forward. The Canadian Jewish Congress, represented by Toronto lawyer

Morris Manning, claimed status as a national umbrella Jewish body with a very large contingent of Holocaust survivors. This was the same basis on which the League for Human Rights had successfully sought standing in Ottawa. Two independent groups of Holocaust survivors, the Canadian Holocaust Remembrance Association and the Montreal-based Holocaust Survivors of Nazi Oppression, also requested standing; as eye-witnesses to Nazi war crimes as well as their victims, they had a direct and special interest in the punishment of the perpetrators. The Jewish Defence League spoke of its own investigations of war criminals and offered to reveal information from its files in private sessions of the Commission. The Canadian branch of the Simon Wiesenthal Centre, named for the world-renowned Nazi hunter, also described its continuing efforts to expose war criminals and its expertise in conducting investigations. All of these bodies urged action by the government and pledged their full co-operation in supplying names and evidence to the Commission.

It was now up to Commission counsel—Toronto lawyer Michael Meighen and Yves Fortier of Montreal—to make recommendations to the Commissioner on the granting of standing. In the end, Mr. Justice Deschênes granted standing to three of the groups heard from in Toronto, although he emphasized that this special status was to be limited to public hearings. No group gained the right to be present at the highly confidential *in camera* hearings of the Commission.

Among his reasons for granting standing to the League for Human Rights two weeks earlier, the judge considered it important that the B'nai Brith counted among its members actual victims of the Nazi persecutions (and as a result, had a direct and special interest in the outcome of the Commission's work). On the same basis, standing was granted to the Canadian Jewish Congress, which was represented during the rest of the inquiry by Irwin Cotler. The Ukrainian Canadian Committee obtained standing as the representative body for all other Ukrainian groups who had appeared before the Commission. This group later came to be represented by Toronto lawyer John Sopinka. And the Galicia Division, which the judge considered to be "in a class all by itself," was given standing to the extent that matters arising in the inquiry touched upon its members. In subsequent hearings, Mr. Yuri Botiuk of Toronto acted as counsel for the division. As a matter of course, the Government of Canada had been given standing before the Commission, without the necessity of making formal application. Its representatives, Department of Justice lawyers Ivan Whitehall and Judith McCann, played an important role throughout the course of the inquiry.

These were the principal players in the difficult two-year process of examining the Canadian response to the Nazi's "final solution," of reviewing Canada's indifference to war criminals, and attempting to uncover clues about persons who had committed crimes in war-torn Europe, and had later fled their homelands to find refuge within our borders. It was an often disturbing process, exposing a series of revelations about deliberate government inaction on the matter of war criminals, the intentional harbouring of known Nazi war criminals, and a file destruction policy that indicated a total absence of any moral sensibility to the horrors of the Holocaust. It was an often painful process, which would, for many Canadians, mean rekindling devastating memories of wartime suffering.

Chapter Two

The Historical Background

"I am Phillip Weiss. I live in Winnipeg since 1948. I was born in 1922 in Poland. I am a citizen of Canada....I am a survivor of three concentration camps [including Auschwitz]....I am just here to give a small episode of my life. Many of us survivors can discuss those individual episodes, and when we take all those episodes together, we create history....That history has to be told....All western civilized world should know what happened in those crucial years of 1939 to 1945."[1]

While it was not within the mandate of the Commission to undertake a comprehensive review of the Holocaust and the Second World War, it is only against this backdrop that one can begin to understand how the issue of Nazi war criminals touches upon so many communities in Canada today. It is a fact of history that the Holocaust, while perpetrated under German direction and control, simply could never have occurred without the active assistance and support of local populations in Nazi allied and occupied countries. Their co-operation was indispensable to the program of extermination carried out by the German government.

The military campaign of the Third Reich began with the invasion of Poland in 1939. With Poland conquered, Hitler's armies marched into Western Europe in 1940. In the summer of 1941 Germany invaded the Soviet Union and began the annexation of Eastern Europe—the Baltic countries of Latvia, Lithuania and Estonia, and to the south, the Ukraine. Throughout the campaign, one objective took precedence above all else: the elimination of the Jews. When the carnage finally came to an end, some six million had been captured, rounded up, confined, deported and murdered.

A simple exercise in logistics indicates that a high degree of collaboration was necessary to carry out an operation of such magnitude. First, the actual number of German personnel and equipment dedicated to carry out Hitler's policies was small. In addition, German military units were unable to communicate easily with the local populations. They were often distrusted, isolated and unfamiliar with the countries in which they were stationed. As well, the ratio of Jewish victims to German organizers of the Holocaust was about one hundred to one.[2]

Throughout the villages and towns of the Baltic states and the Ukraine the mobile killing units of SS troops (*Einsatzgruppen*) "marched the Jews out to nearby forests, forced them to dig their own graves, stripped them naked, lined them up, and shot them." Nearly one million Jews had been killed by 1944. But, there were only about three thousand *Einsatzgruppen* men. They did not carry out the killing alone. They relied on indigenous forces of sympathizers, formed as "auxiliary police" or "militia," and willing to take up arms against Jews.[3]

In all of France, there were three battalions of German police—between two thousand and three thousand men.[4] In the summer of 1942, the collaborationist Vichy regime dutifully assisted in the task of deporting Jews to the east, to the gas chambers and crematoria of Auschwitz—some forty-three thousand were sent to their deaths.[5]

By 1943, the Nazi death factories were churning out corpses at a fevered pitch. Hundreds of thousands of Jews from all over Europe were being crammed into cattle cars destined for annihilation in Treblinka, Sobibor, Maidanek and the rest of Hitler's death camps. Statistics show that the more co-operative the occupied country, the greater was the loss of life. In Poland, 3,000,000 Jews were killed out of a population of 3,300,000, or ninety percent. Ninety percent of the Jewish population of Lithuania, Latvia and Estonia perished.[6] In what is now the Ukrainian Soviet Socialist Republic, the loss of life to the Holocaust was 900,000 out of a population of 1,500,000 or sixty percent. It wasn't much different in Western Europe: in the Netherlands, the loss of life was 105,000 out of a population of 140,000—seventy-five percent.[7]

Many Jews might have been saved—and it would not necessarily have meant the active assistance of local populations in sheltering their Jewish compatriots. Mere passive refusal to co-operate with the Nazis would have sufficed. The Italian authorities, for example, persistently withheld their co-operation. As a result, eighty percent of the Jewish community was saved. In Denmark, where the local community flatly refused to take part in Hitler's genocide, almost all of Danish Jewry survived. And while there were thousands of people throughout Nazi-occupied territories who risked their lives to help Jews, such heroic efforts were sadly overwhelmed by the far greater numbers who collaborated in the Holocaust.

When the war ended in the spring of 1945, Germany and its neighbours were overflowing with homeless, uprooted people—unable or unwilling to return to their countries of origin. Displaced person (DP) camps were hastily set up by the Allied military in over nine hundred centres throughout Germany, Austria and other liberated territory to deal with the millions of displaced persons. The result was a bizarre intermingling of the oppressed and their oppressors: "They were a mass of diverse faces....Ukrainians, Lithuanians, Latvians, Poles, Romanians, Czechs, Jews, with nothing in common beyond a desire never to return to their homelands. Each, for his own reason, had to begin a new life somewhere else....Some were the wreckage of war; some were the makers of war. And many had been the handmaidens of Nazism in their homelands. In the DP camps, the makers of war, their victims, and the bystanders all gathered together."[8]

Indeed, the DP camps were said to be "rife" with those who had favoured the Germans. One reporter for the New York Times characterized them as "camps for collaborators," and a U.S. army major put it even more bluntly: "You've probably got everything in this camp except Hitler and I wouldn't be surprised if you turned up that bastard when you get started on the registration."[9]

Just how many war criminals and pro-Nazi sympathizers or collaborators inhabited the camps will never be known. But for war criminals of whatever nationality, the obvious avenue of escape was emigration. At home they were known, and known for what they had done. Overseas they could hide, assume new identities and lower the odds of being detected. With the staggering number of displaced persons, how simple it was to slip in among the legitimate refugees and sail far away from Europe to foreign shores.

Because DP camps were virtually swarming with perpetrators of the Holocaust desperate to flee and because the pool of prospective immigrants was "polluted," countries like Canada—in the process of selecting their own future residents and citizens—had to be especially vigilant. Canada had to take every precaution to ensure war criminals would not find refuge within our borders. And yet, Canada did no such thing.

The evidence of witnesses who testified before the Commission revealed that government policy and practice showed a disturbing lack of resolve in preventing such persons from entering Canada. Immigration and RCMP authorities were totally unprepared for the pandemonium that followed the war. The staggering volume of immigrants strained a wholly inadequate bureaucracy. In the immediate postwar years, Canada had failed to articulate any coherent immigration policy. Until then, the government, reluctant to let "foreigners" into the country, had resisted opening its doors for as long as possible. Faced with mounting pressure both at home and abroad to assist in the relief effort, a policy began to evolve in piecemeal fashion. As it did, it became evident that immigration and security procedures were filled with gaping holes. Security checks were weak, conducted by scantily trained personnel and often dependent on dubious foreign sources. Lack of communication between government departments led officials to ignore the highly valuable "watch lists" of wanted war criminals circulated by Allied agencies.

Above all, Canada was far more concerned—indeed, obsessed—with screening out Communist sympathizers than suspected Nazi war criminals. In fact, if any consistency was to emerge in Canadian policy, it was, ironically, in the gradual relaxation of entry criteria for members of Nazi organizations. Not coincidentally, the same government departments, and often the very same officials, implementing these measures were responsible for earlier, restrictive immigration policies designed to exclude Jewish victims of Nazism. This is not to suggest that the government purposely devised a conspiracy to admit Nazi war criminals into Canada on a grand scale, but there were specific cases where the highest levels of authority sidestepped the law to harbour known perpetrators. The Count de Bernonville episode, which is recounted later in this book, is a chilling example. But the majority of Nazi criminals came here through all the regular channels, aided and abetted by a filtering system so porous it virtually guaranteed refuge to any Nazi perpetrator schooled in the art of deception.

Under existing immigration regulations at the end of the war, there was an outright ban on "enemy aliens." With its "lurking hostility to 'foreign' immigrants, particularly Eastern Europeans and, most particularly Jews,"[10] , the Canadian government had no desire to make action on the refugee situation a top priority. No machinery had been set up to deal with an influx of immigrants. But the initial onslaught of refugees between 1945 to 1946 exerted on Canada "immediate pressure from international refugee organizations and church groups to admit some of these displaced persons," according to the testimony of George O'Leary, chief of program guidelines for the Department of Immigration. This pressure came precisely at a time when Canada had no immigration offices in most of Europe, no formal application process abroad, and until 1948, no form of security screening whatsoever. But Canada was forced to open its doors. What prevailed, in the words of O'Leary, who prepared a review of postwar Immigration policy and practices at the Commission's request, was "an element of confusion."

By 1946, voices in the Departments of Immigration and External Affairs, and in the RCMP were expressing concern over the security implications of Cabinet's decision to increase the flow of immigrants from Europe when no Canadian organization existed for the security examination of those immigrants at their point of origin. An inter-governmental body was formed on June 24, 1946 to grapple with, among other pressing security matters in the wake of the war, the urgent matter of passport control. Set up as an advisory body with the power to instigate departmental action, the Security Panel of the Privy Council was composed of Cabinet representatives, top officials from the Departments of National Defence, External Affairs and Immigration, and the RCMP. It held highly confidential meetings regularly and would mold Canada's immigration security policies for the next fifteen years. The minutes of those meetings were declassified and made public for the first time during the Deschênes inquiry.[11]

Recognizing the inadequacy of machinery to screen prospective immigrants, the Security Panel set out to develop a long-range plan. But this was going to take "a long time." In the meantime, from 1945 to 1948, anybody who came into Canada came forward without any security screening. That was the evidence of Joseph Robillard, a high-ranking official who had served as chief of the Canadian government Immigration Mission for Germany and Austria. It was confirmed by retired RCMP Deputy Commissioner William Kelly, who testified that security in the immediate postwar years was "much looser" than later on. There were no formal security rejection criteria in place, such as guidelines to prohibit members of the Nazi Party and other offensive organizations. During this highly chaotic period more than 180,000 persons were admitted to Canada— some 65,000 of them from DP camps, many without papers or any form of identification.[12]

Even in 1949 and 1950, when Canada finally began to put a security system in place under the direction of the RCMP, that system was hardly an improvement over the procedures of earlier years. Officially known as "Stage B" of the immigration process, the security clearance procedure was far from satisfactory. A departmental memorandum of the period described security measures of the day as "very patchy." That correspondence continued: "It was often impossible because of limited staff and facilities to complete the security check until after the immigrants had arrived in Canada...." At a 1949 meeting, the Security Panel was blunt about the situation: "If immigration is to continue at its present volume, it must be clearly understood that security risks are involved and must be accepted. Security screening will necessarily be incomplete and it cannot be assumed that an effective screen exists through which all persons coming to Canada must pass." Several years later in 1954, Joseph Robillard, who had recently been promoted to head of Immigration in Germany, gave his assessment of early postwar Canadian screening procedures: "In the days of the International Refugee Organization we took tens of thousands of refugees. In these early days the available Allied Stage B Channels were not as efficiently organized as they are today. In thousands of cases no information of any sort was obtainable....Many Stage B officers decided their cases on information received and/or elicited during the course of their interrogation. Admittedly,...a small number should never have been admitted because of their political views or criminal records of which we were not aware at the time of issuing visas."

Such were the conditions that made it possible for the likes of Albert Helmut Rauca, later extradited for the murder of more than ten thousand Lithuanian Jews, to disguise himself as one of the thousands of legitimate refugees aboard the immigrant ship S.S. *Beaverbrae*. When the ship docked at Saint John, New Brunswick, on December 30, 1950, Mr. Rauca stepped onto Canadian soil a free man. Four years before him, another collaborator with the Nazi regime—Count Jacques de Bernonville, who had served as the right hand man to Klaus Barbie, the infamous "Butcher of Lyon"—managed to slip into Quebec from the United States dressed as a priest.

Canada's ability to screen incoming immigrants accurately was hampered by a series of self-imposed limitations that reflected the low priority assigned to the detection of war criminals. The first was the failure to staff screening facilities properly. According to the minutes of a 1948 Security Panel meeting, "Great difficulty was being experienced...in employing suitably qualified personnel in this work. Existing scales of remuneration and the lack of adequate living allowances contributed to this condition...." By and large, Canadian security personnel were untrained and inexperienced, with no background in war history, no special insight into the Nazi regime and no strong appreciation of the nature of the war crimes committed. They were RCMP officers with an ordinary police background and received only the most rudimentary preparation for their screening duties. For example, Albert Greening, who served as an RCMP visa control officer in Germany from 1954 to 1962, described his own training programme to the Commission as a three-month course given by the American authorities: "They taught us background material on the people we were dealing with....We covered, shall we say, the political situations in...the countries that we could expect to have people from....There was no particular emphasis on the Germans or the make up of the German army, as such. The emphasis was on the political background of each particular country." This experience was shared by Mr. McCordick, a former employee in the Berlin Military Mission between 1946 and 1947, who testified that he had received "no specific training."

The problem persisted throughout the postwar period. In 1957, a Cologne office staff member complained about the quality of Stage B screening and expertise of security personnel: "Stage 'B' procedures are slow, and since Canada has no agreement with the Government of the Federal Republic similar to that of the U.S.A., Great Britain and France, Canadian police have no authority to investigate German nationals or, I understand, other aliens residing in Germany. Stage 'B' is, therefore, thrown upon the mercy of the American, British and French, who obtain our security information for us. The actual function of Stage 'B' people, then, is first to conduct personal interviews of applicants. These interviews are held by privates or corporals, usually with no security background. There are odd exceptions, but in general these policemen receive no specialized training in Canada before coming to Europe."

The Canadian government was not in the dark concerning Nazi atrocities committed during the war. Canada, like every other Western nation, had available to it abundant evidence of the systematic and scientific program of mass murder that had been carried on by the Nazis. Perpetrators were being tried and convicted of war crimes by Allied forces. And yet, surprisingly enough, Canadian officials abroad were not even familiar with the term "war criminal." The testimony of Albert Greening:

"Q: Did the term 'war criminal' at any time creep into your conversation while you were involved in performing your duties in Europe during that period?
A: I think our interpretation of the term 'criminal' would fall back on our interpretation of criminals in Canada. Therefore, we would not really feel that we were dealing with a war criminal, as such. We could be dealing with persons who had carried out activities in other countries outside of Canada, which [sic] could be a crime in Canada, might not necessarily be considered a crime in other countries...But the term 'war criminal' I do not think we dealt with it in that term because it was ambiguous for our purpose."

William Kelly, the officer in charge of visa controls in London, who headed up the entire liaison operation between the RCMP and all other police organizations in Western Europe from 1950 to 1954, concurred: "...the term 'war criminals' was something foreign to our vocabulary at that time, and the first time I think I heard of war criminal, and it is not inconsistent with the term 'major offenders or offender,' but the first time I heard it, I think, was in some correspondence from an ambassador in Europe to External Affairs in dealing with certain matters, but war criminals was not a common term in our vocabulary." (This ignorance about war criminals and their actions was to persist among Canadian immigration officials in Europe for quite some time. Indeed, one of the more striking facets of Commission testimony surrounding the later Mengele incident of 1962 was that the Canadian visa officer in West Germany during the period in which inquiries were being made about Hitler's chief medical experimenter had no idea who Mengele was.)

Nor did the term "war criminal" appear anywhere in Canada's Immigration Act. To this day, the Canadian Immigration Act does not expressly prohibit the admission of war criminals. Instead, the legislation was enacted with exclusions for such categories as "enemy aliens", "Nazis" and "members of the German military." Had these exclusions remained in place, "war criminals" within these categories would have been excluded without a specific reference. But the progressive relaxation of these categories over the years left large loopholes through which a war criminal might squeeze. He would simply have had to keep silent about his deeds.

It is difficult to understand why the Canadian government excluded the term "war criminal" from its vocabulary when the term was in common usage: the Refugee Convention excluded "war criminals" from the definition of "refugee" and the International Refugee Organization Constitution expressly precluded "war criminal" and "persons who assisted in the persecution of minorities" from obtaining displaced person certification. Yet, neither of these categories was specifically referred to in Canadian security criteria as grounds for rejection. The choice of nomenclature by Parliament and security officials responsible for administering immigration policies seemed to be another reflection of Canada's indifference to the seriousness of offences committed by the Nazis.

Even more inexplicable is the evidence given by government archivist Robert Hayward concerning Canada's failure to make use of war criminal lists circulated by international agencies. As a member of the Western Allied occupation forces and a participant in the prosecution of war crimes, Canada was privy to numerous lists of wanted or suspected war criminals prepared and distributed by the Central Registry of War Crimes and Security Suspects (CROWCASS) and the United Nations War Crimes Commission. Mr. Hayward testified that the CROWCASS lists of some forty thousand names were in Canadian hands from 1947-1948 onward. "I believe they would have been provided to the Canadian authorities upon production," he stated. The UN War Crimes Commission developed eighty lists which also found their way to Canada, some by as early as 1946. And yet, these lists were never circulated to Canadian security officers in Europe for comparison against applicants for immigration!

Evidence before the Commission indicated that government practice was not to circulate them. The lists were transmitted to Canada in duplicate, compared with lists of prisoners of war in Canada and prisoners of war who had been returned to England, and then simply filed away for posterity. No further use was made of them. In a 1946 letter, Louis St. Laurent, then Canada's secretary of state for External Affairs wrote: "It is felt that this is the most useful way in which those lists can be scrutinized here and it is not the practice to distribute them to any other Canadian authorities."

William Kelly told the Commission that no lists were ever circulated to his post, nor was he even aware of any lists during his tenure abroad:

> "Q: Did you, sir, as officer in charge in the whole of Western Europe, did you have available for quick reference any kind of a list drawn up by the Department of National Defence of Canada or any other organization giving the names of suspected or wanted war criminals?
> A: No.
> Q: You never did?
> A: Never did.
> Q: So would I be correct in concluding, sir, if you did not have one, your men in the field in all probability did not have one either.
> A: I would say that that is the case."

Albert Greening, during his almost eight years of service in Germany, never had access to or knew of the existence of any lists. He relied solely on his sources to tell him whether a particular applicant was wanted or had been involved in "various activities."

Reliance on outside sources was part and parcel of the screening policy of the RCMP. The force did not set up its own intelligence or security machinery or develop its own sources for checking purposes. Explained Greening, "We did not have an organization over there and it was not our policy to get involved in offensive intelligence." Security personnel at all posts abroad relied heavily, if not exclusively, on foreign sources for security checks. According to a 1949 internal government document, "We are dependent upon the records of those friendly countries which do collect and collate such information." Of course, this policy meant that Canada conducted no independent scrutiny of persons approved by foreign powers. The result? Incidents such as a 1953 episode disclosed during the Deschênes Commission in which what one Commission witness identified as a "friendly" country had duped Canada into admitting immigrants by supplying them with false documents—persons who would never have been approved for immigration otherwise.

The sources on which Canada relied—primarily British and American intelligence, and to some extent the German authorities—were themselves filled with gaping holes. Canada was also reliant upon the often ineffective screening carried out by the independent voluntary relief agencies. Sources from France were quite poor, and as for Eastern European countries, Canada had no sources whatever. And yet, both Kelly and Greening, who were directly involved in the screening process, acknowledged that Canada's screening system–based on a "negative clearance" process–could only work if it had effective sources.

In the immediate postwar years, Canada depended almost exclusively on British intelligence. The Security Panel believed that as an interim measure, the United Kingdom "would provide reasonable facilities." But screening techniques employed by the United Kingdom were amateurish. There was neither an indexing system nor an investigating body to interview the hundreds of thousands of displaced persons in British controlled camps. Instead, the army actually recruited German refugees to carry out the interrogations—and they were instructed to look for security risks, not war criminals.

An Austrian Jew named Roger Elliott was recruited, nominally as an interpreter, in June 1945. After four weeks training he was sent to Paderborn internment camp. Within an hour of arriving he discovered that he and a Dutch recruit had been made responsible for the interrogation of no less than twenty-five thousand internees. Said Mr. Elliott, "They just left us amateurs all alone....For all I know, the biggest war criminals could have got through our fingers. My only criteria was whether the German was a danger to security or of interest to intelligence. I never had anything to do with war crimes...."[13]

American screening was no better. Training was haphazard and techniques were slipshod. According to Allan Ryan, Jr., former head of the U.S. Office of Special Investigations, the American Counter Intelligence Corps (CIC), to which Canada deferred for most of its security data, was a questionable source of intelligence, and "had no access to the records that would indicate that a Ukrainian, Baltic, or other Eastern European applicant had been a Nazi collaborator." Apart from a check with the Berlin Documentation Centre, CIC investigations were "limited to an applicant's behaviour since he entered the camp, or at least since he had entered Germany." In other words, the CIC had no greater access to information than the Canadians in many cases. It was a case of the blind leading the blind.

More alarming was the CIC's use of the Gehlen organization, headed by a former Nazi intelligence chief with special expertise on the Soviets. General Gehlen co-operated closely with the Americans after the German surrender and eventually became chief of West German intelligence. That he held onto his Nazi convictions was evident from the high-ranking Nazis included among his staff. The CIC employed former collaborators and Nazi war criminals as informants and for intelligence purposes, the most notorious case being that of Klaus Barbie, the "Butcher of Lyon," who escaped to South America through American complicity. William Kelly himself acknowledged that the CIC "might well have" used the Gehlen, which he called an "offensive organization." Although he admitted that such information was not likely to be reliable, neither he nor Mr. Greening had any qualms at the time about relying on U.S. intelligence that emanated from suspect sources.

The International Refugee Organization (IRO), along with other voluntary relief agencies and church groups, assisted in the resettlement of refugees and provided financial assistance for their passage abroad. These groups were authorized by Ottawa to issue travel documents after conducting a pre-screening on behalf of Canadian authorities in accordance with Immigration guidelines. While in theory, only *bona fide* displaced persons were eligible to receive certification under the IRO mandate, Ryan asserts that IRO investigations were "superficial, and in the eyes of some, corrupt." One person who worked closely with the IRO charged that many staff members "were former collaborators themselves who coached the applicants in the techniques of successful deception or who simply filled out the papers on behalf of applicants, submitting them for rubberstamp approval by unsuspecting IRO officials."[14] Moreover, reports of racial discrimination within the IRO led to an internal investigation in 1948, which uncovered instances of collusion between IRO personnel and Canadian officials abroad to exclude Jews from certain bulk-labour schemes, such as woodworking, railroad maintenance, hardrock mining and domestic workers programs.[15]

Internal government documents released during the Deschênes Commission revealed that at least some high-ranking officials in Ottawa were aware of corruption within the IRO. In 1947, members of the Security Panel observed: "Officials of the International Refugee Organization administering these camps do not co-operate in screening DP's presenting themselves for selection. In fact, if a DP is rejected by one country on account of his political or criminal record, the IRO will conceal this fact and have the DP present himself to the screening team of another country. There are grounds to believe that IRO have facilitated the movement of high-ranking Nazis from Germany." By 1949, the Security Panel had no doubts: "Communists abroad are doing everything possible to infiltrate Communists into this country. Other groups are doing the same for former Nazis and Nazi collaborators. There is proof that such operations have been planned and in a number of cases have been successful."

It is most likely that security checks by voluntary relief organizations were cursory at best. Their primary purpose was to move hundreds of thousands of people out of camps and see to their resettlement. They were not interested in cumbersome investigations and exerted a great deal of pressure on Canadian officials to speed up the process. According to former visa control officer Albert Greening, "There are [sic] many occasions when our teams...were pressed to proceed as quickly as possible because various groups would be brought forward, church organizations would be pressing for a certain number of cases."

In the final analysis, for the purposes of security, emphasis was on what organization a person belonged to, rather than what that person had done. Given this state of affairs, it is hardly surprising that Helmut Rauca, mass murderer, managed to enter Canada through a voluntary agency. His own passage was aided by the Canadian Christian Council for the Relief of Refugees.

Canada had no facilities for access to Eastern European sources, which proved to be a great obstacle to the screening effort. When Soviet forces had replaced the Nazi troops retreating from Eastern Europe, they captured vast quantities of Nazi documentation pertaining to the Holocaust. All of the Nazi death camps had been in Eastern European countries. After the war, surviving victims and eye-witnesses were scattered throughout Communist countries. But because of cold war politics, Canada refused to make any effort through diplomatic or other channels to gain access to such sources in Soviet territory. William Kelly testified, "We had no sources at all in places like Poland, Bulgaria, Romania, Yugoslavia and that sort of thing, none at all. That made it difficult, of course, for us in dealing with the people who came from there as refugees." At a 1949 meeting, the Security Panel expressed fears over the severity of the problem: "The RCMP have now advised Immigration and the Department of External Affairs that attempts to screen persons who desire to come forward from 'Iron Curtain' countries are proving impossible to carry out. No security information is obtainable in the country of origin; there is only the London check. This is a hit-and-miss method which may only catch one in several hundred or a thousand and would only show up well-known Communists or Nazi collaborators. The RCMP therefore consider that screening of applications behind the 'Iron Curtain' is now impossible. The only exception is Czechoslovakia for which there are good sources outside the country itself. These sources will eventually disappear but for the present are useful." The Security Panel concluded, then, that "if such immigrants are to be admitted to Canada at all, it must be on the basis that no opportunity exists for adequate screening."

As for information from German authorities, Canadian officials were, according to a 1951 Immigration Department memorandum, "largely at the mercy of the local police chiefs who may or may not be inclined to assist." Albert Greening, who worked at the Nuremberg Refugee Camp from 1954 to 1962, stated that Canadian officials were not in a position to assess the adequacy of information processing on refugees from East Europe by West German officials. As far as he knew, West German sources did not use official Soviet sources, just as the Canadians did not. He considered this a definite impediment to the accuracy of screening. He also admitted that the desire of German officials in the Nuremberg refugee centre to "dispose" of hard-to-place persons may have led to misrepresentations of their security status. William Kelly testified that the RCMP "often wondered...if we were getting the right information from the German authorities."

Immigration and RCMP officials also made security checks through the Berlin Documentation Centre (BDC)—the repository of Nazi party and SS personnel records. Because an unknown portion of files had been taken over by the Soviet Union following the war, BDC information was severely limited in scope—covering only German or Austrian applicants, and not persons from Eastern European areas. Berlin had no records on members of the Ukrainian militia, Latvian political police, Estonian *Selbstschutz*, Croatian *Ustashi* or Hungarian Arrow Cross, who were usually not members of the Nazi Party of Germany, but of their own fascist organizations. A BDC check on such individuals would have been absolutely useless. For Canadian authorities, this meant another gaping hole in the security net. Testified Albert Greening: "There was a gap we could not judge. If a person was being processed by us, we could not decide whether, if we got a negative reply from the BDC, it was because of the gap or because he had never come to the attention of the German authorities as being within the military or party ranks. We just had to accept that the gap was there and we could not assess it."

But even where records were available in the Berlin repository the evidence suggests they were checked in a rather offhand manner. During the 1983 extradition hearing of Helmut

Rauca, his complete BDC file—intact as it had been since the war—was reproduced as evidence against him. It is truly mystifying that the Canadian officials responsible for his admission into Canada could have overlooked the Rauca file. Unfortunately, this is a puzzle for which there will never be an answer. Certainly, none of the witnesses who testified before the inquiry were able to offer any explanation.

One likely explanation is that the sorely understaffed Canadian immigration posts were simply overwhelmed by the sheer volume of immigrants and the unrelenting pressure to process their applications with utmost dispatch. Even as late as the 1950s, only twenty-five or thirty visa control officers were stationed in all of Europe to screen the hundreds of thousands of refugees being processed annually. Stage B became a bottleneck. Screening facilities were overloaded. By April 1949, there was a backlog of some thirteen thousand cases.

Outside relief groups were not the only voices pressing the RCMP teams to hurry Stage B inquiries in order to speed up the flow of immigrants. Pressure was also exerted from within government. William Kelly, in his frequent meetings with head immigration officials in Germany (first Mr. Bird, and after 1953, Mr. Robillard) discerned that "Immigration was more concerned with numbers than security," and as a result, he continued, "they certainly quarrelled with us often enough because we were not producing results quickly enough...." The pressure filtered down to every visa control officer, according to Albert Greening: "The volume was heavy....So we had to spread out our resources and deal with them as well as we could....Yes, there were many times when we were pressed."

To alleviate the ever-mounting backlog, the "fourteen-day procedure"—the issuance of a conditional visa, subject to a security check—was effected in the early postwar years to deal with cases other than displaced persons from Communist states or suspicious individuals. How this fourteen-day procedure worked was described in minutes of a 1949 meeting of the Security Panel: "This procedure is that applications are received at the Immigration Offices in Canada and providing the applicant meets all requirements other than security screening the application is then forwarded to RCMP Headquarters for security screening of the sponsor in Canada and proposed immigrant overseas. 14 days after the application has been forwarded to the

RCMP for security screening and regardless of whether a security report has been received or not, the Visa Officer in the country concerned is advised by the Immigration authorities in Ottawa that the application has been approved. In short, this gives the RCMP 14 days only in which to screen the sponsor in Canada and the proposed immigrant overseas. If no report is received within that period from the RCMP, and it practically never is, the immigrant can come forward. It is absolutely impossible for the RCMP to complete this screening in the prescribed time of 14 days."

So, if a visa officer did not receive an adverse report from the RCMP, that visa officer was free to issue a visa to the immigrant—the only catch was that the RCMP did not always have a chance to look at the case until over fourteen days had passed. Checks were then completed even though the immigrants had already gone forward to Canada! In effect, the fourteen-day procedure was as good as having no screening at all, concluded the Security Panel: "The only useful purpose therefore which this screening under the 14-day scheme serves is to provide the RCMP eventually with a record of who have come into Canada who may be considered subversive."

George O'Leary testified that immigrants were permitted to come forward on this conditional basis before the completion of Stage B "in order to go ahead under pressure from refugee organizations and other interested groups." While he had no idea how many immigrants came forward in this way, discussions of the Security Panel show that the practice was occurring on a wide scale: "Of the backlog of 13,000 cases now under review by the U.K. authorities, some 11,000 applications are from Eastern European countries. It is very difficult to assess the real meaning of this backlog as many of the applications are already in Canada and, of the remaining number, it is impossible to state how many might eventually obtain exit permits from their countries of origin."

In theory, a person found to be a security risk following admission to Canada would be removed. In practice, no one ever was: "It is believed that a very large percentage of the present London backlog consists of persons who are already in Canada and concerning whom no screening report will be available for months. If an unfavourable report comes forward after entry, there are apparently no legal provisions under which the persons involved can be deported as they have already been granted a permanent landing." For anyone with the ability to conceal his status as a suspicious individual, the fourteen-day procedure was an automatic ticket of admission into Canada.

And what of immigrants from the Soviet Union and other Communist states? Because of the absence of information from Eastern Europe, these people had to be handled differently. To deal with the problem, the RCMP implemented a screening device that came to be known as the "two-year residence rule." Under its provisions, where no security information was available about a prospective immigrant, that individual was required to reside for at least two years in a country where security screening facilities were set up. The hope was that any undesirable tendencies would manifest themselves within this time or that a source might come forward. But the officers who administered it were not convinced of its usefulness. Albert Greening admitted, "We accepted the two-year rule as the lesser of two evils. It was not satisfactory but under the circumstances it was what was decided could be done for these people." Even the officer in command of the whole operation had little faith in the procedure. The two-year rule, testified William Kelly, "helped us a little bit, but we did not think it was the answer to the problem." Under further questioning, he conceded that, in effect, the rule was a pointless exercise:

"A: ....Actually, I think it was a stalling tactic mainly because we had to do something with them, and yet, we had no basis for clearing them for security, but if, within the two years, there was still nothing against them, again, it was a negative clearance; they came to Canada.
Q: Did that sometimes happen, that within the two years you would get information?
A: I cannot think of any case where we did, but the two-year residence rule was established on that basis, that there was a possibility of something turning up against these people.
Q: Did it sometimes happen that you would get information even after they had come to Canada?

A: I cannot think of any case where that was so...we could not expect any sources [from Communist countries] to give us the information."

Of what practical effect, then, was the two-year rule? Absolutely none. Did Canadian authorities believe that war criminals hiding in camps might re-enact their crimes, and thus reveal "undesirable tendencies"? Did they expect information to turn up when all channels to sources were closed? If anything, the rule seemed to reward patience rather than elicit relevant facts about prospective immigrants. Applicants from Lithuania, Poland, Romania and other Eastern European nations who were prepared to wait out the two-year period could gain admission to Canada, even if no sources were available to check their security status.

With such a flimsy intelligence network in place, visa control officers responsible for discharging the Stage B security clearances had, in reality, little more information to go on than what they could glean from a personal interview. Overburdened as they were—witnesses at the Commission estimated between ten and thirty-five interviews were held daily, many with one or more interpreters—officers would be forced to rush through interviews, devoting only a fraction of their time to matters of security.

To make matters worse, interview procedures were not standardized. Immigration forms and documents contained no direct questions about membership in the Nazi party or actual activities during the war. There was nothing on the forms to indicate that such questions were asked orally during the interview. Even after the application forms were amended in 1953 to include military records, still no direct questions were posed as to a person's actual wartime duties, nor did the forms specifically ask the applicant to state whether he or she had been a concentration camp guard. (It is true that asking applicants whether they are war criminals is not likely to produce a positive response. A person who has murdered innocents is not likely to hesitate about telling a lie. But this line of questioning does serve an important purpose, later on. If a person was asked the question, and lied, he could subsequently be deported for gaining entry to Canada by fraud. Failure to pose the question makes it extremely difficult to prove entry by fraud, and thus eliminates a subsequent ground for deportation.)

As for the actual physical examination of applicants—again, no standard procedure was in place. While their American counterparts fingerprinted all applicants for immigration, the RCMP chose not to, in spite of a CROWCASS directive. "Personally," testified Albert Greening, "I was in favour of setting up a fingerprinting system, but it was never condoned by our Headquarters in Ottawa." Witnesses at the Deschênes Commission gave conflicting testimony as to the procedure followed, if any, for identifying the SS blood mark, tattooed under the armpits of every member of Hitler's sinister, elite guard, which was responsible for many atrocities during the war. Albert Greening said he only advised the medical officer to check for the mark when he had reason to be suspicious and that the examining doctor would advise him if a mark came to his attention. On the other hand, Joseph Robillard testified that he issued verbal instructions to check for the SS mark in every case. However, there is no written documentation to suggest any standard routine was ever followed. In fact, actual incidents of undetected SS marks have been documented. In *None Is Too Many*, authors Irving Abella and Harold Troper cite an eye-witness account in which twelve men about to board an immigrant ship were stopped after a last minute medical examination revealed the mark tattooed under their armpits.[16] A similar incident in U.S. screening was described by Allan Ryan in *Quiet Neighbors*: In one group of twenty immigrants, "there were twelve former SS officers who bore the SS mark on their arms. All were approved for DP status. Each claimed he had received the identical mark from a burn, wound or accident and the American interrogator accepted the explanation."[17] According to the background study prepared for the Deschênes Commission by historian Alti Rodal, there were even instances where Canadian officials decided to overlook SS tattoo marks on individuals applying for entry to Canada.

And so, the general format of the interview and physical examination was left up to the discretion of individual screening personnel—RCMP officers who lacked specialized training, did not have the benefit of war criminals wanted lists, were dependent on unreliable sources and worked long hours to keep up with the unending stream of applicants. The chances for error were very high. William Kelly elaborated on just how easy it was for slip-ups to be made by screening officers. If someone was not within a listed exclusion category and happened to be a war criminal, he explained, "unless we got some indication from our sources there was nothing we could do but just clear it with security." Screening officers, stated Albert Greening, had no way of checking whether information given on an application was false unless there was other information brought to light from the interrogation or intelligence sources—sources which were often non-existent. By misrepresenting the fact of his Nazi involvement, a person could have passed through Stage B. By the time adverse information turned up, it would be too late to do anything about it. It was as simple as that. Any Nazi war criminal who could tell a lie or avoid the subject of his past could just as easily come right through Canada's doors.

Then there were the cases in which Canadian officials were deliberately misled by foreign powers. Alti Rodal's study sheds light on evidence that U.S. and British intelligence services may have spirited known Nazi collaborators from Eastern Europe into Canada, unbeknownst to federal authorities, in an effort to build up anti-Soviet intelligence networks. (This study is entitled *The Nazi War Criminals in Canada: The Historical and Political Setting from the 1940s to the Present.* Despite Mr. Justice Deschênes' recommendation that the report receive wide distribution, Ottawa considered the document too sensitive because it presents a stinging indictment of postwar government policy on war criminals and because it could lead to identification of suspects. As a result, it was kept secret by the government for months, until a heavily censored copy was obtained in August, 1987 by *Toronto Star* reporter David Vienneau under Canada's Access to Information Act.)

According to that study, American intelligence officers "withheld information from and misled Canadian authorities as to the true background of prospective immigrants to Canada." These immigrants were "persons who had rendered postwar service to U.S. intelligence and who would have been inadmissible on grounds of moral turpitude—the category for undesirable Nazi collaborators." In his testimony before the Deschênes Commission, William Kelly raised the question of an Allied nation falsifying documents in 1953 to smuggle otherwise unacceptable immigrants into Canada. Before he could identify the "friendly" power to which he was referring, he was requested by Mr. Justice Deschênes to continue his testimony behind closed doors in order to protect national security. Without revealing any names William Kelly did manage to confirm his belief that the incident had occurred: "I must say that it is quite possible that had they been presented in the right way, they might well have been cleared for security....Yes, we think that before we caught on to what was happening, some of them did pass through the screening based on false information and information which had been established so that when we checked our sources, it would not reveal anything adverse against such people." It became clear with the release of the Rodal study that he had been referring to the United States government. In the study, he is quoted as saying that a number of "suspicious applications" for security screening had come to his attention, "all neatly typed and emanating from an address in the American zone of occupation." That quote was followed by three pages that were completely censored. In an interview immediately following the study's release, Kelly told reporters that he had no doubt the U.S. was providing false histories for undesirables. The Americans were putting these individuals forward for immigration, he said, "on the basis they had worked for the U.S. and were therefore not the type of people Canada would keep out. They [the Americans] were the last people we thought would deceive us. They felt because they were anti-Communist we should follow them without question."[18]

Other indications that Canada had been hoodwinked were given by an American source in 1985. John Loftus, a former attorney with the U.S. government's war crimes inquiry unit, the Office of Special Investigations, said that British intelligence resettled Nazi war criminals in Canada in the 1940s.[19] Although Rodal could find little evidence of British intelligence relocating alleged Nazis in Canada, she indicates in her study that this might have been due to a mysterious "disappearance in the early 1970s of files relating to the subject of Nazi war criminals." (In any case, to say that the Canadian security system was duped is naive. Canada was by no means an innocent victim. If the government did not know that certain sectors of the U.S. and Britain were trying to smuggle in Nazi mass murderers, it is because it did not want to know. As Rodal pointed out, "Canada was not all that innocent in the way that it placed a very low priority on screening of Nazis after the war."[20]

Under these conditions, one can only conclude that slip-ups were inevitable; it is clear that Canadian officials in the field were well aware that serious mistakes were being made, as a 1952 report outlined: "The modus operandi followed by local Stage B officers during the last 12 months became stricter perhaps as a result of a few cases which went wrong...." (Of course, it is hard to imagine that only a "few" cases went wrong!)

Human error was not the only factor that poked gaping holes in the screening process. A combination of many factors—the progressive relaxation of immigration regulations, departmental policy directives, ministerial discretion, and sometimes executive abuse—made it common practice for the entire screening process to be altogether dispensed with or waived. As Joseph Robillard noted in his 1954 assessment, "50% of the immigrants we take annually are not even subject to Stage B inquiries."

By virtue of immigration regulations, certain categories of immigrants were entirely exempt from screening. Immediately following the war, persons in certain "close relative" categories—first degree relatives of persons in Canada, such as spouses, parents and children—were not subject to screening. In sponsored cases such as these, Canadian sponsors would be screened, but not the applicants abroad.

With the passage of time, as the immigration regulations were eased, categories exempt from screening were expanded to include a broader range of "close relatives" and a variety of nationalities. By 1955, the "close relative" categories had been extended substantially. At the same time, it was proposed that the two-year residence rule be waived for these exempt categories. This policy change was debated by the Security Panel: "The Deputy Minister of Citizenship and Immigration explained that on humanitarian grounds security screening of immigrants was waived for certain categories of close relatives of Canadian residents. The present proposal was that these waivers for close relatives of Canadian residents should be extended: first, to include all parents, children, husbands, wives and fiancees of Yugoslavian nationality wherever they might make application; secondly, to include all parents, children, husbands, wives and fiancees of Soviet or satellite nationality making application at a

Canadian immigration office outside their country of birth. In neither case would the two-year residence rule (which requires applicants to have lived for two years in a country where there is a Canadian immigration office) any longer apply. In all cases a satisfactory security clearance of the sponsor in Canada would be required." The exemptions were adopted, in spite of the security risks acknowledged by the Security Panel: "In general discussion, it was observed that there were some obvious weaknesses in the present Immigration Act, including provisions which would allow persons in the exempt categories, but with backgrounds likely to make them undesirable persons, to enter Canada. It was noted that once such persons had obtained access to the Canadian courts, it was very difficult to find grounds on which they might be deported."

Even where screening was mandatory under the regulations, it could be dispensed with by the exercise of ministerial discretion. The minister of Citizenship and Immigration had power to override a security rejection and that power was used—orders-in-council were passed quashing rejections or minister's permits were granted to overcome security test failures. Ministerial reviews of security rejections meant that in some cases clearance was given to an individual who had failed Stage B, without a further screening check, according to an internal government memorandum: "...When after rejection on security grounds, the minister decides to admit the person, the immigration officer is to grant the visa immediately upon receipt of this information without further reference to the RCMP." George O'Leary acknowledged that a person who had been rejected by screening officials as a member of the SS, for example, might be cleared without further security checks on the orders of a Cabinet minister. Albert Greening recalled actual cases in which the minister's permit was in fact granted to overcome Stage B. In this way, persons who had been rejected by the RCMP later immigrated to Canada.

Ministerial override was not always necessary. In a variety of cases, immigration officials convinced the RCMP to withdraw security objections and the individuals in question were processed as if they had passed security. Sometimes these withdrawals occurred in response to the progressive relaxation in screening criteria. As exclusion criteria covering service in the German army and membership in the Nazi Party and Waffen SS were loosened, Immigration would request the RCMP to review and reverse dispositions on persons who had previously been rejected on security grounds—and the RCMP were required to yield. This meant that earlier restrictions on entry were of no effect. People who had been rejected under the old guidelines simply waited, re-applied when the criteria were relaxed and were admitted. Immigration correspondence of May 1951 noted that "the number of applications for review covering persons previously rejected for [service in the German army] is steadily increasing and favourable reviews are being effected in nearly all cases." The RCMP Security Section kept a log of statistics on the withdrawal of security objections, which confirmed that this practice occurred on a wide scale. An excerpt from 1951 statistics showed that membership in the SS during the relevant period had accounted for forty percent of all security rejections. Fifty percent of those rejections were reviewed and of the fifty percent reviewed, sixty-five percent had their security rejection withdrawn.

Screening was also a problem where persons were brought forward to Canada to fill labour shortages as part of bulk labour schemes. On an "as-needed" basis, Cabinet brought in large groups of labourers—agriculturalists, domestics, farming labourers, persons experienced in mining, lumbering, logging and others with specialized training. In general, they were presented by the IRO to Canadian immigration teams and dealt with on the spot by a security officer. In some cases, no screening whatsoever took place. In others, applicants who had previously been rejected were passed through. The Security Panel addressed itself to this problem in the context of at least two labour schemes:

> "(a) *Mine Workers Scheme (1949)*
> There have been cases of men who have applied to come forward with a group on, for instance, the Mine Workers' Scheme and have been turned down for security. Some of these men have immediately departed for another section of Germany and made application to join, for instance, a group of lumber workers coming forward to Canada and the IRO file at the point where they made previous application does not follow them forward. On arrival at the new point of application IRO

make up a new file which does not disclose that the man
was previously rejected on security grounds. He is now
better prepared to face interrogation and quite frequently is passed. Similarly there have been cases of
men having been rejected as DP's and who, under similar circumstances have made application to come forward under a Labour Scheme and have been accepted
due to there being no record of their previous screening.
The RCMP are endeavouring to overcome this by the
circulation of a black list among all Security Officers
overseas. Any man rejected is immediately circularized
on this black list. Quite frequently, however, the second application takes place within a matter of days and
before the names on the black list can possibly get to all
Security Officers.
(b) Farm Labour Scheme (1956)
Lt. Col. [Laval] Fortier [deputy minister of Citizenship
and Immigration] stated that approximately 150 ur-
gently-needed farm labourers were to enter Canada
from refugee camps in West Germany and from Austria. They were required before September and therefore security screening would have to be waived if they
were to arrive in time."

Tragically, any careful screening that did take place in the
bulk labour programs was most often directed at excluding
Jews, in keeping with a discriminatory policy issuing from the
highest levels of government.
A highly fragile security net had been set up, containing
great potential for human error, with endless ways around the
system and with built-in loop-holes that facilitated the entry of
Nazi war criminals. But if an ineffectual screening system left
room for Nazis to slip into this country, Canadian immigration
policy almost guaranteed that they would come. The only real
consistency in Canadian postwar immigration policy on suspected Nazi war criminals was the progressive relaxation of entry restrictions for classes of immigrants in which the numbers
of Nazi supporters were the greatest. Between 1950 and 1954 the
government gradually lifted restrictions on Nazi organizations.
By 1955, any Nazi except for a former camp guard—even an SS

member—was allowed in. By selectively easing up on prohibitions against these groups Ottawa ensured that the criteria of eligibility would be all too easy to fulfil by war criminals.

Following the initial outright ban on enemy aliens, a 1947 order-in-council lifted the enemy alien exclusion for nationals of Finland, Hungary, Italy and Romania. The next year, nationals of Austria were also removed from the enemy alien list and became eligible for admission. As of March 1950, German nationals with first degree relatives in Canada were able to enter under the "close relative" category. Eight months later, in November 1950, the blanket exclusion was lifted for all German nationals— they were now to be dealt with on the same basis as any other European immigrant. All remaining restrictions on enemy aliens were revoked in July 1952.

In the four years immediately following the war, Ottawa had no specific guidelines for the rejection of Nazis or the German military on security grounds. It was not until 1949 that the first security rejection criteria issued forth. They provided for an automatic rejection of members of the Nazi Party, SS or German Wehrmacht, of persons bearing the mark of the SS blood group and of collaborators. Eight months later—and only a month after the ban on German nationals had been lifted—the Security Panel put into effect the first in a long series of relaxations, this time in favour of Nazi party members. An Immigration Department directive dated December 1, 1950,was circulated to the European immigration posts advising that "membership in the Nazi Party will not in itself be a cause for exclusion." Each case was henceforth to be dealt with on its own merits. And indeed, according to internal immigration correspondence of January 1952, "very few" Nazi party members were rejected as applicants.

But pressures to slacken the rejection criteria further were coming from both within the government and from outside. George O'Leary testified that a considerable number of submissions "were made from the posts abroad, based on representations they had received from the International Refugee Organization, church groups, and so on...."

Similar sentiments were echoed at home. Inter-departmental correspondence in 1951 indicated that immigration authorities were pushing for fewer restrictions. It was recommended that membership in the Waffen SS in itself no longer be a blanket cause for security rejection and that in collaboration cases, a more relaxed view be taken providing the degree of collaboration and surrounding circumstances warranted leniency.

Taking these views into consideration, the Security Panel began a gradual process of whittling away at the prohibition against members of the Waffen SS—an organization that had been declared criminal by the International Military Tribunal at Nuremberg in 1946: "Units of the Waffen SS were directly involved in the killing of prisoners of war and the atrocities in occupied countries. It supplied personnel for the *Einsatzgruppen*, and had command over the concentration guards after its absorption of the *Totenkopf* SS, which originally controlled the system."[21]

On July 6, 1951 the Security Panel implemented its first relaxation for non-German members of the Waffen SS, based on the date and coercive nature of membership: "Members of the Waffen SS, who joined after the 1st day of January, 1943, will not be rejected automatically if it can be established a prospective immigrant was forced to join that group." In its inexplicable haste to lift restrictions against non-voluntary members of the Waffen SS, the Security Panel may well have opened the doors to those who had volunteered to serve in the Waffen SS. Its choice of January 1, 1943 as the cut-off date was disputed by later RCMP opinion. On January 21, 1953, William Kelly, at that time an RCMP liaison officer, wrote: "For all practical purposes the opinion of all Security Officers in Germany is that there was no conscription or coercion in the Waffen SS until September 1944, and as a guiding date which is clearly on the safe side, we have suggested the date of 31st December, 1943, as the date before which we are quite satisfied there was no conscription or coercion." The Security Panel had been off by a year.

In fact, one year earlier, Cabinet had already made an exception to the blanket exclusion against the Waffen SS. On May 31, 1950, in response to lobbying efforts at home, Cabinet passed an order-in-council to admit several thousand men of Ukrainian origin who had served in the Galicia Division of the Waffen SS. The unit was composed of volunteers who had enlisted in the Ukraine in the spring and summer of 1943 and fought briefly on the Eastern front before surrendering to the British occupation forces. At their time of entry, they were being held in the United Kingdom as prisoners of war. The order-in-council   provided   that   this   group   be   admitted "notwithstanding their service in the German army provided they are otherwise admissible. These Ukrainians should be subject to special security screening, but should not be rejected on the grounds of their service in the German army."

Additional relaxations in favour of the Waffen SS followed—although not without some debate among the policymakers. In a memorandum dated May 12, 1952, recommendations to the Security Panel maintained that the Waffen SS was "at best, a dubious group and unless there is reason to envisage serious grounds for consideration on their behalf they should be refused visas. The large backlog of eligible German applicants does not suggest the need to select from this group." Over these objections, exceptions to Waffen SS exclusions were extended—that very week—to German nationals who were under the age of eighteen at the time of conscription and to ethnic Germans (*Volksdeutsche*) who were naturalized and/or conscripted under duress.

Political considerations led top Canadian officials to press for further relaxations of SS exclusions. On April 22, 1955, Joseph Robillard, then chief of the Canadian Immigration Mission in Germany, wrote Canadian Ambassador to Germany Charles Ritchie, suggesting that it might now be "politic" to reconsider even persons who had voluntarily served in SS Divisions: "After West Germany becomes a member of NATO, the German authorities will no doubt take a very dim view to the fact that we welcome their new soldiers in our family of nations but still refuse to declare eligible for migration to Canada those who in former times joined the elite of their Armed Forces in order to serve the Fatherland....Our recommendation only concerns those who served and fought with the SS Divisions in an honourable manner and whose only impediment to migration is their previous voluntary service with such units."

Ambassador Ritchie took strong exception to this proposal and wrote to Lieutenant Colonel Laval Fortier on May 20, 1955: "I am afraid I cannot agree with Mr. Robillard's suggestion that the present ban on the immigration of former members of SS battalions be lifted. I find it hard to believe that we are so short of suitable candidates for immigration that it is necessary to start recruiting in a portion of the German and Volksdeutsche population whose war records are of the worst."

The Security Panel nevertheless met to consider the proposal, expressing the hope that such modifications "would not allow a sudden increase in the number of these persons being granted entry to Canada." In fact, it would be impossible to calculate just how many might get into the country, according to minutes of that meeting: "Mr. Dougan enquired if there were some means by which the Canadian Ambassador to the Federal Republic of Germany could be periodically informed of the volume of persons coming forward as a result of the proposed relaxation....Mr. Smith replied that the complexity of present operations was such that he knew of no means by which this could be reasonably done."

It did not seem to matter—political expediency won out. The Security Panel decided in favour of extending immigration privileges to voluntary members of Nazi organizations. After a meeting on October 18, 1955, a sub-committee of the Security Panel (the Security Sub-Panel) endorsed a three-fold policy:

> "(a) that former members of the SS, Waffen SS, SA [Storm Troops], *Abwehr* [Military Intelligence] and SD [Security Service] should no longer be automatically rejected as applicants for immigration to Canada;
> (b) that these cases were to be considered on the basis of political and humanitarian considerations and that the Department of Citizenship and Immigration be asked to consider applying these considerations only in close relative and meritorious categories; and,
> (c) that former members of the Gestapo, concentration camp guards and persons, who in the opinion of an examining officer, would be considered major offenders under Allied Control Council Directive No. 38 should continue to be automatically rejected as applicants."

In communicating these recommendations to the deputy minister of Citizenship and Immigration, however, the Security Panel failed to state explicitly that the modifications were intended to apply to voluntary members. Not realizing the scope of the policy, the assistant deputy minister gave his approval in the absence of the deputy minister. Only later was it realized exactly what had been agreed to. After a great deal of confusion and a flurry of correspondence to clarify the situation, the recommended changes were ultimately approved by both the minister of Citizenship and Immigration and the minister of External Affairs. The new policy was announced on March 21, 1956: "Henceforth, notwithstanding their membership in the Waffen SS, SS, SD, SA, or *Abwehr* was voluntary, such ex-members coming forward to close relatives in Canada or who may be deemed cases of exceptional merit, may be eligible for immigrant visas. Security officers will continue to refuse clearances in those cases where the persons were major offenders, concentration camp guards, etc., but will refer other cases to the visa officer." Exactly what criteria determined whether a case was of "exceptional merit" were not elucidated in any written guidelines.

In 1962, the blanket prohibition was withdrawn altogether. Former members of the Waffen SS, SS, SD and SA would no longer be automatically rejected as candidates for immigration, whether or not sponsored by close relatives in Canada and without having to show a case of exceptional merit. Further relaxations meant that former members of the Nazi Party would only be rejected if an individual was deemed a real security risk by the RCMP. Moreover, collaboration would not in itself be considered grounds for automatic rejection, except for those collaborators who were:

> "(a) actively engaged in fighting against Allied forces or in activities harmful to the safety and well-being of the Allied forces;
> (b) implicated in the taking of life or engaged in activities connected with forced labour and concentration camps;
> (c) employed by German police or security organizations and who acted as informers against loyal citizens and resistance groups;
> (d) charged with and found guilty of treason."

Had Parliament been truly determined to keep out collaborators, however, it could have included a specific ban on persons who had served in police auxiliary units—local forces who collaborated with the Nazis in many areas of German-occupied Europe. Aside from the *Einsatzgruppen* and the SS themselves, police auxiliary units employed by the Nazis played the most direct role in perpetrating the Holocaust. These units did not form part of the German military. Yet, they enthusiastically assisted the Nazis in rounding up Jews for the concentration and death camps, and carrying out executions. Canadian immigration guidelines completely overlooked them. Without an explicit prohibition, there was nothing to alert screening authorities to conduct more assiduous investigations of applicants from the ranks of the auxiliary police. Someone who admitted openly to serving in an auxiliary police unit but failed to disclose his actual duties might easily be granted a visa. The case of Haralds Puntulis suggests that this was a highly probable scenario. A platoon commander in the semi-military Latvian rural police, Puntulis was alleged to have offered his services to the Nazis when they marched into Latvia in 1941, helping to round up and murder hundreds of Jews in several towns and villages. He made his way to Quebec City in 1948. He was later tried by a Latvian court, *in absentia*, for treason.[22]

Quite apart from their step-by-step dilution over the years, the security rejection criteria were weak measures to keep out Nazi war criminals by virtue of their very format. They were mere statements of policy, rules of thumb. Because the criteria were not incorporated into the Immigration Act or its regulations, they lacked the teeth of binding laws. Further, no mechanism existed to ensure their enforcement. The criteria could be waived, ignored or applied in an altogether subjective manner according to the whims or biases of screening personnel— whose own attitudes reflected the anti-Communist, anti-Jewish sentiment that prevailed during the postwar immigration wave and formed the basis of official government policy.

As Professor Irwin Cotler observed in his submission to the Deschênes inquiry: "The Klaus Barbie affair vividly portrays the lengths to which Western powers were prepared to go in their Cold War strategies. Havens were provided to high-ranking Nazis and their collaborators in exchange for information concerning Communists, the new security priority. While the precise degree of Canadian involvement in these pursuits is not made clear by the evidence presented in public hearings before the Commission, there are good and substantial reasons to believe that an emphasis was placed on detecting Soviet sympathizers over other 'undesirables,' and that this emphasis, inadvertent or otherwise, had the effect of shielding those applicants with a Nazi past."

It did not seem to matter that the government steadily cut back measures to exclude those groups most likely to be laced with Nazis and their henchman, as long as it kept out Communists. In the words of a 1951 Immigration document, "Naturally we cannot anticipate any relaxation under this category." The introduction of security screening measures was primarily geared towards keeping out Communists—not war criminals. "Security screening of immigrants was designed to impede the entry of foreign agents and particularly to prevent an influx of Communists into the country." This was one of the very purposes of screening devices such as the two-year rule, a point reiterated during a 1952 meeting of the Security Panel: "Residents of Israel, from among whom there were many applicants, could not be checked against Israeli records; many of them had changed their names on entering Israel, and this fact alone made the infiltration of agents by the Soviet [sic] particularly easy. It was to meet this kind of problem that the two-year residence rule was proposed." As well, the training of screening personnel emphasized the political background Communist countries to allow them to make informed decisions on the security status of Eastern European applicants.

The evidence of William Kelly confirmed that the system was aimed at screening out persons who posed future security risks for Canada, rather than those who had committed war crimes in the past:

> "Q: So you were not as such looking for war criminals;
> you were looking for security risks.
> A: Oh, that is true, that is very true...."

Collaborators, too, if screened out as undesirable immigrants, were rejected not for their involvement in war crimes, but purely as security risks: as nationals of German-occupied states who had betrayed their homelands, their allegiance to Canada could not be assured. The RCMP, concerned for "the internal security of Canada," doubted that "prospective immigrants who were disloyal to the country of their birth would in fact be any more loyal to the country of their adoption."

One high-ranking immigration official, chief of admissions P. T. Baldwin, emphasized the political nature of screening decisions in a 1951 internal memorandum: "In my personal opinion, Waffen SS rejections in accordance with present regulations have been based, with some exceptions, on public sentiment in Canada as a result of World War II, rather than the fact that the authorities would consider the individual concerned a security risk in Canada at the present time." A "security risk" was defined by the Immigration Act as a person loyal to another government or likely to be a threat to the security of Canada. Evidently, suspected Nazi war criminals posed no such threat to Canada. Indeed, as historian Alti Rodal aptly stated, "If you could prove you were a Nazi, you had proved you were not a threat."[23] The Nazis had already lost the war—what possible security risk could they now pose? On the contrary, certain government sources were more inclined to regard them as security assets: anti-Communists with a wealth of information on Eastern Europe. Political considerations such as these also led Ottawa to admit, without any screening, several hundred refugees after the Hungarian uprising in 1956. It did not matter that some may have collaborated with the Nazis. Their flight from the Soviet take-over, proof of their staunch anti-Communism, was enough.[24]

Most abhorrent of all was the startling contrast between the government's growing leniency towards Nazis and its unwavering resolve to restrict the entry of Jews. Canada's notorious closed-door policy in relation to Jewish immigration from the early years of Nazi persecution in prewar Germany, throughout the Holocaust and in the aftermath of the war has been documented as one of the most dismal chapters in this country's history.

In *None is Too Many*, a comprehensive study of Canada's policy on Jewish immigration, Professors Abella and Troper expose the prevailing climate of anti-Semitism giving rise to the restrictions that so successfully thwarted the victims of Nazi oppression in their quest to find a new home here.[25] Confronted with the anti-Jewish problem in prewar years and later, as war broke out, the mounting evidence of Hitler's systematic campaign to wipe out European Jewry, the response of Canadian officialdom—reflecting the general public mood—was to fortify barriers to Jewish immigration. Jewish cries for rescue were met with indifference, even open hostility by immigration authorities, who remained unmoved by humanitarian considerations.

That Canada succeeded in its deliberate strategy to stave off Jewish immigration is painfully manifest, say Troper and Abella, in the pitiful numbers permitted to enter: "The single-mindedness with which the Nazis murdered the vast majority of European Jews was seemingly matched by the determination of Canada to keep out these same people. Only a tiny handful were given permission to enter the country. During the twelve years of Nazi terror, from 1933 to 1945, while the United States accepted more than 200,000 Jewish refugees; Palestine, 125,000; embattled Britain, 70,000; Argentina, 50,000; penurious Brazil, 27,000; distant China, 25,000; tiny Bolivia and Chile, 14,000 each; Canada found room for fewer than 5,000."

Even after the Nazi defeat, while the gruesome details of the Holocaust were still vivid, Jewish survivors found themselves out in the cold. Like other western Allies, Canada continued to insulate itself from the European refugee crisis. When international pressure and economic self-interest drove Canada to bring in displaced persons, the government carefully imposed controls designed to keep Jewish immigration to a bare minimum. According to *None is Too Many*, "In opening the door to displaced persons, the Cabinet was still concerned about the degree to which this movement might become a Jewish one. It was understood, it was beyond debate, that to whatever extent possible, this should be prevented; immigration preference should be given to other groups—especially British and northern Europeans."

And so, the policy of "selective discrimination" persisted. When Cabinet approved increased immigration under expanded "close relatives" categories, it did so with the sound knowledge that relatively few Jewish refugees would benefit. In displaced persons camps, visiting Canadian officials ranked ethnic groups in descending order of preference—usually beginning with the Balts and almost always ending with the Jews. Bulk labour schemes implemented to fill vacancies in the Canadian labour market were by and large structured in such as way as to virtually exclude Jews. Quotas were inevitably applied to limit Jewish participation and, in some cases, programs were strictly designated as "Non-Jews only." In a 1948 scheme to bring forward one thousand women as domestics and hospital workers, for example, Jewish applicants were rejected out of hand, deemed unacceptable for domestic work. An IRO resettlement officer assigned to the project was quoted in *None Is Too Many* as reporting, "Forty Jewish candidates were interviewed. All were rejected. Four Jewish girls (the first interviewed) were accepted by Labour and cleared by Security Officer, Major Howells. The latter then withdrew security by writing 'not' above the words 'cleared for security' on the grounds that he had received a cable from Ottawa stating that no Jews were to be accepted." The anti-Jewish bias in the Canadian bulk labour programs, state Troper and Abella, led one Jewish community leader to charge that it seemed easier for war criminals to get into Canada than for Jews.

It is certainly no coincidence that those responsible for placing insurmountable obstacles in the way of Jewish refugees seeking shelter in Canada were the very same politicians and civil servants whose progressive laxity towards Nazis paved the way into Canada for perpetrators of the Holocaust.

How? By giving preference to groups which had Nazi collaborators among their members and then failing to set up an effective filtering system. With each successive relaxation of its security requirements, Canada opened its doors a little bit wider to the oppressors, while standing firm in its repudiation of the oppressed. It is impossible to say how many Nazi persecutors entered Canada as a result of these relaxations, or to estimate which ones among them were directly involved in war crimes.

In 1952, after it was discovered that certain individuals who should never have been passed through security, had entered Canada on the strength of false documents, one immigration official reported in a somewhat defensive tone, "The best system in the world would never prevent the odd bad case from slipping through occasionally...." From the evidence that came to light at the Deschênes Commission, Canada's screening system was far from the "best system in the world"—it gave war criminals plenty of opportunities to slip into the country. Of course, the actual number will never be known. No written documentation exists, nor are there any reliable statistics. None of the witnesses at the inquiry could even guess. There is simply no conclusive data. But precise numbers are not necessary to prove beyond a reasonable doubt that Canada—unwittingly or otherwise—practically extended an open invitation to people who had taken part in some of the most ghastly crimes in history.

Chapter Three

Sanctuary?

On October 9, 1985, Member of Parliament and former Cabinet Minister Robert Kaplan, was sworn in before the Deschênes Commission in Ottawa. An important witness in the inquiry, the federal politician had served as solicitor-general in the Trudeau Cabinet from 1980 to 1984. During his tenure he began to look seriously into the presence of Nazi war criminals in Canada. His probings eventually led to the precedent-setting trial and extradition of war criminal Helmut Rauca. More than this, they unearthed a variety of startling revelations about the Canadian government's role in creating what Simon Wiesenthal has called a haven for war criminals.

Much of the testimony Kaplan gave over the next two days of hearings was based on his earlier top secret exchanges with the RCMP and other government officials—classified information that had never before surfaced publicly. Though Mr. Kaplan took the witness stand to tender answers, his testimony raised a number of disturbing questions about this country's involvement with Nazi war criminals and collaborators.

One such question was whether Canada willingly and knowingly co-operated in any schemes to harbour war criminals. By now the evidence was clear on the feeble screening structures which facilitated their entry, but did the government actively participate in deliberate plots to resettle war criminals within our borders as a result of Cold War paranoia?

This unsettling prospect first occurred to Kaplan in 1983, when headlines reported a shocking admission by U.S. authorities that the Americans, whatever their policies of keeping war criminals out of the country, appeared to have allowed certain war criminals in. At the centre of this scandalous revelation was Klaus Barbie, one of the most wanted Nazis in the world. An investigation was launched by the U.S. Justice Department war crimes unit, the Office of Special Investigations, into the relationship between American security and intelligence officials and Klaus Barbie in the immediate post-World War II era. In a letter of March 30, 1983 to RCMP Commissioner Simmonds of the RCMP, Kaplan wondered whether a similar policy had been followed by the Canadian government: "The evidence which led to the present decision by U.S. authorities raises questions in my mind as to whether any war criminals were settled in Canada with the support or co-operation of the Canadian government." Around the same time, a major television newscast aired a feature containing allegations of Canadian complicity in shielding war criminals.

Kaplan ordered an investigation by the RCMP into a possible government policy of accommodation. RCMP Corporal Fred Yetter was charged with this task, and when finished, promptly handed over his report, which induced Kaplan to make still further inquiries. To this end, he approached certain public servants and politicians who had taken part decades ago in the very meetings where postwar immigration policies were made. "I had hoped that I would be able to interview some of them, just get them to come up to my office....And, unfortunately, right at the top of our list, the first person who we approached...wanted to have some legal advice about the situation and that took two or three months and the meeting never occurred. So I was never able to get information that, I think, should be obtained...."

The question remained: Did Canada ever deliberately open its doors to war criminals? Explained Kaplan in his testimony, "In the middle of the 1950s the government narrowed the exclusion criteria for persons who might have been involved in war crimes...and I wanted to know why they did that. Was there some individual who was pressing for that change? Was there a group of prospective immigrants, a large group or a small group, waiting to have these criteria changed so that they could come to Canada? And, I never was able to get to the bottom of it."

If Robert Kaplan was unable to learn the complete story in 1983, by the time the Deschênes Commission was wrapped up, there could be little doubt that Canada had, on more than one occasion, sheltered known war criminals. It should be scrupulously pointed out that such actions were likely not part of any general plan to import Nazis into the country. Nonetheless, specific incidents of government complicity were not only alluded to by various Commission witnesses, but serious allegations turned up in the politically explosive Commission study prepared by historian Alti Rodal.

Links were revealed between Canadian authorities and then-British spy Kim Philby. In his role as a senior British intelligence officer, Philby was in charge of sending Nazis into Canada under new identities. (Philby later defected to the Soviet Union.)[1] An equally shocking discovery was the government's "direct and willing" participation in a British-U.S. plan to settle up to seventy-one German scientists and technicians in the West to keep them from falling into Soviet hands immediately after the war. Between 1946 and 1949, Canada actively competed with its western Allies in what was described as a race to recruit the scientists, without checking into their wartime activities. During that period, when official policy barred German nationals from immigrating to Canada, the government bent its rules by permitting these men to enter as temporary contract workers. When the ban on German nationals was lifted in 1950, they were eligible to apply for permanent residence and later, for citizenship. It was hoped that the Germans would make a contribution to the establishment of new industries in Canada. The precise number still in Canada could not be ascertained, and Mr. Justice Deschênes recommended further investigation.[2]

Moreover, the report revealed that in December, 1952, the government set up a committee on defectors. That committee permitted the entry into Canada of "defectors" who did not meet normal security requirements, at the request of a friendly intelligence service. The term "defector" was simply a convenient euphemism for former Nazis posing as anti-Communists. How quick the government was to forget the menace of Nazism because of the newer Communist foe. (It was learned in the 1970s that the RCMP files on re-settlement of former Nazis were missing and had been replaced by a false docket. American documents on the subject remain classified. A three-country agreement between the U.S., Britain and Canada provides that no information about about these "defectors" can ever be released without the joint consent of all governments. I have written to the Canadian government on behalf of the League for Human Rights, requesting that Canada give its consent and seek the consent of the U.S. and Britain.)

In another case, Prime Minister Louis St. Laurent admitted Nazi collaborator Karol Sidor into Canada in 1950 "after the direct intervention of Pope Pius XII", according to the Rodal study. Sidor was the first commander-in-chief of the Hlinka Guard, the Slovakian stormtrooper equivalent of the Romanian Iron Guard and the Arrow Cross in Hungary and had served as Nazi Slovakia's ambassador at the Vatican. He was granted entry into the country—albeit reluctantly—upon the request of the Apostolic delegate to Canada, who wrote to the Prime Minister in August, 1949: "Considering the delicacy of the situation, it is not opportune for Mr. Sidor to protract his residence in the Vatican any longer: while, on the other hand, he cannot settle down anywhere in Europe without undergoing serious inconveniences and vexations." His Nazi background had made him *persona non grata* throughout Europe. As a result of the letter, St. Laurent asked Deputy Minister of Immigration Hugh Keenleyside to overlook Sidor's past activities. "Keenleyside, clearly uneasy, emphasized the difficulty of obtaining security clearance for Sidor," explains the report, but admission was granted all the same. Sidor died in 1953.[3]

Perhaps no episode so vividly depicts the moral depths to which Canada under Prime Minister St. Laurent sank as a result of its anti-Communist phobia than the story of how the government played host to a network of convicted French collaborators who slipped into the country on false passports shortly after the war. The most notable among them was Count Jacques de Bernonville, who, as an official of the collaborationist Vichy government, had served faithfully at the side of Klaus Barbie in German-occupied Lyon. There is a certain historical irony in the fact that some four decades later, as the "Butcher of Lyon" was held to account for his brutal reign of terror, in Canada the Deschênes Commission was recalling the shady details of the de Bernonville affair.

The case of Klaus Barbie is by now notorious. Under Barbie's orders, thousands of Jews—many children among them— and Resistance fighters were tortured and deported to Nazi death camps. When the Germans surrendered in May 1945, Barbie remained at large and was recruited in 1947 by the Americans to spy on Communists for the next four years. The U.S. government then secretly arranged his safe passage to South America where he lived as a free man and a fugitive of justice for thirty-three years. His 1983 expulsion from Bolivia and subsequent trial in France in 1987 continue to dominate the news around the world.

By contrast, relatively few people are familiar with Barbie's right-hand man or with his privileged treatment by Canada. But the lesser-known story of the Count de Bernonville and the Vichyites lends weight to the theory that there was an underground railway by means of which these collaborators were smuggled into this country. Moreover, the government's decision to harbour de Bernonville and his fellow collaborators reveals executive abuse at the highest level and the obstruction of justice by Prime Minister Louis St. Laurent and his Cabinet in refusing to turn these wanted Nazi supporters over to the French authorities. According to Rodal's study, "St. Laurent and his aides were personally involved in communicating with the alleged war criminals, their protectors, and those that would have had them expelled from the country."

A survey of de Bernonville's wartime deeds lends a particular repugnancy to his connection with Canada.

The Vichy government headed by Pierre Laval, set up shortly after Germany's occupation of France in 1940, proved to be an enthusiastic collaborationist power. A top priority for the SS was to neutralize the Maquis—the French Resistance movement—whose capital was Lyon, France's second-largest city. When the SS moved into Lyon in 1942, Klaus Barbie, then twenty-nine, was appointed head of the Gestapo there. His assignment was two-fold: first, to take care of the city's Jews and, second, to go after the leaders of the Resistance. He carried out both tasks with cold-blooded determination, and among his crimes, Barbie is blamed for the savage beating murder of Resistance leader Jean Moulin, one of France's greatest heroes. The Gestapo chief carried out his mandate by skilfully manipulating a network of French informants, among them none other than nobleman Count Jacques Charles Noel Duge de Bernonville.

De Bernonville, who was numbered among "the cream of Lyon society," had been decorated in the First World War. But when the Nazis occupied France, he went to work for them. During the North African campaign he established Gestapo units to gather information among the French behind Rommel's lines. After the defeat of Rommel, de Bernonville escaped to

France. There, the Germans appointed him military comman-
dant of Lyon, second in command to Barbie—a post reserved
for only the most tried and true supporters of the Nazi cause.
His special task was to set up a counter-resistance police to
combat the French Maquis. He was also second in command of
Jewish affairs and a top training official of La Milice, a kind of
"French gestapo."[4]

The ardour with which he worked for the Nazis earned him
the praise of the Vichy leader Pierre Laval, later shot as a traitor
in France. Horrifying incidents of torture and death were directly attributed to de Bernonville and the orders he gave. Subsequent testimony of survivors and relatives of de Bernonville's
victims painted a grisly picture of the man who was later to become a Canadian immigrant.

One widow described how her husband had been
wounded in 1944 and taken prisoner under the command of de
Bernonville. "...he went through terrible tortures, namely, [he
was] hanged by the feet regardless of his severe wounds, then
turned over to the Germans who left him forty days in the
Chalon prison without any care and shot him....I add that de
Bernonville was perfectly aware of the tortures inflicted by his
men on the French...."[5]

Maurice Nedey, head of a leading Resistance group, was
called one of the most remarkable figures of the Resistance by
General Charles de Gaulle. He received the Croix de Guerre in
1945. Captured by de Bernonville's men in June, 1944, Nedey
was horribly tortured and then deported to Buchenwald concentration camp. He eventually escaped and later described the
vicious treatment he received at the hands of de Bernonville:

> "After having been slapped and insulted, they brought
> me to the...headquarters of the Milice....They tied my
> feet with electric wire, after having handcuffed me, and
> permitted me to lie down on the floor of the guard
> room....The next morning...they brought me to a large
> room...and de Bernonville sat down behind his desk
> which was in a corner. They cleared the tables and
> chairs and made me strip....De Bernonville, seated be-
> hind his desk, did not sully or tire himself to torture
> me; he merely gave the orders and lead the course of
> interrogation. All the staff...rivalled each other in cru-

elty....They spat on me, hit me with their fists, kicked
me in the stomach...one of them lashed me with a whip
across the stomach and I thought I would vomit out my
guts. I dropped to the floor time after time but they immediately made me get on my feet again by kicking me
in the sides....They stood in a circle and pushed me
from one to the other....Then I got a tremendous blow
which broke my lower jaw and I spat out bits of teeth
broken by the shock....Having been completely unsuccessful in the interrogation, [de Bernonville] com-
manded my torturers to use electricity on me. They
took a wire, which they spliced, attaching half to my
handcuffs and pricking me with the other half, thus
causing burns to my right arm and to the entire right
side of my body and to my legs. This process of torture
was the most unbearable that I suffered during that unhappy year. It gave you the feeling of a knife turning in
your breast, close to the heart. I curled up like a worm,
crying out like a madman....De Bernonville was im-
passive. I begged him to have pity and I recited
prayers....These various tortures lasted all day with
three-quarters of an hour of rest at noon and ended at
seven o'clock at night....When interrogation had been
completed de Bernonville told me I was a traitor and
that it was a disgrace to work for England....I had the
strength to [request that De Bernonville] promise me at
once not to turn me over to the Germans....He acquiesced....They took me then to prison....The
guard...later said he had never seen a man in worse state
enter the prison....I could no longer open my mouth
because of the fracture. My hands were completely
dead and insensible. For a time it was even thought I
would go mad....On June 22...I heard a guttural voice at
the door of my cell and a militiaman turned me over to
the gestapo, despite the promises of de Bernonville."[6]

Such was the character of the man who, dressed as a priest,
quietly made his way into Quebec from the U.S. in 1946 under a
phony name. For five years he managed to stave off deportation,
through the help of the Catholic Church and other powerful

sectors of Quebec society and supporters in the House of Commons.

But the de Bernonville case was not an isolated incident. He was only one of four other French collaborators who gained entry into Canada by disguising their true identities—and the fact that they had actively assisted the Nazi forces during the war. All had been convicted *in absentia* at trials in France of crimes relating to their work for the Nazi regime. The Count de Bernonville, living in Montreal with his wife and three daughters, had been sentenced *in absentia* to death for treason by a court in Toulouse. He and the others were wanted by the French authorities.

Their presence in Canada eventually came to the attention of the RCMP, but by then "they had succeeded in establishing themselves amidst Quebec's religious and social elite and could count on its support," says Rodal. Prime Minister St. Laurent was "in a quandary" because of the political implications of trying to have them deported from Quebec. Cabinet passed an order-in-council granting permission to all of the collaborators, except de Bernonville, to remain in the country as "political refugees." "An RCMP investigation of de Bernonville concluded that de Bernonville had engaged in 'particularly despicable' acts of collaboration during the occupation of the country." It was "even suspected that he may have had some part in the death of Jacques Benoit, a member of the Canadian Parachute Battalion killed in action in August, 1944." In fact, de Bernonville had assumed the identity of Jacques Benoit until he sought landed immigrant status in December, 1947, when he decided to apply under his own name. By now, the government felt it had little choice but to at least mount an effort to have him expelled.

Pressure to crack down on de Bernonville mounted when he was recognized by a former Resistance fighter living in Montreal. Punitive action was demanded by the Royal Canadian Legion, trade unions and the United Jewish People's Order. The campaign to deport him was frustrated though, by powerful French-Canadian nationalists who wanted to keep him in Canada, and by the federal government's reluctance to offend the Quebec hierarchy. De Bernonville was, according to one former French Resistance fighter active in the campaign to expose him and have him deported, "the darling of the ultra-Catholic aristocracy," and therefore well-protected. Among his staunchest supporters were several Quebec members of Parliament, members of the National Assembly, Montreal mayor Camillien Houde (who was also an M.P.), and various high-ranking church officials. A defence committee raised $72,000 on his behalf and a battery of lawyers dragged out the legal battle to deport him.[7] Each time de Bernonville was ordered deported, the decision would be overturned, much to the delight of his defenders.

In the House of Commons, only one member of Parliament spoke up against him. Alistair Stewart, the Winnipeg CCF representative, charged the government with allowing known supporters of Nazism to enter and stay in Canada. His demands for a crackdown on the French collaborationists were met with outrage. He was accused by several Quebec MPs of harbouring sentiments against French people. Camillien Houde denounced the requested deportation of de Bernonville as "a crying injustice," and "infamy." Another ardent supporter, Montreal businessman Jean Bonnel, called de Bernonville "a great Roman Catholic, a great Frenchman and a war hero." Independent MP Frederic Dorion commented, "I am sure that if it had been Communist Jews who had come here instead of French Catholics we would not have heard a word about them."

At first, the ministers responsible for permitting the collaborationists to stay in Canada attempted to hide their exercise of discretion in favour of these men, claiming that they had been properly screened and approved as proper applicants for entry by immigration officials. The powerful C. D. Howe, acting Prime Minister at the time, not only stated his agreement with the decision to regularize the entry of these Nazi collaborators, but went so far as to raise doubts about the validity of the legal processes by which they had been convicted in France, calling them "hasty trials." (De Bernonville's supporters claimed that the death sentence he was given was an act of revenge by French Communists. But A. L. Joliffe, the director of immigration dismissed this view, saying that de Bernonville was convicted by a competent court recognized by the French government.)

Months went by and, despite Stewart's persistent questioning, the government still refused to address the matter in Parliament or explain the basis of its decision to permit these undesirable immigrants to remain in Canada. In December 1949, the best response Minister of Mines and Resources Colin Gibson could muster in the House of Commons was evasive: "I can only say that the government at the time went over the material and decided that it would be justified in admitting certain ones and not admitting the others....They found they were not collaborators who should be sent back."

The sad, ironic counterpoint to this affair was the Cabinet's refusal around this time to grant asylum to a group of Jewish immigrants who had come over with falsified papers. Stewart had made an unsuccessful bid on their behalf: "I remember last year when seven unhappy Jews were deported from this country because they had come in illegally," he told Parliament on February 22, 1949, "I wanted to see if there were any grounds for clemency in their cases, in view of what they had suffered. The then minister said no; that if we should allow them to stay we would establish a precedent. That precedent had been established. I suppose the minister knew that all these fascists were here, but he deported those Jews who apparently had no very important friends." Months earlier, he had asked the Cabinet: "What circumstances prompted the government to permit these men to stay here, knowing that they had come on false passports, knowing that they had deported 7 Jewish people for exactly the same reason? What was the distinction between the seven Jews and these collaborators?" Whatever the distinction, Cabinet wasn't prepared to talk about it.

Officially, says Rodal, the government expressed its hopes that de Bernonville would be deported. On the unofficial level, St. Laurent and his aides were attempting to convince him to seek asylum elsewhere. Eventually, time ran out for de Bernonville. After stretching out the legal battle for more than three years and exhausting every avenue of appeal, he was again ordered deported in 1951. France was demanding his extradition. Incredibly, Prime Minister St. Laurent tipped him off, warning him to flee the country before he could be extradited.[8] St. Laurent's motives, other than a strong allegiance to the Quebec Roman Catholic church, remain puzzling. On August 17, 1951 de Bernonville escaped to Brazil, where he became a vocal activist for the extreme rightwing. A 1956 attempt by France to extradite him was unsuccessful. Twenty-one years after his flight from Canada, at seventy-four, Count de Bernonville was found strangled to death in his Rio de Janeiro apartment. Some commentators have theorized that de Bernonville's plan to publish his memoirs may have alarmed some of his wartime political allies and that he was killed on the orders of Brazilian Nazis.[9]

At least three of the other French collaborators were permitted to remain in Canada. One of them, Dr. Georges Benoit Montel, eventually became a medical professor at Laval University. Practising under his name, Montel was considered an ideal citizen by the local community, according to Rodal, but the RCMP had information showing that he "collaborated in every respect with the Germans and was instrumental in denouncing his French compatriots." When, during the course of the Deschênes inquiry, *Toronto Star* reporter David Vienneau requested the government to release the files of the Vichyites, he was advised that they had mysteriously disappeared from the archives and were nowhere to be found.[10]

Not surprisingly, speculation arose that these collaborators had been smuggled into Canada through an "underground railway".[11] Certainly, the actions of the Prime Minister and his Cabinet did nothing to refute that theory. Moreover, Jean Bonnel, who had admitted to being one of the main sources of aid to the collaborators upon their arrival in Canada, implied at the time that this was indeed the case: "The four are not the only ones here. I could name you twenty living in Montreal. I have one working for me now. There was another here in this office this morning, a man under sentence of death with no passport at all. Nearly all the rest are here under false passports—naturally...."[12] Certainly the Americans were secretly harbouring Klaus Barbie and using him as a spy throughout this period. Was Canada involved in a similar scheme? Were Barbie and de Bernonville in contact with one another at that time? Did the French collaborators provide intelligence on Communists? These questions have never been answered.

I am loath to implicate the Canadian government in any widespread plot to smuggle Nazis. Canada was certainly not a major player in the international intelligence community. Yet— whether for purely domestic political considerations or otherwise—Canada, regardless of stated government policy, willingly participated more than once in harbouring war criminals. In the words of historian Alti Rodal, "There was often a gap between what government policy was and what actual practice was."[13] Whatever the extent of that gap, it is shocking to think that this country's leaders were so insensitive to the horrors of the

Holocaust that pressures to provide refuge to its perpetrators took precedence over every moral consideration.

Chapter Four

Forty Years of Inaction

Upon their arrival in this country, Nazi war criminals unobtrusively built new lives for themselves, taking cover among a population unconcerned by their presence. For the better part of forty years, successive governments and private citizens alike preferred to turn the other cheek and ignore the fact that the killers of innocent people might have found refuge within our borders.

Whether the Canadian authorities failed to appreciate the gravity of the atrocities perpetrated or simply did not care, they chose a deliberate policy of inaction. Their indifference was widespread. It was manifest in the haphazard destruction of immigration records; in the advice of government legal advisers who persistently argued that nothing could or should be done to prosecute war criminals in spite of the precedent set by the trial of major Nazi criminals at Nuremberg; and in the RCMP's "hands-off" policy in force for almost four decades.

In its haste to sweep aside the horrors of the Holocaust, Canada may well have taken a cue from Britain. The occupying Allied forces had failed miserably in their postwar efforts to de-Nazify Germany. In fact, historians argue that Nazis, among them those who had given orders for extermination, deportation, plunder and enslavement, had been appointed by the British and Americans to head up the rehabilitation of Germany. The Allies also feared that Germany's support for the West would be inhibited by continuing prosecution of German soldiers. So, with Europe's political future in mind, the British government deemed it expedient, in late 1947 and early 1948, to wind up its war crimes program in Germany and drop the prosecution of Nazi criminals from its list of priorities. Some commentators say this was the price West German Chancellor Konrad Adenauer demanded from the Western allies in return for his promise to rearm Germany and make it an anti-Soviet bastion.[1] As a result, thousands of suspected war criminals held by the British in Germany were let loose without being tried.[2] How quickly the United Kingdom had turned its back on Winston Churchill's 1941 pledge in the House of Commons: "We have but one aim and one single, irrevocable purpose. We are resolved to destroy Hitler and every vestige of the Nazi regime." [3]

On July 13, 1948, the British government issued a secret cable to the seven Dominions of the Commonwealth detailing the newly developed policy, which was produced before the Deschênes Commission. It directed that "as many as possible of cases which are still awaiting trial should be disposed of by 31st August, 1948 [uncompleted trials which began before that date would continue]." Also, "no fresh trials should be started after 31st August, 1948. This would particularly affect cases of alleged war criminals, not now in custody, who might subsequently come into our hands." The message continued, "In our view, punishment of war criminals is more a matter of discouraging future generations than of meting out retribution to every guilty individual. Moreover, in view of future political developments in Germany envisaged by recent tripartite talks, we are convinced that it is now necessary to dispose of the past as soon as possible."

My own reaction to this telegram is utter dismay. The notion that we can discourage future generations by letting the guilty go free is a perversion of justice. If we are genuinely committed to the principle of deterrence, we must arrest, prosecute and convict those who have perpetrated crimes in the past. The adage that "those who ignore history are condemned to repeat it" suggests that in order to avoid the repetition of tragedies, we cannot simply ignore them. There can be only one way to truly dispose of the past—by dealing with it, not by turning a blind eye to it.

In any event, Canada did not challenge the edict. When invited to respond, the government had "no comment to make." Whether the British directive actually thwarted the Canadian government from bringing war criminals to justice or simply confirmed Canada's own inclination to do nothing is a matter of speculation. Up until then, Canadian forces overseas had launched their own prosecutions and held public trials in the

British occupied zone of Germany. The army convicted General Kurt Meyer and sentenced him to death by shooting. His sentence was later commuted to life imprisonment, and Meyer was imprisoned in Canada. He was eventually sent back to Germany, where he died. Six more accused were found guilty of war crimes at three separate trials and further cases were pending. No Nazi war crimes trials had been conducted in Canada. But at the behest of Britain, the matter of war criminals faded into oblivion and our government did not lift a finger to seek out and prosecute offenders for the next forty two years.

At the outset, the decision not to pursue Nazis in this country was not enunciated. From 1945 to 1962, Canada's law enforcement agency, the RCMP, had no formal guidelines relating to the investigation of war criminals, but its unwritten policy was clear: hands off. Neither this country's elected representatives nor its civil servants possessed the resolve or moral sensibility to initiate action. And, other than from the Jewish community, pressure was not forthcoming from a public that for the most part chose to remain unaware of Nazi criminals hiding within our borders. Canadians, it seemed, were enveloped by a sense of insularity: war criminals were primarily a foreign problem, of concern only to European nations. Other priorities, including the perceived threat of Communism, meant that the prosecution of Nazis was relegated to the back burner.

Indeed, by the mid-fifties, the Holocaust was a closed chapter. In Canada, as in many countries, a self-imposed silence had fallen on the worst genocide in history. The international community was only too anxious to forget its capacity for human depravity, and Canada was no exception.

Then, with the advent of the 1960s, came the sensational news that Israel had captured Adolf Eichmann, who, as architect of Hitler's Final Solution, had directed the murders of Europe's six million Jews. Eichmann, a former vacuum cleaner salesman, joined the Nazi Party in 1932 and quickly worked his way up the SS. In 1940, he was appointed head of the Gestapo's Jewish affairs department, responsible for the liquidation of Jewish communities throughout occupied Europe. One year later, Heinrich Himmler, Hitler's lieutenant, and Reinhard Heydrich, head of the Gestapo, promoted him to the rank of major and put him in complete charge of "the final solution of the Jewish problem." From this platform he directed the Jewish extermination program over the next six years. His 1962 trial and execution in Israel's Ramlah prison made headlines around the globe. For the first time since the immediate postwar period, the events of the Holocaust emerged under the glaring lights of public scrutiny, giving birth to a new popular awareness which would grow slowly over the years. Israel's chief prosecutor Gideon Hausner observed later in his memoirs, *Justice in Jerusalem*, that Eichmann's trial had served to unite, around the world, Jews and Gentiles, humanitarians, and morally sensitive individuals in the determination that there would never be another Holocaust. (Hausner also noted that the very countries who fought Hitler on the battlefield turned a blind eye to death and concentration camps and continue to do so to this day.)

But even as the Eichmann affair became the focus of international attention, at home, apathy prevailed when it came to dealing with the reality of war criminals within our borders. The same year that Eichmann was put to death, Prime Minister John Diefenbaker and his Cabinet were faced with the prospect that a major Nazi war criminal had turned up in a small Ontario town. The alleged sighting was of Joseph Mengele, the infamous Nazi doctor. Given the obscenity of the genocidal experiments carried out by Mengele—Hitler's "Angel of Death"—one might have expected a decisive response from the government and a serious probe into the matter. But it seemed that Canada's unwritten "hands-off" policy had a stultifying effect on the entire investigation of this incident. Unwarranted delays and bureaucratic bungling plagued the case from the outset. For over nine months the RCMP refused to launch an investigation. It became mired in a long chain of correspondence among senior public servants more concerned about the political ramifications of pursuing the matter than about the punishment of war criminals.

On January 14, 1962 a private informant tipped off the Ontario Provincial Police (OPP) that a man named Joseph Menke residing in Washington, Ontario, was really Nazi war criminal Joseph Mengele.[4] In reality, the suspect's name was George Menk, but the investigating officers proceeded under the mistaken assumption that his name was Joseph Menke. In fact, both names were aliases of Mengele's. A report was made the following day:

"Provincial Constable J[ohn] McPherson, Woodstock Detachment, reported by telephone that he had received the following information from a reliable person who wishes to remain anonymous.
Joseph Menke, since 1960, has resided on a farm at Washington, Ontario, in the County of Oxford about 12 miles from Woodstock. It is suggested that *Joseph Menke* actually is *Joseph MENGELE*, a German War Criminal, who fled Germany to South America and then to Canada.
It is believed that he was born in Germany, March 19, 1911. He has a stepson 21 years of age and several dogs. He drives a 1957 General Motors car, make unknown. Visitors are not welcome at his farm."

The OPP passed this information over to the RCMP. The RCMP, at a loss over what to do, sought instructions from the Departments of Justice and External Affairs. Over the next three months, as the RCMP sat on the case, a flurry of internal memoranda went back and forth. By April 10, the OPP, dismayed at the lack of action, alerted the RCMP that the informant was becoming impatient. On April 19, 1962, RCMP Superintendent C.W.J. Goldsmith, officer in charge of the Criminal Investigations Branch, responded to the OPP:

"We regret the delay in pursuing this investigation, however, we feel that a definite policy in handling suspected war criminals must be established by the government, particularly the Departments of Justice and External Affairs, in view of the international and political implications involved. Pursuant to this opinion we have corresponded with the Department of Justice requesting that some definite policy be established for guidance in such delicate investigations.
2. As you can appreciate, if enquiries were conducted and it was established that MENKE is in fact MENGELE, we should know in advance what we can do with him legally. Enquiries of this nature, of course, involve interpretation and application of Treaties, which, in turn, implicate the government. We feel it is essential that we know where we are going and what we intend to do

when we get there, prior to conducting extensive enquiries, which although conducted discreetly, could
result in publicity.
3. We appreciate the apparent anxiety of Constable
McPherson, however, hope that you will explain our
position and feelings on the problem and assure him
that we are pursuing the matter with the intention to do
everything possible to successfully conclude the en-
quiry. We will advise you as soon as we have received
definite instructions from the Department of Justice.
The interest and assistance of your Force is very much
appreciated."

The RCMP wanted to know "where we are going and what
we are going to do when we get there" before even considering
whether to mount an investigation. But this request for direction
in handling the file created a tizzy among senior federal policy
advisers about what should be done and led to numerous inter-
departmental meetings and memos to consider the options. In
1985, the contents of those top secret exchanges were released
to the *Toronto Star* through Canada's Access to Information Act.[5]
Although the names of the two suspects under consideration
were blacked out it is fair to conclude one was Mengele because
of the timing of the correspondence, the terminology used and
the description of one suspect as being wanted by West
Germany, Poland and Israel. With the release of these
documents, it became all too apparent just how little the concept
of justice meant to those handing advice to Diefenbaker's
government.

The Cabinet of the day was counselled not to prosecute
Nazi war criminals. To do so, went the opinion, would appear to
be pandering to Jewish groups seeking revenge. One senior official opposed the opening of any investigation into the identification of two alleged Nazis by Jewish groups because "it smacks
very strongly of a witch-hunt." In a classified memo dated May
25, 1962, John A. Donald of External Affairs European division
wrote to the consular division, "Both cases have been brought to
light in what looks like a spirit of revenge instigated by Jews;
And in my view anti-Jew-baiting by the Jews is just as reprehensible as Jew-baiting by the Nazis." Donald added that the interest
of the Jewish community in the pursuit of war criminals "should

not be allowed to carry any weight—political or otherwise—in arriving at a decision in respect of possible war crimes committed by [suspects' names blacked out]"

Donald M. Cornett, an External Affairs official in the consular division, took much the same approach in his memo of June 1, 1962: "Our view is that it does not rest with the Canadian government to determine whether war crimes have been committed or whether Canada is harbouring war criminals."

Officials also warned about the dangers of straining relations with West Germany and Third World countries that had, in fact, little interest in Nazi atrocities. Jean Fournier, of the legal division of External Affairs felt that the RCMP were wise to move cautiously and await guidance from the government before going forward. "An investigation", he wrote on May 17, 1962, "might well be inimical to our relations with the German Federal Republic and should therefore be undertaken only for good cause. He did point out, however, "If the government were to take no action, it might be subject to some criticism by the Jewish community. This consideration must be weighed against the one set out above."

On June 30, undersecretary of state for External Affairs Norman Robertson sent a memorandum to the External Affairs minister of the day, Howard Green, outlining the political realities confronting Cabinet. The advantages of an investigation included demonstrating to the world that "we were not prepared to tolerate people of this kind in Canada" and providing a strong response to claims by the Soviet Union that Canada was harbouring war criminals. On the other hand, by exposing suspected war criminals here, Canada would be providing the Soviet Union and its allies with ammunition for their anti-German propaganda campaign. Robertson added that Canada "would be unlikely to make any great impression on the governments of under-developed countries to whom Nazi atrocities of 20 years ago seem less important than their own recent experiences." And finally, even though West German authorities "could scarcely refuse to ask for the extradition of a war criminal, they were not likely to be pleased with their past: If they were given a choice, they would probably prefer that we let sleeping dogs lie."

The general consensus was that no completely effective legal remedies were readily available to take measures against suspected war criminals. At best, if the case were of "crucial importance", it might be possible to extradite one of the suspects to West Germany. This was the type of negative thinking that prevailed over the next twenty years, and which would thread its way through the highly pessimistic Low Report of 1981.

I cannot continue with this story and Cabinet's reaction to the memoranda without some comment on the views they express. First, I reject the notion that the pursuit of Nazi war criminals is a witch-hunt. What is wrong with a witch-hunt is that it seeks to find something that is not there: there are, after all, no witches, and innocent people suspected of sorcery are victimized. Nazi war criminals and their crimes, on the other hand, do exist. To equate the two is a form of Holocaust denial. It implies that the criminals do not exist. Labelling the search for Mengele a witch-hunt is a way of saying that Mengele committed no crimes.

Secondly, the desire for justice has nothing to do with revenge. Vigilantism would constitute revenge, but invoking the Canadian legal system to bring murderers to trial is not vengeance. Rather, it is the quest for simple justice. Nor is the punishment of Nazi war criminals is not merely in the interest of the Jewish community. When we prosecute murderers we do so in the interest of society as a whole—not just for the benefit of the victims' relatives. A society that considers murder a solely private matter between the killer and the family of the victim is not a society governed by law.

To suggest that the prosecution of Nazi war criminals is anti-Jew-baiting is a travesty of logic. Jew-baiting is the provocation and bullying of Jews because of their religion. There is all the difference in the world between prosecuting someone for a crime and persecuting someone because of his religion. To blur that distinction is to blur the distinction between innocence and guilt.

Any suggestion that Canada should take no responsibility for Nazi war criminals found here flies in the face of international law and our own obligations to the global community. In the United Nations, Canada has repeatedly spoken up for the principle that the prosecution of war crimes and crimes against humanity constitutes a universal commitment for all states. How could we urge other nations to prosecute war criminals and do nothing at home? Arguments that Third World countries or West

Germany would prefer Canada to do nothing are equally false. Most of these nations have consistently supported United Nations resolutions denouncing Nazism and calling for prosecution of war criminals. West Germany has its own mechanism in place to deal with Nazi war criminals.

The pursuit of Nazi war criminals in this country does not provide ammunition for Soviet propaganda. In fact, the reverse is true. Our refusal to take measures against war criminals in Canada serves as much better grist for the Soviet propaganda mill. What a field day the U.S.S.R. would have had if the man in Washington, Ontario, had turned out to be Joseph Mengele, and Canada had decided to put the matter to bed.

Whatever the logic of the arguments used by officials at the time, they convinced Cabinet to adopt its first formal policy on Nazi war criminals: a definitive "do-nothing" approach. Nevertheless, before any final conclusions were reached on the precise wording of the policy, the RCMP was given the go-ahead to accumulate information about Mengele's appearance. By now it was late June. George Bailey, at that time chief visa control officer in Cologne, wrote to the Central Registry of the U.S. Army Europe (USAEUR) requesting descriptive information on "Joseph Menke, alias of Mengele." Bailey, now retired, testified before the Deschênes Commission that inquiries concerning alleged Nazi war criminals were routine during that period. Yet, neither the name Mengele nor Menke meant anything to him in 1962. One can only speculate whether his lack of familiarity led to a more cursory investigation by the visa control office than was warranted for a criminal of Mengele's magnitude. On June 26, Bailey received the USAEUR file on Mengele. Additional European sources were also checked.

Two weeks later, on July 10, OPP Constable McPherson took RCMP officers Daniel Webster and Harvey Blythe to the Woodstock farm of Menk, only to find he had departed for destinations unknown. Menk was later located by Officer Blythe in Kitchener, Ontario. On July 20, the OPP file was closed on the recommendation of Constable McPherson . From the end of July until early September, the RCMP continued its investigation, conducting title searches on the Menk farm (which had been sold earlier) and showing photographs of Mengele to locals. Not until September, some nine months after the allegation was first made, did the government come to a decision about what should be done. In a letter dated September 11, 1962, Norman Robertson advised External Affairs that there should be a "cautious and confidential" investigation to see whether at least one of the suspects under consideration could be deported to West Germany to stand trial.

The authorities ultimately determined that the person in Washington, Ontario, was not Joseph Mengele. While it appears they were right in concluding that Mengele had not come to Canada, given their methodology, they might have come to the same conclusion even if he had. Their finding was made on very weak bases, including the fact that Menk had made several trips to Germany and was actually in that country as the investigation was winding up. "His trips to Germany would suggest that he is not Mengele as he would no doubt be recognized if he returned", stated a report made August 16 by the RCMP to the Justice Department. That the RCMP lost track of their suspect during the investigation, enabling him to leave the country without their knowledge, hints at the sloppiness of the investigation. On September 6 the RCMP reported that identification of Menk by photographs of Mengele had proven negative. The final document remaining in the RCMP Mengele file, though, was not entirely conclusive on the issue of identification. That correspondence stated that "inquiries to date suggest that Menk was not identical to Dr. Joseph Mengele. However, further inquiries were being conducted to verify this matter." And that is where the file ended. There was no evidence before the Deschênes Commission to suggest the investigation was ever definitively completed—it simply faded away.

Because the suspect in Washington, Ontario, did not turn out to be Mengele, it is of no consequence that he eventually left the country for good. But it remains disturbing that any person alleged to be a notorious war criminal should the subject of such a tentative investigation delayed for months on end. The investigating officer on the case, Harvey Blythe, was unable, when testifying before the Deschênes Commission more than twenty years later, to offer any explanation:

> Q: Can you, from your involvement in July '62, explain that time gap?
> A: No, I am sorry, I can't. I really can't.
> Q: Does it surprise you?

A: It seems like a bit of delay, I would suggest, although the correspondence may have come in, I suppose to—it may have even gone to headquarters in Ottawa and back through to Toronto. But it seems little excessive.

One other factor is also troubling. The police investigated the suspect for the purpose of determining whether he was Joseph Mengele. But Joseph Menke is the actual name of another senior Nazi wanted as a war criminal. At no time did the RCMP make any checks into the possibility that the suspect, if not Mengele, might indeed be Joseph Menke. They were not even aware that a war criminal named Menke existed. It was just one of many stones left unturned.

The only result of the Mengele affair was a clear decision by the government that it wanted no part of cases like these. Within weeks, an explicit policy was handed down to all RCMP personnel through a circular dated September 28, 1962, entitled "War Criminals":

"1. In view of the possibility that individuals or organizations may attempt to employ the Force as an investigational agency for groups engaged in locating and punishing individuals suspected of war crimes, unless otherwise instructed by Headquarters, Ottawa, investigations into allegations of this nature are not to be conducted by the Force.
2. Although some of the alleged offences may have been committed in territory now under the control of West Germany, the majority of the offences will have taken place in the areas now under Communist control. Even though it may be shown that persons now resident in Canada were responsible for war crimes, Canadian Courts have no jurisdiction over such offences and Canada has no Extradition Treaty with Germany, the U.S.S.R. or Poland.
3. When a complaint or information is received that a resident of Canada is guilty of war crimes, our jurisdictional position should be explained and the informant advise that, if he wishes to pursue the matter, he should contact the Department of External Affairs.

4. Information of this nature may be of interest from the Immigration or Security and Intelligence aspect and further enquiries along those lines may be feasible; however, enquiries are not to be conducted for the primary purpose of determining whether or not a person is responsible for a war crime."

It is truly incredible that a complaint about a Nazi war criminal in Canada would be considered an attempt to divert the RCMP from its true purposes or that an investigation of this type amounted to a personal or private matter. One of the primary functions of the RCMP has always been to look into serious allegations of murder. The RCMP are mandated to investigate murder suspects. Why should Nazi murderers have been treated differently?

Yet this "hands-off" policy of the RCMP and a firm resolve not to deal with war crimes in Canadian courts was to persist for the next twenty years. As a consequence, no specific resources were dedicated to investigating allegations against suspected war criminals. And so, any individual cases, regardless of their merits, were simply left to gather dust. From the period of 1946 until 1982, when the policy was amended, only forty-two allegations were pursued. Of those, five were investigated by the RCMP's Criminal Investigation Branch, and the rest were handled purely as non-criminal security matters by the Security Service of the RCMP.

The interest in the Holocaust generated by the Eichmann trial continued to grow throughout the 1960s and 1970s. The Nazi genocide could no longer be dismissed as a historical aberration perpetrated by a group of madmen. Instead, as an event which involved widespread collaboration, the Holocaust slowly took on a new dimension as an integral part of Western history. An enormous body of scholarship developed. No longer merely a "private Jewish agony," the Holocaust became a concern to the community at large.[6] Jews and non-Jews alike were ready to look directly at the Holocaust.

Many factors were responsible. Brushes with neo-Nazism in Canada and elsewhere presented a real and immediate threat to a whole new generation of people who were too young to have lived through the Second World War. Holocaust survivors began to speak out as, little by little, they emerged from the trauma of their tragedy. Jewish activism in North America gained momentum in the wake of Israel's triumph in the 1967 Six Day War. In the early seventies a small number of vocal advocates in the United States began a seven-year struggle to set up a mechanism to bring to justice Nazi war criminals in that country.

A growing Canadian awareness that something had to be done about Nazi war criminals in our midst was not reflected by any change in the government's stance. Nonetheless, by the late seventies, the matter of war criminals had crept onto the parliamentary agenda at the urging of concerned individuals and groups. In 1979, the impetus to take action at home grew out of the pending expiration of the German Statute of Limitations, which would have meant an end to further war crimes prosecutions in that country. A world-wide protest convinced West Germany to extend its deadline indefinitely, and Canada's ambassador to Bonn lent his voice to that international outcry. The same year, another important development occurred south of the border. The Carter administration took definitive action against war criminals by setting up the Office of Special Investigations, a permanent organization within the Justice Department. Canadians, dismayed that their own government did nothing in the face of affirmative steps elsewhere, and fearful that Nazi criminals fleeing the U.S. might seek refuge here, began to apply pressure.

Public consciousness had thus been awakened by the time the Liberals swept back into power in 1980 after Joe Clark's short-lived Conservative government. Robert Kaplan, the newly-appointed solicitor-general, had long been a spokesman for action against war criminals, and armed with a firm resolve to address the issue and the very real power to direct the RCMP, Kaplan undertook a number of initiatives.

Within three days on the job, he requested a full briefing from both the RCMP and the Justice Department on the various options available for dealing with Nazi war criminals. Their bleak report was hardly news: in keeping with past opinion, the prospects for action were viewed as extremely dismal. Government legal experts continued to rule out all remedies, although they did leave the door open ever so slightly to the possibility of extradition to another country. But Kaplan learned soon enough that extradition requests involving war criminals had just stopped coming because of Canada's long-standing failure to co-operate. In short, he said, when it came to the matter of war criminals, "the results were there for anyone who got the inside story, as I did very quickly, which was that nothing was happening." Kaplan pursued the extradition option, and later toured Western Europe in an effort to determine whether any of those countries would be prepared to request the extradition of war criminals residing in Canada. "I wanted...to convince countries which might have given up...that Canada would respond and would co-operate, according to our treaties, to move war criminal extradition requests forward." Kaplan would continue to explore the route of extradition throughout his time in office.

Early in his mandate, Kaplan also led a team of senior government officials to meet with Simon Wiesenthal in Washington, D.C. On the same visit, he established personal contact with the director of the newly established Office of Special Investigations, Allan Ryan. According to his testimony before the Deschênes Commission, these meetings generated a great deal of attention among Canadians. "There was a lot of publicity—an amount that surprised me—that confirmed to me that there was a large public interest in the issue....Another outcome of [the meetings] was a great series of representations to me and, in general, to members of Parliament and to the Government of Canada from Canadian citizens about alleged war criminals in Canada. Without our yet having confirmed the basis on which the government would proceed to deal with war criminals, we were already getting quite a lot of names put forward and allegations put forward about people said to be in Canada."

Despite Kaplan's strong personal commitment to taking measures against Nazi war criminals and a surge of optimism on the part of the public, the Trudeau Cabinet remained unresponsive. Strong factions within the government maintained that the original "do-nothing" policy needed to be reasserted. Kaplan was placed in an untenable position. On the one hand, he was fighting an uphill battle inside Cabinet for action on Nazi war criminals. At the same time, the principle of Cabinet solidarity forced him to act as apologist to a disappointed electorate for a government that refused to act.

In an effort to overcome the resistance of his Cabinet colleagues, Kaplan initiated an inter-departmental committee in the spring of 1980 under the chairmanship of Department of Justice lawyer Martin Low, then executive assistant to the deputy minister of Justice and deputy attorney-general of Canada. Representatives of the Secretary of State, the Departments of Justice, External Affairs, National Defence, the Solicitor-General, and from the Employment and Immigration Commission, the Privy Council Office and the RCMP were asked to review Canadian law thoroughly and examine the routes for legal action against Nazi war criminals. After one full year of deliberations, the committee came out with a report, entitled *Alleged War Criminals in Canada*, which only reaffirmed the government's long-standing tradition of inaction. In the words of Martin Low, who testified before the Deschênes Commission, the committee's work was intended "to reconcile any differences that might have existed" with respect to the issue of Nazi war criminals. Its effect, in my words, was to bring Robert Kaplan into line.

The discussion paper that the committee delivered in February 1981 was long, detailed, technical—and extremely one-sided. The Low memorandum argued, in effect, that no legal remedies existed to bring Nazi war criminals in Canada to justice. This fresh examination of the law after more than thirty years of continual negativism had come up dry! Worse, in reaching the conclusion that nothing could be done, the report had irresponsibly left out every contrary legal argument and all the laws and precedents that offered a contradictory view. The historic Nuremberg Trials, which represent the strongest precedent in international law for trying war criminals, were not once referred to in the entire document. Because the discussion paper was treated as top secret, its views were never given a public airing, a virtual guarantee that it would never be rebutted openly by legal minds outside the narrow confines of government. The memorandum remained classified until its release in 1985 as an exhibit in the Deschênes Commission.

The study may not have been specifically designed to squelch Robert Kaplan and bamboozle the entire Cabinet. But that had to be the inevitable result of how the Low committee carried out its mandate. Faced with a document devoid of alternative approaches, what could Cabinet possibly do? The elected executive are not technical experts in the area of international law. When the Low committee wrote its very limiting report, it virtually painted Trudeau's Cabinet into a corner. The government's path was clear: continue to do nothing.

Barren as the Low memorandum was, it had not, as mentioned, completely slammed the door on extradition. Kaplan, now trapped by a document which provided cold comfort for those concerned with the punishment of Nazi murderers, seized upon this one opportunity for action. At the same time, Cabinet expressed a new willingness to co-operate in extradition requests from other nations with which Canada shared a treaty. If a second nation were prepared to point its finger at a suspect living in Canada, the government would play ball. The RCMP were ordered to step up their investigations of allegations that had been flowing in for some time. At meetings between Kaplan and the RCMP specific allegations were examined to determine whether they could form the basis of extradition requests.

These initiatives eventually led to the trial of Helmut Rauca in the spring of 1982. Rauca had been sought by the West German authorities for years, and in fact, they had requested his extradition from Canada as early as 1973. At that time, Canadian authorities seemed incapable of locating him. When Kaplan first became involved with the case he was informed by the RCMP that Rauca had been discovered in his suburban Toronto home, packing. Following a tense period of around-the-clock surveillance while the crucial documents needed to make the arrest were being gathered, Rauca was apprehended, brought to trial and extradited to West Germany. He died shortly after his arrival in that country.

The Rauca case will be remembered as the first time in Canadian history—after a delay of more than thirty years—that this country took a firm stand against one of an uncounted number of war criminals hiding among its citizens. From the legal standpoint, the case is rife with irony. Only one year before, the Low memorandum had emphatically maintained that no remedies existed in Canadian law to prosecute Nazi war criminals. Yet, Rauca's lawyers rested their entire defence on the argument that there were plenty of alternative legal avenues in Canada that precluded the court from ordering their client's extradition, which they considered a solution of last resort. In the meantime, the Canadian Jewish Congress war crimes committee, which I was heading at that time, had just completed a comprehensive study outlining every possible legal means to deal with war criminals in Canada. Ironically, in listing all the options, our own paper appeared to support the very position put forward by Rauca's lawyers! Our timing could not have been worse. We fervently believed that action by the government was urgent, but at the same time, we were not prepared to add fuel to the Rauca defence by handing our brief over to his lawyers. This absurd coincidence forced us to hold off on making our report public until the legal process in the Rauca matter was exhausted.[7]

In the wake of Rauca's extradition came about a long overdue change in the RCMP's policy, finally making the investigation of war crimes allegations obligatory. In April 1983, the policy manual was amended to include the following provision: "Upon receipt of information that a suspected war criminal is in Canada, an investigation *shall* be conducted to substantiate the information." (emphasis added) Mandatory investigation of complaints has always been routine in every other area of RCMP activity, and now, for the first time, its war crimes policy was brought into conformity with standard practice. Since that change, some 252 investigations were initiated up until the Deschênes Commission began its work. Yet the new, broadly worded policy may have been severely restricted by official interpretation indicating that "ultimate extradition appears to be the purpose of the investigation." Whether one was to presume from this that individuals not considered by the RCMP to be extraditable were never pursued did not emerge during the course of the Deschênes inquiry.

Inconceivably, that very year, two alleged Nazi war criminals were allowed to enter Canada by a senior Mountie who believed the war crimes issue was no longer relevant. At least one of the pair had a Waffen SS background. The incident became public knowledge for the first time with the release of the Rodal study in August, 1987. It is hard to believe that the country's law enforcement agency was deliberately defying the expressed will of the government to take action against Nazi war criminals. But, according to the Rodal report, the Mountie in question and other key officials "whose sympathies inclined them towards leniency with regard to alleged Nazis" facilitated the entry of the two suspects by destroying records and disregarding regulations. "It is noteworthy," adds Rodal, "that this officer, described by another RCMP officer as 'quite right-wing,...and who regards the war criminals issue as blown all out of proportion by the

Jewish lobby,' would have been assigned the task of security screening prospective immigrants from Germany." He was transferred to other duties when the incident came to light within the government. It was as Ms. Rodal aptly described later, "a replica of what was happening in the 40s and early 50s when people who had sympathetic leanings towards people with Nazi backgrounds"[8] were in positions to make decisions on individuals' entry into Canada.

• • •

Like Canada's quiet code of inaction, the official record retention and destruction policies mirrored the government's apathy when it came to banishing war criminals from this country. Admission records are invaluable tools in identifying and locating persons who applied for immigration, and in finding evidence about what they did in the past. The judicial process of deporting or revoking the citizenship of a suspected war criminal involves a comparison between his actual activities during World War II, and his declarations to Canadian authorities in applying for immigration or citizenship. The purpose is to uncover fraud, false representations, or the concealment of material circumstances. Any of these are grounds for expulsion. Unfortunately, immigration file destruction policies have left huge gaps in the records that can only hamper efforts to bring suspected war criminals to justice.

Completed application forms were routinely destroyed in accordance with file "retirement" schedules which had been in effect since the Second World War up to the Deschênes inquiry. Copies of documentation circulated between Canada and immigration posts in Europe, and whether at home or abroad, all files were destroyed in due course. The typical retention period was two years. Application forms were slated for destruction whether the prospective immigrant was accepted or rejected. These files could have been retained on microfilm, a brand-new development in the immediate postwar years. The Americans did microfilm their records, but Canada chose not to.

A long string of archivists and records administrators from External Affairs, Immigration, Public Archives and the RCMP outlined to the Deschênes Commission their file retirement schedules in minute detail. They brought in mounds of paperwork itemizing the thousands of files destroyed over the years. Then some surprising news surfaced concerning the recent destruction of a large batch of immigration files which had accumulated since the war.

The story unfolded through the testimony of Robert Kaplan. As the extradition case of Helmut Rauca made its way through the courts, the RCMP began working up cases against other suspected war criminals throughout 1983 and 1984. "I was told," said Kaplan, "and I believe, in any event that the Mounties felt that they had two winners and another one that was in the works". During the course of their inquiries, the RCMP were informed that a significant number of immigration files which had been earmarked for destruction had not actually been destroyed. They believed that these files held information pertinent to the cases they were investigating. When the RCMP sought access to those files, Kaplan testified, "they found that in the very recent past a tremendous number of them had been destroyed."

Kaplan learned the reasons from RCMP Commissioner Simmonds in April 1984: "After we had been under the impression that almost total file destruction had occurred on a routine basis since the end of the War, it turned out that a large number of files had been shipped to National Archives and that in 1982 someone had determined that those were documents of only historical interest, not of any operational interest, and that therefore the quantity should be reduced in order to save something like 680 feet of shelf space. So in July of 1982 a representative sample was taken out, namely all of the cases that began with 'F', and every other letter of the alphabet was destroyed."

The file destruction occurred in the midst of the highly publicized Helmut Rauca affair, and during that same period, the inter-departmental committee on war criminals was also active. Mr. Kaplan and his officials could not believe it. "We were absolutely furious about it. It just seemed incomprehensible at that particular time that my officials and the RCMP would be foiled that way, if I can put it in that expression, by a file destruction policy working in thin air." Incredulous, Kaplan wondered, "How could you apply a good housekeeping measure to files whose utility was the matter of the earnest attention of the government at the time?"

On May 22, 1984, Deputy Solicitor-General Fred E. Gibson, wrote to Kaplan: "The [RCMP] Commissioner's correspondence does not offer an opinion upon whether such destruction involved á culpable act, or was 'simply' a monumental blunder. What is clear is that the loss of these records, whose destruction should not have taken place, has seriously impaired the ability of Canadian authorities, notably the RCMP, to investigate and take effective action against war criminals in Canada."

In response to this "strange situation" elicited by the evidence, the Commission probed further, under what Mr. Justice Deschênes described as "a cloud of rumours of a conspiracy to destroy files which might have compromised people suspected of war crimes." Mr. Justice Deschênes called a new round of witnesses to explain what had happened to the files. Upon reviewing all of the evidence, the Commissioner came to the conclusion that the 1982 file destruction had been neither a "culpable act" nor a "monumental blunder." Rather, his report concluded, the incident occurred "in the normal course of the application of a routine policy duly authorized within the federal administration." Even if it was a blunder, he continued, "it would only point to a case where the right hand does not know what the left hand is doing. Here is a group of employees performing their task under schedules approved by the proper authorities. They have never been advised that other authorities may wish to retain the files that they are instructed to destroy."

This, however, is precisely the point. Had the government been serious in its desire to deal with war criminals, guidelines would have required employees to check for immigration forms which might be useful in identifying suspected war criminals. Orders would have issued from the top levels of authority to preserve any pertinent information in those files. And yet, none of the witnesses who participated in the destruction, including those archivists responsible for scanning files to pick out significant information, ever received any instructions to that end.

"Regrettable as the destruction may have been," reported Mr. Justice Deschênes, "those files did not contain material which would have been very helpful in the hunt for Nazi war criminals." With all due respect, there is much evidence to suggest otherwise. For one, they contained names and addresses of immigrants. This was the testimony of Anthony Keenleyside, a solicitor retained by the Commission to examine the remaining "sampling" files. These would have helped to locate and identify Nazi war criminals in Canada. They contained documents signed by immigration applicants agreeing to repay loans made by the Canadian authorities immediately after the war to enable their transportation to this country. Because these forms were completed before the immigrants came into Canada, they could have been used to establish fraud on entry.

Any determination about the relevance of these files should have been made prior to the destruction, not after the fact. In routinely destroying files, the government failed to consider their significance, in terms of the information they might contain on Nazi war criminals, and for their potential contribution to social history. It was argued by one witness that keeping immigration files would have created a mountain of documents in storage at enormous cost. Yet the Americans have managed to overcome this obstacle by microfilming every immigration file and destroying the original. Canada could have done the same.

The destruction of documents continued well into the mandate of the Deschênes Commission, leading me, on May 3, 1985 to introduce a motion requesting that the Commission order all remaining immigration documents to be preserved. It was quite possible that a small number of the older immigration forms had survived, but also, that more recent forms which might contain valuable information would now be destroyed in the normal course, according to routine destruction schedules. It seemed inconceivable that any further proceedings against suspected war criminals should be stymied by newly lost files.

Although counsel for the Government of Canada initially opposed the motion, the following week Department of Justice lawyer Judith McCann gave an undertaking that the government would not destroy any files "which the Commission identifies as relating to war criminals or any files which the Government of Canada identifies through its ongoing review of its records as being relevant to the work of the Commission."

That undertaking gave me some concern. First, it was limited to files identified as relating to war criminals. The Commission may have already identified some people as possible war criminals, but others might not be identified until later. According to the undertaking, their files might be destroyed. Secondly, the undertaking left it up to the Government of Canada to determine whether a file was relevant to the inquiry. Given the govern-

government's position that most immigration applications were not relevant, the risk remained that some useful documents might be lost.

The Commissioner agreed: "As a result of the development of the work of this Commission, it may be that two months from now we might come to the conclusion that indeed we are interested in Mr. X., about whom we have today no information. Then two months from now, we come across information pointing to Mr. X as being a suspect war criminal. Then, if we want to look into the record of Mr. X, in the absence of any other indication today, we may run into the situation where the relevant documents could be destroyed tomorrow by pure bad luck."

A better-defined undertaking was drawn up, which became a new government policy that still stands on the record. It ensures that immigration applications from overseas posts will not be destroyed if the applicant's date of birth is 1927 or earlier which would make the individual eighteen years of age at the end of the war, and where the country of birth of the applicant is a European country, including countries now absorbed by the U.S.S.R. The retained applications would relate only to persons who were granted visas and gained entry to Canada. Instructions will be sent to all posts abroad asking them to review the files which they have on hand and new files, and to note and forward any that contain information that may pertain to war criminals.

Some records do remain. Landing records dating back to 1921 have been retained on a permanent basis, as have pre-1952 ship's manifests. These contain helpful information, including the immigrant's name, age, place of departure and arrival, destination in Canada, accompanying family members and previous occupation. But the records that were lost would have added immeasurably in the effort to bring Nazi war criminals to justice.

This completes the historical account: a sad chronicle of inactivity, obstruction of justice, obfuscation of the law and destruction of valuable documents. It is that history whose course must, for once and for all, come to an end.

Chapter Five

The Nuremberg Tribunal

The International Military Tribunal at Nuremberg represents one of the most important sources for determining what acts were criminal at international law in the period leading up to and during the Second World War. If the Canadian authorities ever doubted the legal basis on which to seek redress against the Nazi fugitives from justice, they would have found ample guidance in turning to the judgment at Nuremberg.

On October 1, 1946, twenty-two accused Nazis were sentenced by the Tribunal: twelve were sentenced to death by hanging; seven received prison terms varying from ten years to life. Three were acquitted. Three of the six organizations on trial were found to be criminal. Described by President Harry Truman as "the first international criminal assize in history"[1] , Nuremberg represented an innovation. Never before had an international court been set up to judge and punish persons guilty of war crimes and crimes against humanity.

The trial had its roots in the declaration of Nazi atrocities by Churchill, Roosevelt and Stalin at the Moscow Conference on November 1, 1943. By virtue of the Moscow declaration, "major criminals, whose offenses have no particular geographical localization...will be punished by the joint decision of the Governments of the Allies." The rest were brought to justice, in accordance with the first part of the declaration, before individual Allied military tribunals. Established by the London Agreement of 1945 under the signature of twenty-three nations and the Charter of the International Military Tribunal, the trial was conducted by the United Kingdom, the U.S.A., France and the U.S.S.R.

Nuremberg established a new procedure, but it did not state new law. In the words of Mr. Justice Robert Jackson, who led the prosecution for the U.S.A., "This Tribunal, while it is novel and experimental, is not the product of abstract speculations nor is it created to vindicate legalistic theories. This inquest represents the practical effort of four of the most mighty of nations with the support of seventeen more [two more joined subsequently], to utilize International Law to meet the greatest menace of our times—aggressive war." World War II was a Nazi war of aggression not only against the Allies and military combatants from the other side, but against innocent civilians, using the military conflict as a cover for its attempt to exterminate the whole Jewish people. The world demanded immediate action against the Nazis, and the Tribunal was a response to that demand.

In 1946, the United Nations General Assembly passed without dissent or abstention a resolution reaffirming the principles of international law recognized by the Charter and the judgment of the Nuremberg Tribunal. This universal acceptance gave Nuremberg a unique quality. Its pronouncements on the international law of war crimes and crimes against humanity must be regarded as authoritative. Any statement by a Tribunal whose judgment has been accepted by all nations of the world must carry more weight than any declaration on international law made by the courts of a single state.

While its principles have been integrated into international law, there are critics who attack the foundations on which it is based. Criticisms generally fall into three areas: one is the notion that Nuremberg unfairly applied "victor's justice"; a second relates to limitations imposed on the defence of the accused; and a third raises the argument that the convicted were punished retroactively. Each of these calls for a response.

Field Marshal Goering, one of the defendants sentenced to hang at Nuremberg, complained that the Tribunal did not measure up to the standards of justice because it failed to call for judges from the neutral and vanquished countries.[2] "Unfortunately," responded Mr. Justice Jackson in his opening speech to the Tribunal, "the nature of these crimes is such that both prosecution and judgment must be by victor nations over vanquished foes. The world-wide scope of the aggressions carried out by these men has left but few real neutrals. Either the victors must judge the vanquished or we must leave the defeated to judge themselves. At the very outset, let us dispose of the contention that to put these men to trial is to do them an injustice entitling them to some special consideration. These defendants may be hard pressed but they are not ill used."

Goering's statements simply cannot be given any weight, not merely because of his crimes or because it was in his interest to undermine the credibility of the Tribunal. More importantly, Goering, who committed suicide hours before his death sentence was to be carried out, viewed the Nuremberg Tribunal as a platform for Nazi propaganda, an opportunity to speak to future Nazi generations. He tried to portray himself as a martyr to the Nazi cause.[3]

In any event, at law, belligerent states have habitually assumed jurisdiction to prosecute captured enemies who have committed war crimes. The legal competence of one country's criminal military courts to try aliens for offences against the Law of Nations has never been questioned. While sovereign states cannot be forced to submit to the laws of a foreign jurisdiction, individuals can. The Nuremberg Tribunal did not exercise jurisdiction over Germany, but over certain German individuals, and as such it was perfectly in keeping with the rule of law.

Criticism that the judges at Nuremberg came only from four victor states is erroneous, for it ignores the mandate given to the Tribunal with the consent and approval of the whole international community. In signing the London Agreement, the governments of twenty-three countries provided the legal basis on which the Tribunal assumed its powers. The subsequent UN resolution affirmed Nuremberg, and neither the Federal Republic of Germany nor the German Democratic Republic have since questioned the legal basis or fairness of the Nuremberg Tribunal.

The independence of the judiciary at Nuremberg is beyond reproach. Although it was set up as a military tribunal, the French, British and American judges were civilians. Only the Soviet judge and one alternate were officers. If the Soviet judiciary was controlled, certainly the judicial traditions of the three Western members of the bench were all based on individual integrity, detachment and learning. No conviction or sentence was handed down without an affirmative vote of at least three of the four judges, ensuring a majority vote of the judges from the United Kingdom, France and the U.S.[4] A parallel situation exists in Canadian domestic law, where Crown counsel, appointed and maintained by the government, regularly litigate before judges also appointed and maintained by the government. Yet the independence of our own judiciary, and the justice they mete out, is never doubted.

Perhaps the strongest proof that Nuremberg was in no way marred by "victor's justice" was the trial itself. The court remained autonomous from the prosecution all the way through the trial, often ruling against it. In the end, two defendants were acquitted. All but six of the accused were acquitted on one or more counts. Said Mr. Justice Jackson in his closing submission, "Of one thing we may be sure. The future will never have to ask, with misgiving, 'What could the Nazis have said in their favour?' History will know that whatever could be said, they were allowed to say. They have been given the kind of trial which they, in the days of their pomp and power, never gave to any man."

Critics also claimed the trial was less than impartial because the statutes adopted by the London Agreement frustrated the defence of *tu quoque* (you also). The Nazis were not the only ones to breach the laws of war, charged the defendants—the Allies were equally guilty. True, the Allied forces did, on occasion, violate the laws of war. But how can one compare their acts with the monstrosities of the Nazis in organizing and perpetrating genocide? By and large, the Allies did not also do what the Nazis had done, leaving very limited scope for the accused to point a finger at their prosecutors and argue *tu quoque.*

In fact, the defence of *tu quoque* was not altogether prohibited. The Charter of the Tribunal permitted each defendant to give any explanation relevant to the charges against him. The *tu quoque* argument was actually raised successfully by the defendant Admiral Doenitz, who was charged with waging unrestricted submarine warfare. He pleaded that the U.S. and Great Britain had also violated the laws of war as they applied to submarine warfare and his defence on this count was accepted.[5]

As for the criticism that Nuremberg retroactively punished people for acts that were not offences when committed, it is best addressed in the words of Chief Prosecutor for the United Kingdom, Sir Hartley Shawcross, who anticipated this concern in his opening speech. "There is no substantial retroactivity in the provisions of the Charter....It fills a gap in international criminal procedure. There is all the difference in saying to a man, 'You will not be punished for what was not a crime at the time you committed it,' and in saying to him, 'You will now pay the penalty for conduct which was contrary to law and a crime when you executed it, although, owing to the imperfection of the international machinery, there was at that time no court competent to pronounce judgement against you.'" The Charter of Nuremberg was not "an arbitrary exercise of power on the part of the victorious Nations", stated the Tribunal, but "the expression of international law existing at the time of its creation."

It is vastly unfair to claim that Nuremberg fell short of the true measure of justice. The trial itself was a triumph of the rule of law over politics. The extraordinary fairness of the proceedings—before independent judges according to international legal standards—stands in stark contrast to the inhumanity of the deeds committed.

Some may debate the historical value of Nuremberg. But its contemporary relevance in setting important precedents for the development of international law is beyond dispute. The Charter of the Tribunal codified the definition of the crimes of aggressive war and the criminal liability of persons acting on behalf of a state, whether under official orders or as members of criminal organizations, such as the SS, the SD, and the Gestapo. It stands as a solid point of reference for international jurists. The judgment at Nuremberg serves as an invaluable guide to Canadian judges in deciding what the law requires and, in some ways, a model on which to base action.

Chapter Six

Remedies

The Nuremberg Tribunal came into being within a year of war's end, while the blood was still fresh on the Nazi murderers' hands. Fewer than eight months earlier, the very courtroom in which the trials took place was an enemy fortress held by the German SS. The sound of the goosestep still reverberated throughout Europe, and horrifying evidence of the Holocaust was all around. Millions of wretched souls were left to wander, displaced by wholesale deportations, enslavement and slaughter—all of them eye-witnesses to the Nazi campaign of terror. Thousands of official German documents attesting to the atrocities buttressed the case for the prosecution. When the trials came to a close, more than seventeen thousand pages of oral evidence and argument had been heard by the court.

Decades later, everything has changed, and yet, nothing has changed. The flux of time, the migration of peoples around the world to build new lives and, in some cases, new identities, the destruction and loss of records and documents, the waning of memories—all of these blur the details of past crimes. But time cannot wash away their brutality. Nuremberg provided a model to bring Nazi war criminals to justice in 1945. It has been left up to future law enforcers to apply that precedent in the context of current realities. And while it may be difficult, it is by no means impossible.

For years, Canadian authorities have chosen to focus only on the obstacles. Yet, against the backdrop of Nuremberg, both domestic and international law offer Canada a number of measures to root out war criminals in this country. Because of the widely varying circumstances surrounding the crimes, their location and the evidence available, no single response will address every case. Despite the problems, there are three legal remedies: extradition to the country where crimes were committed, revocation of citizenship and deportation, and prosecution in Canada under a variety of laws. Each approach has distinctive features and requires different sorts of proof.[1]

All three options require specific evaluations to determine their suitability to a given case. Extradition may hinge on the cooperation of a foreign country in making a request or on the existence of an extradition treaty with a requesting state. To launch a successful prosecution in Canada may mean searching for incontrovertible evidence on crimes perpetrated many years ago on another continent. In some instances, immigration records could be pivotal in attempting to deport a war criminal. It is for the Canadian authorities to select the most appropriate legal mechanism for each individual case.

Over the course of time, every available option has been presented to the government, but each has been met with overwhelming resistance. By contrast, the Commission of Inquiry on War Criminals considered all three upon close scrutiny, to be viable approaches for dealing today with the horrendous crimes committed in the first half of this century.

Extradition

Extradition is a legal procedure designed to facilitate the surrender by one country of a person accused or convicted of a crime committed in the jurisdiction of another country. The formal process is initiated when a foreign country requests that the government of another country arrest a fugitive and hand him or her over for trial. Extradition reflects the time-honoured principle that a criminal should not escape justice in one country by fleeing to another. If Canada accedes to the request, as it did in the case of Helmut Rauca, the fugitive is apprehended and must appear in a Canadian court to determine whether the request is valid. Evidence presented in the extradition hearing must not only set out a crime which corresponds to a crime in the Canadian Criminal Code, but must be strong enough to warrant the initiation of a trial under our own laws, or *prima facie* evidence. All the safeguards and procedures of an ordinary criminal trial are imposed. For Nazi war crimes, extradition offers the distinct advantage of prosecuting persons in the European countries where the crimes actually occurred and witnesses reside.

When available, extradition is by far the most appropriate remedy for dealing with war criminals, as the Rauca case exemplifies. Canadian advocates have proposed a number of ways to expand the scope of this remedy, which in practice, has been limited. First, the procedure depends on the willingness of a foreign country to initiate a request and second, on Canada's willingness to acquiesce. All nations may choose or refuse to enter into operative extradition treaties with other countries. In Canada, the final decision is made by Cabinet under its treaty-making powers. The Canadian government has entered into treaties with Western European countries, but as a matter of policy has declined to negotiate treaties with most Eastern Bloc countries, on the grounds that accused persons sent there might not receive fair trials. If a request were made by one of these countries, Canada would turn it down.

Canada does have operative treaties with four Communist states where Nazi war crimes were committed: Czechoslovakia, Yugoslavia, Romania and Hungary. If previous policy were followed, Canada would likely refuse to extradite Nazi war criminals to these countries, despite the treaties. But a recent case suggests a shift in that position. In 1981, Yugoslavia asked Canada to turn over Dr. Svetislav Rajovic for trial on charges of rape and fraud. He was arrested by the Canadian authorities and later that year surrendered to Yugoslavia where he was prosecuted. Canada would be imposing a double standard if it were prepared to extradite for the offence of rape but not for Nazi war crimes—some of the most atrocious crimes mankind has seen. In 1985, a United States court ordered Nazi war criminal Andrija Artukovic extradited to Yugoslavia for the mass murders of Serbs and Jews. Canada could follow suit and honour an extradition request from any country with which it has an operative extradition treaty.

The vast majority of Nazi war crimes were committed in Poland and the U.S.S.R., with which Canada has refused to enter treaties. One way to expand the extradition remedy to cover crimes committed in these countries is to ask the Federal Republic of Germany to assert broad jurisdiction over war crimes committed in territory that was under the control and direction of Nazi Germany during the Second World War. West Germany did just that when it sought the extradition of Helmut Rauca for crimes he committed in German-held Lithuania. Unfortunately,

Germany has made a practice of seeking extradition only of German nationals, such as Rauca. Local collaborators who committed war crimes in Nazi-occupied Poland, the Ukraine or the Baltic states, for example, have not been pursued by West Germany. As a result, the large number of suspected war criminals in Canada who were not German nationals have not been extraditable under current West German policy. In the United States, this very difficulty led the American government to seek the cooperation of West Germany in requesting the extradition of non-German Nazi war criminals living in the U.S. In a formal statement on February 12, 1982, Germany's minister of Justice acknowledged that his country had the power to do so "in appropriate cases" and agreed to leave the door open to that possibility. Although West Germany has yet to demand the surrender of any non-Germans, Canada could enter into similar cooperative effort with the West Germans to facilitate the extradition of all Nazi war criminals to that country.

Another possibility is for Israel to claim jurisdiction and request extradition of war criminals as a representative of the victims, although the existing Canada-Israel treaty presents problems. Unlike other treaties, it applies only to offences committed within Israeli or Canadian territory and committed after the date the treaty was ratified, March 10, 1967. Nazi war crimes of World War II would not fall under the treaty with its present cut-off date. However, two simple amendments to the treaty would enable Israel to request the extradition of any Nazi war criminal in Canada. The first is would require removing the restriction which limits the treaty's application to crimes committed after 1967 so that it can be invoked for earlier offences. Second, a change in wording would permit Israel to have jurisdiction over offences considered to be universal in nature. War crimes and crimes against humanity fall into that category. Israel has both the political will and a large population of witnesses to the events of the Second World War which make it a suitable arena in which to bring Holocaust perpetrators to justice. In recognition of this reality, the United States has entered into an extradition treaty with Israel that is free of the Canadian restrictions. That enabled the American government to extradite to Israel John Demjanjuk, accused of being "Ivan the Terrible," the brutal gas chamber operator at Treblinka death camp.

Regrettably, the history of the Canada-Israel treaty demonstrates that the Canadian government fully intended to prevent war criminals from being sent to Israel for trial. When Canada signed its treaty with Israel in March 1967, no cut-off date was written in to the agreement. The Canadian government waited two years before bringing it into effect, and then in February 1969 it proposed an amendment to the treaty, incorporating the March 1967 cut-off date. Israel accepted it, and the treaty went into operation as of December. Cut-off dates are a rare feature for Canadian extradition treaties. In fact the only other one is the treaty with Austria, Eichmann's homeland, which was signed and ratified around the same time as the Israeli document. Canada, unlike the U.S., wanted nothing to do with sending the likes of Eichmann or Mengele to Israel. The attitudes manifested in the secret 1962 correspondence in the Department of External Affairs must have led to the unnecessary restriction on the Canada-Israel treaty. These biases have no place in present reality. Canada could amend the treaty to remove the arbitrary cut-off date, and to permit Israel to take extraterritorial jurisdiction over persons who have committed universal crimes.

Advocates have urged that the potential use of extradition should not be limited by hair-splitting over the wording of offences. When a fugitive is sought, Canada should look to the acts alleged to have been committed, and not to the actual wording of the charge by a foreign jurisdiction. Legal language can vary from country to country, and this should not defeat a suitable extradition case. Ottawa has already refused a 1981 extradition request from the Dutch government for the surrender of Jacob Luitjens, a Vancouver resident convicted *in absentia* in 1948 in Holland as a Nazi party member responsible for two deaths and sentenced to twenty years in prison. The Dutch asked that Luitjens be extradited for "aiding and abetting the enemy in time of war." Canada's extradition treaty with the Netherlands, signed in 1899, refers only to the crime of murder, and not complicity with foreign occupation in general. Despite the fact that Luitjens' alleged crimes were considered by the Dutch court that convicted him to be complicity in murder, the Canadian government was not prepared to accede to the extradition request. Canada needs to reassert a fundamental principle of law that "it is the essence of the offence that is important." Suspected Nazi war criminals should not be afforded protection simply because the wording of the extradition request does not strictly adhere to the terminology set out in the treaty.

Denaturalization and Deportation

Deportation is an altogether different method for removing Nazi war criminals from Canada. It is a unilateral measure by the Canadian government expelling an undesirable alien because he did not enter Canada legally in the first place, or because he has done something since his admission to disqualify him from staying. In no way related to extradition, deportation is a civil procedure, calling for proof that the alien in some way violated our immigration laws. His ultimate destination is not the primary focus of a deportation hearing, and is only considered once he has actually been ordered deported. Under the Immigration Act, a deportee is entitled to leave Canada voluntarily and select the country he wishes to go to, provided the minister of Immigration agrees with his choice. If he makes no choice or the Immigration minister does not honour his request, he may be deported to the country of his birth, the country from which he gained entry to Canada, or, if all else fails, to any other country prepared to take him. Unlike extradition, deportation provides no guarantee that a war criminal will be put on trial and punished. It is strictly an internal concern of the recipient country. A deportee who goes to Paraguay and Panama, for example, would likely find his stay all too pleasant. Portugal, where the United States deported Nazi war criminal Valerian Trifa, never showed the slightest interest in prosecuting him. Nor does Canada have any control over the conduct of any trial a deportee might receive in, say, an Eastern Bloc country. The fairness of the justice system in the state of destination is not a valid concern for Canadian immigration authorities in making their determination. The whole point of deportation is to rid the country of someone who should not be here.

A war criminal who was a landed immigrant but who never acquired Canadian citizenship could be brought to deportation proceedings as soon as he or she is discovered by the authorities. However, since most of the suspected Nazi war criminals in this country became naturalized Canadian citizens, they would have to be stripped of their Canadian citizenship before being deported. The entire process, therefore, would actually take place in two stages: first denaturalization, or revocation of citizenship, then deportation. Advocates have urged the government to follow the lead of the United States, which has launched over fifty proceedings through its Office of Special Investigations, a unit of the Justice Department set up to pursue Nazi war criminals.

A person may be denaturalized under our Citizenship Act if he obtained either his citizenship or his admission into Canada under false pretenses. The Citizenship Act of 1946 required an applicant for Canadian citizenship to satisfy a judge that he was of "good character." That statute remained in force until 1977, when it was replaced by the present act. A Nazi war criminal could only have passed the character test by hiding his past activities and could now be denaturalized for fraudulent concealment. When Helmut Rauca applied to become a citizen of this country, the Citizenship judge signed a declaration that stated, "Having examined and heard the applicant herein, the court has concluded and hereby declares that the said applicant is of good character." It goes without saying that had Rauca disclosed the thousands of murders he authorized as an SS master sergeant, that declaration would never have been signed. Because he had fraudulently misrepresented himself as a person of good character, Rauca, like many other war criminals in Canada, was a candidate for denaturalization.

An applicant for Canadian citizenship must also demonstrate that he was lawfully admitted to Canada for permanent residence. If, at the time of landing, he fraudulently concealed or misrepresented facts that would have made him ineligible to enter the country, his later acquired citizenship could be revoked. The prerequisites and prohibitions for entering Canada after World War II were spelled out in the existing Immigration Act, the various regulations and directives of the Immigration Department and Cabinet orders-in-council.

While we have already seen how inadequate the immigration regulations were—they did not specifically exclude "war criminals" as such—a Nazi war criminal would have been prohibited from entry into Canada under one of several categories. German nationals were automatically rejected until November, 1950, and a blanket exclusion for members of the Nazi party remained in place until December, 1950. All members of the Waffen SS were excluded until July 1951 and, after that, members who had joined before January 1943. Persons who were implicated in the taking of life or engaged in activities connected with forced labour and concentration camps were also ineligible to enter the country. All of these people would have failed security clearance had they revealed their true backgrounds.

Any Nazi war criminal who gained admission to Canada, unless granted specific permission by Cabinet order-in-council to override these prohibitions (which, regrettably, did happen) could only have done so by fraudulently concealing his past. Wartime visa control officer Albert Greening and immigration official Joseph Robillard both testified that if a war criminal entered the country without an order-in-council, he must have lied. John McCordick of External Affairs confirmed, "If a person did get through the filter system and got into Canada and had a past of the worst sort of activities, then I'd be sure that part of his success was due to his lying. A pack of lies was part of it." The mere presence in this country of a suspected Nazi war criminal would point to the conclusion that he committed fraud on entry. He could be denaturalized by a court even without documentary proof of fraud.

But documentary evidence is available. Every postwar immigrant to Canada is listed either in a landing record or on a ship's manifest. All landing records and every ship's manifest prior to 1952 are still on file in government archives. These contain important background information which sheds light on other misrepresentations made by Nazi war criminals. Landing records posed the question, "Have you ever been convicted of or do you admit having committed any crime involving moral turpitude?" Any Nazi war criminal who answered "No" was obviously lying. Any immigrant who was not required to fill out a landing record was, at the very least, listed on the ship's manifest. Included among the background questions on this record was, "What trade or occupation did you follow in your own country?" The answer given by Helmut Rauca, for example, was "commercial clerk." Now while it is true that as a teenager he held that occupation, in light of his later career in the Nazi army, that answer was a fraudulent representation designed to conceal his true past, and would have been a ground for denaturalization.

Because all applicants for immigration and citizenship have a duty to disclose their past activities, it may not even be necessary to prove that a person told an out and out lie in response to specific questions asked by an immigration official or contained on a landing document. Under Canadian law, a person who knowingly suppresses facts that affect his eligibility for admission or citizenship can be denaturalized even if he was never directly asked about that information. A Nazi war criminal could be guilty of fraudulent entry simply by failing to volunteer information about his past involvement in persecution. Every person who enters the country or acquires citizenship must accept responsibility for any known gaps in his answers. It would stretch all bounds of belief for any person who took part in the Nazi genocide to claim that he had no idea that the grisly details of his past might bar him from Canada.

Since denaturalization proceedings are not criminal, it is not necessary to present *prima facie* evidence (strong enough evidence to warrant a trial) of war crimes in court.[2] All that must be shown is that a Nazi war criminal residing in Canada "fraudulently foreclosed" or stopped inquiries by immigration or citizenship officials which would have led them to discover his wrongdoings. In the United States, Feodor Fedorenko was deported to the Soviet Union in 1984 because, on entry to the U.S., he failed to tell authorities that he had been a guard at the Nazi extermination camp, Treblinka. Had he done so, officials would have been able to ascertain through further questioning the fact that he had committed war crimes. A U.S. court found that his failure to disclose this fact was sufficient grounds for deportation. The situation is identical in Canada.

Even after 1950, when membership in the Nazi party was no longer grounds for automatic rejection, immigration officials continued to routinely ask applicants about past Nazi involvement. Acknowledgment of Nazi party membership would have led officials to ask additional questions to determine whether an individual was a war criminal. Concealment of this fact would have stopped any further inquiries. On that basis alone, a Nazi war criminal could be denaturalized. This is where information on records would be of use. Even if one could find no direct lies on landing records or ships' manifests about whether a person belonged to a prohibited class, it would be possible to show that the partially true answers given prevented officials from digging deeper to discover the truth about a person's criminal past. For example, Helmut Rauca's statement on the ship's manifest that he had been a commercial clerk in Germany was the kind of half-truth that would have put an end to further questioning. It was not a lie, but it was not the whole story. With these records, it is possible to tell whether an individual prevented further inquiries by withholding information or whether his answers were complete enough, but that immigration authorities missed the truth about his past through their own oversights.

Apart from the landing records and ships' manifests, many immigration records of the immediate postwar period have been destroyed. Some still remain, however, due to the government's policy of retaining a random sampling of those files. Immigration files for persons who came to Canada in more recent years may still be in existence. Other sources of records would also be fruitful, such as those maintained by the many outside agencies on which Canada relied for security screening. British intelligence, the Nuremberg Refugee Centre, and the International Refugee Organization all maintained records which might still be available to prove the fraudulent foreclosure of inquiries. For the purposes of a denaturalization hearing, it does not matter that any misrepresentations on these records were not made to Canadian immigration officials, so long as it can be shown that they led to a person's fraudulent admission into Canada.

Although war crimes justice advocates have clearly identified many ways to prove false pretenses and denaturalize under the existing Citizenship Act, the destruction of immigration documents has raised a great deal of controversy about the strength of available evidence. As a result of the gap in records, the onus of mounting sufficient proof may be very difficult in practice, at least in the eyes of government. Because of the controversy surrounding the availability of evidence, advocates have for years been urging the government to amend the statute to make participation in Nazi persecution a distinct ground for denaturalization and to eliminate the need to prove that a person committed fraud on entry or on obtaining citizenship. Robert Kaplan introduced a private member's bill to this effect in Parliament in 1978 and again in 1979, but it was never enacted. With this type of amendment, all war criminals and criminals against humanity would lose the rights and privileges of Canadian citizenship for the very reason of their horrendous actions, and not because they happened to be caught telling lies about them.

Only after citizenship has been revoked, can the process of deportation begin. Under the Immigration Act, the primary ground on which a Nazi war criminal might be deported is for making a misrepresentation of any material fact on entering Canada. Unlike denaturalization, the deportation process does not require proof of fraud. Even an innocent misrepresentation or non-disclosure is sufficient grounds for removing an alien from Canada. A person may be deported even if he had no intent to deceive—his liability is absolute.

Like denaturalization, it is not necessary to prove that a person was a Nazi war criminal to deport him. All that need be established is that through deception, he turned aside inquiries that might have led officials to discover his Nazi past. Opponents of this legal option have complained that, as a civil procedure, it fails to protect suspected war criminals adequately. The standard of proof is lower than that of criminal proceedings. *Prima facie* evidence of war crimes is not necessary. All that need be shown is that, on a balance of probabilities, the person lied on entry. He is entitled to none of the protections of the Canadian Charter of Rights and Freedoms which would be accorded to a defendant in an extradition hearing or a criminal trial. As a result, he may be compelled to testify himself, and he cannot benefit from the presumption of innocence. While the protections to an accused are higher in criminal proceedings, it must be remembered that the penalties are potentially greater as well.

When all is said and done, denaturalization and deportation proceedings are not inherently unfair, even though they may have harsh results at times. Canada has been deporting aliens from Canada for failing to disclose far less damaging information, such as their marital status or the fact that they have children. By themselves, being married or having children do not put persons into a prohibited class, but they are relevant facts that must be revealed to immigration authorities. Since the government has consistently applied its rules to less serious non-disclosures, it would be perverse to act more leniently towards persons who omitted to reveal facts that might suggest they were mass murderers, Gestapo or SS officers, concentration or extermination camp guards—in short, that they had a Nazi past. Yet government has been reluctant to invoke the full force of immigration law against war criminals in the past. War crimes justice experts have been advocating that the Canadian authorities let go of this double standard and use the existing deportation laws to deprive Nazi perpetrators of the benefits of our society.

In addition, the Immigration Act could be amended to add in a separate ground of deportation for persecution of minorities. In the United States, Congresswoman Elizabeth Holtzman, one of the driving forces behind American initiatives to take measures against war criminals, introduced an amendment in 1978 to the Immigration and Nationality Law to permit deportation of persons who had participated in Nazi persecution. Passed through Congress that year, it became known as the "Holtzman amendment." By incorporating this principle into Canadian immigration law, it would be necessary only to establish proof of participation in persecution, and not misrepresentation on entry into Canada. Making persecution a ground for deportation would also be consistent with the constitution of the International Refugee Organization, which Canada signed and ratified in 1947. It provides that neither a war criminal nor a person who assisted the enemy in persecuting civil populations was eligible for refugee status or displaced person's status. Legislation to this effect, albeit late in time, would reflect Canada's earlier commitment to this concept.

A step in the right direction has been the government's recent proposal to alter the definition of "refugee" in the Immigration Act specifically to exclude those who have committed war crimes, crimes against peace or crimes against humanity. In June, 1985 the government released a report by immigration expert Rabbi Gunther Plaut, who recommended that the exclusion and cessation clauses of the UN Convention on Refugees be incorporated into Canadian law in that way. This proposal was designed to overcome the difficulty which led Canada to refuse assistance to the United States earlier that year, in sending convicted war criminal Karl Linnas back to the Soviet Union. Linnas, sentenced to death in 1963 after being tried *in absentia*, was accused of supervising a death camp in Tartu, Estonia where he took part in the abuse and execution of thousands of prisoners. The United States government, which revoked his citizenship in 1981 and ordered him deported in 1983, wrote to the Canadian Embassy in Washington on January 8, 1985, requesting that the government assist in the removal by transiting Linnas through Canada en route to the Soviet Union. The authorities feared that

Linnas might claim refugee status the moment he landed on Canadian soil, resulting in a protracted immigration hearing and possible appeal. By interpretation, the operative refugee definition probably did not protect any war criminal, but it was not explicit. The amendment, proposed by the government in Bill C-55 in May 1987, will clear up all doubt when passed and will prevent Nazi perpetrators from claiming refugee status in Canada.

One final change to deportation law would substantially speed up the process, which can drag on for years. As the law stands, a Nazi war criminal who is a Canadian citizen would actually have to go through two different courts to be denaturalized and deported. Denaturalization is carried out in the Federal Court of Canada, Trial Division. The deportation process is handled by a Department of Immigration adjudicator. In both sets of proceedings, the same facts may well be the subject of the hearing—whether a person lied on entry. The only difference is in the standard of proof for each. Denaturalization requires proof of intent to deceive (or fraud), while deportation simply depends on proof of a misrepresentation. Advocates in the United States have suggested a consolidation of the two procedures because of the lengthy delays experienced by the U.S. Office of Special Investigations. In a number of cases, Nazi war criminals managed to live peacefully and comfortably in their homes until the end of their days as the multiple proceedings and never-ending appeals went on and on. By eliminating what amounts to double litigation of the very same issues and speeding up the process, Canada would go a long way to ensuring that justice is done.

Prosecution in Canada

A third legal remedy is to prosecute Nazi war criminals found here in the Canadian courts. Precedents for domestic prosecution can be found both in customary international law and under Canadian law. The advantages of bringing a Nazi war criminal to trial in Canada are many. Rather than exporting suspected individuals to another country, they are guaranteed to be brought to justice and receive punishment for their crimes. Moreover, accused persons would be sure to receive all the protections of the Canadian legal system, including undisputably fair trials. For these reasons, many advocates prefer this remedy. There has, however, been a great deal of opposition on the grounds that any prosecution for war crimes would involve the implementation of retroactive legislation. Misguided as these objections are, in light of the precedent set by Nuremberg, they have consistently been raised by the government to justify continuing inaction. Nonetheless, Canada has a number of options by which criminal prosecutions might be launched, either under present law or with new legislation.

a) Customary international law

The sacrosanct laws of warfare have developed over centuries. They are based on a belief among nations that war should be avoided except if absolutely necessary to enforce rights, and once undertaken, it should be conducted "within the bounds of law and good faith."[3] These principles, codified in the regulations of the Fourth Hague Convention of 1907, which included provisions for the protection of civilian populations, have long been accepted as rules of customary international law. Their incorporation into the Charter of Nuremberg reaffirmed this, and emphatically contradicted the charge that the war crimes set out in the Charter were retroactive and unfair to the accused Nazi war criminals brought to trial by the Allied powers. Crimes against humanity have also been recognized as offences independent of war crimes and punishable in their own right as international law offences.

As a member of the community of nations, Canada could invoke customary international law to prosecute suspected Nazi war criminals residing within our borders. Offences under international law are considered Canadian "common law offences," in contrast to most Canadian offences which are spelled out in the Criminal Code. Although the Criminal Code contains a rule against prosecuting common law offences, that prohibition does not apply to offences under international law. The Supreme Court of Canada has ruled that customary international law, unless it conflicts with a Canadian legal principle, forms part of domestic law. The Canadian Charter of Rights and Freedoms also incorporates customary international law as a primary source of Canadian criminal law. It provides that anyone charged with an offence has the right to be found not guilty, unless at the time the act was committed, it was an offence under Canadian or international law, or was criminal according to the general principles of law recognized by the community of nations. This Charter provision is an implied recognition that customary international law offences are domestic offences, giving Canada jurisdiction to prosecute these crimes, even in the absence of specific criminal legislative provisions.

b) Private prosecutions

Even if the government refuses to launch proceedings, any citizen has the right to mount a private prosecution for violations of the general principles of the laws of war recognized by the community of nations. At common law, a private citizen is entitled not only to initiate a prosecution without government approval, but to carry out the proceedings without any involvement or support from the attorney-general. All provincial attorneys-general do, however, have inherent power to intervene to stop a private prosecution from continuing. In the absence of official interference, a private prosecutor could bring a Nazi war criminal to trial and conduct the entire case, from start to finish.

c) The War Crimes Act

The War Crimes Act, passed by Parliament in 1946, directly incorporates the principles of customary international law. Enacted for the very purpose of prosecuting war criminals, it was specifically drafted to apply retroactively to crimes committed from 1939 onward and to govern no matter where the crimes took place. Its significance lies in a clear acceptance of the principle that retroactive procedural law, together with extra-territorial jurisdiction and customary international law can be used to determine the nature of a "war crime" and to punish guilty parties. Canada utilized this statute to try seven war criminals in four military trials in Aurich, in the British zone of occupied Germany immediately after the war. The act has never been used to bring Nazi war criminals to justice since.

Because of this, a number of reservations have been expressed about the application of this legislation to try war criminals in Canada today. The primary objections are based on the military nature of proceedings provided for under the War Crimes Act regulations. Opponents have argued that the statute was only intended for the dispensation of military justice in the battlefield and that military trials are not appropriate so long after the war. Moreover, they would be unfair to many defendants who were, in the strict sense of the word, "civilians" and not members of any armed forces during the war, such as "enthusiastic volunteers" in local populations who perpetrated war crimes. Unlike criminal proceedings, military tribunals do not provide for trial by jury. Critics have taken the view that this violates the guarantee to trial by jury set out in the Charter of Rights and Freedoms. Other complaints have focussed on the evidentiary standards, which are lower than in regular criminal trials and, some argue, unfair to accused persons.

In spite of these criticisms, the clear wording of the statute makes it applicable outside of the strict confines of wartime military operations in the field. Military tribunals are, in fact, quite appropriate to deal with Nazi war criminals, given their unique expertise in trying persons who have violated the laws and usages of war. They are no different than the many other expert tribunals that Canada has established to deal with specialized areas of the law. Tax disputes, for example, are decided by the Tax Appeal Board, and immigration cases before an Immigration Appeal Board. Expert tribunals are relied on throughout the Canadian justice system.

As for the standards of evidence, it is true that the War Crimes Act and its regulations provide for a relaxation of the strict rules that apply in other criminal proceedings. But when it comes to the prosecution of war crimes and crimes against humanity, there is nothing unfair about this divergence. These standards neither violate Canada's Bill of Rights nor the Charter of Rights and Freedoms. The Nuremberg Tribunal, the Israeli court that tried Eichmann, and every British and American war crimes tribunal set up after the war employed rules of evidence like those in Canada's War Crimes Act. These rules are of value to ensure that justice will be done. As International Law Professor Leslie Green explains, "In such cases the best evidence against the accused often consists of official documents, not always signed by him, emanating from his national headquarters or other command offices. In addition, there are the statements, implicating the accused or describing events from which his offences are alleged to have arisen, made by persons who have been tried and perhaps executed in earlier trials. Apart from this type of evidence, documentary material has occasionally been found in the ruins of concentration camps and ghettos, and this, together with photographs found on German soldiers is often the only evidence of what occurred....To have insisted on verbal evidence only, would have meant that in many cases no evidence of any kind was possible....It may well be said that there is now a generally recognized principle that in such trials any evidence may be admitted that is likely to assist the court in ascertaining the truth."[4]

With minor technical improvements to relieve some of the procedural concerns, the War Crimes Act could provide a solid footing on which to base domestic prosecution of war criminals in Canada today.

d) Geneva Conventions Act

On August 12, 1949 at Geneva, more than sixty nations, including Canada, put their signatures to four conventions respecting the laws of war. Among the Geneva Conventions was one concerned with the protection of civilians in time of war. Directly linked to the Fourth Hague Convention of 1907, these provisions were designed to protect nationals of any country bound by the Conventions who find themselves in the hands of an enemy occupying power. All "protected persons", as they are referred to, are entitled to "respect for their persons, their honour, their family rights, their religious convictions and practices and their manners and customs." The Geneva Conventions also established a framework for punishment of anyone responsible for a "grave breach" of the conventions, including willful killing, torture, inhumane treatment and unlawful deportation of protected persons. In agreeing to be governed by the Conventions, each contracting nation was obliged to put domestic legal sanctions into effect for those guilty of grave breaches, and actively to seek out and bring perpetrators before its own courts, no matter what their nationality.

Canada fulfilled its international obligations more than fifteen years later on March 18, 1965, when it enacted the Geneva Conventions Act. This statute gave Canada the jurisdiction to prosecute all violators of the Geneva Conventions, as long as the accused is found in Canada. War criminals in this country could be brought to trial for any war crimes committed after the statute came into effect. Unlike the War Crimes Act, though, the Geneva Conventions Act does not expressly state that its application is retroactive to 1939. As a result, opponents to this legal option have raised doubts as to whether it covers offences perpetrated during the Second World War. Critics have also argued that the "protected persons" category did not include victims who were victimized before the Conventions were ratified.

The rule against retroactive legislation stems from a fundamental democratic belief that individuals should be protected from arbitrary government moves or policy changes so that they can plan their own actions with a clear idea of the legal consequences. This principle is applied with particular vigour in criminal law because of the potentially severe penalties involved, and has been embodied in the Canadian Charter of Rights and Freedoms. It is intended to prevent unfairness to an accused person, ensuring that he will not be punished for any act that was innocent when it was committed.

The Geneva Conventions Act did not create the offences of war crimes and crimes against humanity. They were already well-recognized, internationally and domestically. The brutal Nazi mass murders were punishable at the time they were committed under every law imaginable, including German law, the laws of the occupied states, Canadian law and international law. Could any Nazi war criminal be heard to say that when he savagely killed and plundered ordinary civilians he thought his deeds were innocent? The Geneva Conventions Act did not make war crimes punishable for the first time in Canada. It simply set up new machinery to prosecute crimes that were already on the books. According to statutory interpretation rules, when a piece of legislation is neither explicitly retroactive nor prospective, any provision that is strictly procedural, like those in the Geneva Conventions Act, are to be interpreted as having retroactive application. Based on this principle, the statute also would cover the crimes committed by a national of any country that became a party to the Geneva Conventions, regardless of when it joined. So, the government could prosecute Nazi war criminals under the Geneva Conventions Act, which has never been used since its passage.

e) New legislation

The federal government could introduce legislation which makes Nazi war crimes and crimes against humanity offences under the Criminal Code. Perhaps more than any other remedy, new prosecution provisions would demonstrate Canada's genuine resolve to seek redress against Nazi war criminals living here. Given the wealth of existing legal opinion about the other prosecution options, lawmakers have an opportunity to develop Criminal Code amendments free of the many alleged pitfalls plaguing the other options.

Any new legislation should allow for the prosecution of war crimes and crimes against humanity whether or not committed during any war in which Canada has been or may be engaged. To ensure its effectiveness in dealing with Nazi war crimes, the new legislation should be expressly retroactive. Canada's Charter of Rights, incorporating customary international law, specifically envisages retroactive legislation to permit Canadian law to set up machinery to punish any act that was criminal at international law or according to the general principles of law recognized by the community of nations at the time they were committed. In fact, the history of the Charter clearly indicates that at the time it was enacted, it anticipated criminal legislation to bring Nazi war criminals in Canada to justice.

In addition, it will have to be specifically worded to apply to offences committed outside Canada. Although the application of Canadian criminal law is generally restricted to within the country's borders, the Criminal Code endows the government with extraterritorial jurisdiction for certain offences regarded as threatening to the world community. This incorporates an accepted principle of international law. The Criminal Code already extends universal jurisdiction to Canadian courts over offences relating to aircraft hijacking, piracy and offences against diplomats. The recent Criminal Law Amendment Act, Bill C-18, added two more crimes to this list of international offences, or "universal crimes": theft of nuclear materials and hostage taking. When Bill C-18 was tabled before the House of Commons in 1984, war crimes justice advocates requested that war crimes and crimes against humanity be included, but were turned down on the basis that the proposal was not germane to the subject of the bill. Despite this technical issue, the merit of this approach remains.

Canada has signed and ratified the International Convention against Torture, which required our government to enact extraterritorial legislation to prosecute for the crime of torture. Parliament fulfilled its obligation by enacting a provision in the Criminal Code. To leave out war crimes and crimes against humanity is an anomaly.

On a technical level, any new criminal legislation should permit prosecutions to be launched without the consent of the attorney-general of Canada. Most offences under the Criminal Code do not require such consent and individual citizens have the right to make charges against other citizens in court on their own initiative. Some critics have suggested that imposing the requirement of consent by the attorney-general would temper revenge with mercy. In fact, it would have the effect of confounding justice with politics. The Department of Justice has historically been opposed to Nazi war crimes trials. Requiring the federal attorney-general to give his consent to any upcoming prosecutions would only add scope for a continued reluctance to mount cases. It would be highly unjust for politics to enter any further into the question of bringing war criminals to trial.

An example of this can be seen in Canada's laws on hate propaganda. The hate propaganda sections of the Criminal Code require the consent of the provincial attorney-general before any prosecutions can be launched for that offence. For years, attorneys-general across the country have used their power to forestall proceedings against known offenders. It was only after an outraged Toronto resident named Sabina Citron—herself a Holocaust survivor—launched a private prosecution against hate-monger Ernst Zundel under another Criminal Code provision, that provincial consent was forthcoming in other cases. Soon after, Alberta's attorney-general agreed to proceed against Eckville school teacher Jim Keegstra, who was convicted. The attorney-general of Ontario also consented to prosecutions against Donald Clarke Andrews and Robert Wayne Smith for the same offence. Both were convicted. Without the initiative taken by a private citizen in the Zundel case, these state prosecutions would never have been launched. By the same token, the possibility of private prosecution of war criminals could be an important factor in mobilizing the government into action. Moreover, to suggest that revenge is a factor in war crimes justice misses the entire point. War criminals are put on trial for justice, not vengeance.

f) Office of Special Investigations

The Canadian government can follow the example set by the United States in 1979 and establish an Office of Special Investigations to investigate and prosecute Nazi war criminals. A specialized unit of the Department of Justice would not only permit the development of the expertise needed to effectively pursue war criminals, but would also guarantee the kind of concerted effort which is absolutely crucial at this late stage. The Canadian justice system is replete with precedents for this type of machinery. The narcotics unit within the RCMP and the Combined Investigations Branch of the Department of Consumer and Corporate Affairs are just two examples.

g) Investigations and Records

War crimes justice advocates have urged the Canadian government to undertake other initiatives to back up any legal action. For years, opponents to action have complained about the problems of evidence involved in prosecuting war criminals. Several measures could add greatly to the background information available and facilitate the pursuit of Nazi war criminals in this country.

For starters, Canadian authorities could cross-check the lists of Nazi war criminals compiled by CROWCASS, the OSI and the UN War Crimes Commission against our own lists of immigrants, citizens, taxpayers, drivers licence holders and many others in the hands of various government departments. Although it is a mammoth task, a systematic look at every available listing can be fruitful. In the United States, the OSI has launched more cases in recent years as a result of cross-checking than on the basis of tips or allegations from informants. Nazi war criminals, typically, have kept silent about their past. Reliable informants are highly unusual and the information from lists is likely to be far more reliable. The enormity of the job and the need for a sustained effort by an informed bureaucracy lends further support for an office of special investigations. The federal government could also acquire from the United States Justice Department rosters of death camp and concentration camp personnel compiled over a number of years by the OSI. These represent an invaluable tool for rooting out Nazi perpetrators here, and are available on request. Australia, which began a serious effort to pursue Nazi mass murderers hiding within its borders in 1986, has already made use of them.

In addition, the Immigration Department could and should be preserving the application form of every landed immigrant born in Europe before January 1, 1927. Until the advent of the Deschênes Commission, Canada routinely destroyed these forms two years after landing. The remaining application forms, with extensive background information on immigrants, may contain misrepresentations that would be useful in deporting any Nazi war criminal who surfaces in Canada in the future. In fact, once an immigrant is accepted into Canada, the application form should be retained until the death of the applicant.

Federal authorities must co-operate with police investigators by releasing any information that might point to the whereabouts of a suspected war criminal. The case of Helmut Rauca was delayed for four and a half years by the refusal of the Department of Health and Welfare to provide the RCMP with his old age pension file. Although the Department confirmed in September of 1977 that it held a record on Rauca, officials declined to release any further information than that. Rauca was not tracked down until February, 1982. Obstruction of this nature has only thwarted any efforts to pursue Holocaust perpetrators. Legislation to correct the situation is needed and should be passed.

The names of Nazi war criminals could be added to Canada's immigration look-out lists. As we have seen, the Allies' lists of some forty thousand Nazis which this country obtained after the war has gathered dust in Canadian Archives. During the Deschênes Commission, the national public archivist attempted to assemble them in usable form for the very first time. These and other rosters compiled by Western governments could now be used for what they should have been used for from the start—to keep any late-coming Nazi war criminals out of the country. This can be accomplished by circulating them to all immigration posts and ports of entry into Canada.

Conflicting testimony was presented at the Deschênes Inquiry about the nature of questions asked to applicants for immigration into Canada. Former officials at postwar immigration centres all indicated that they asked refugees about their wartime activities. But two of the suspects examined in private hearings of the Commission claimed they were never asked about their military service when seeking admission to this country. Every immigration official could be instructed to inquire about past military, para-military, political and civilian activities during the Second World War, or any other conflict, as a matter of course.

In 1948, the United Nations became the repository of thousands of files prepared by the War Crimes Commission. The existence of these documents only became widely known with the eruption of the "Waldheim Affair" in 1985, when the newly elected president of Austria was charged with being a Nazi war criminal. His record was among the many compiled by the War Crimes Commission and available to member governments of the UN on a confidential basis. However, until recently, only three other requests had ever been made for access to these valuable documents: one in 1962 by Israel for the Eichmann file, and two by the U.S., first in 1983 for Klaus Barbie's file and then in 1985, for the Mengele records. Canada, which has never made any requests, could be routinely checking with the UN on any suspects under investigation here, to determine if any information is available through that source.

Canada does have the capacity to take actions against Nazi war criminals. A variety of legal options, each of which can be substantiated on solid grounds, have been available for years. With any real commitment to bring Nazi war criminals to justice, Canada could have taken the steps necessary to correct any technical difficulties in the law and to coordinate its bureaucratic resources. Historical and legal precedents have provided every opportunity—indeed, every imperative—for dealing with the monstrous henchmen of the Third Reich.

Chapter Seven

The Reasons for Inaction

Canada's deliberate policy of inaction on war criminals was a well-kept secret, meticulously hidden from public view through closed-door meetings and confidential reports. But its results were plain for all to see. Not a single case was prosecuted in four decades, no extradition requests were entertained until 1982, and few allegations were investigated. In short, Canada became an attractive haven for war criminals.

Not so obvious were the reasons why the leaders of this country remained determined to do nothing about mass murderers in our midst. Until recently we could only speculate. However, the Deschênes Commission of Inquiry has shed light on the factors that lay behind Canada's deplorable policy. The background papers, the internal memoranda, the ministerial orders—heretofore strictly classified—have been brought forward for close scrutiny.

The release of Martin Low's discussion paper provided one of the most telling insights into government indifference. For the first time, we were able to analyze the legal basis on which those in power justified their ongoing refusal to move on this issue—and to refute its narrowly drawn arguments. Indeed, Mr. Justice Jules Deschênes specifically disagreed with many of the report's conclusions. It is unfortunate that the discussion paper stood publicly undisputed for five years—valuable time wasted in the struggle for justice. The government had chosen to classify the document as "secret," the second-highest level of security classification.

By divulging the Low memorandum, the Deschênes Commission finally lifted the legal smokescreen that for years shielded the government from action. Its lop-sided analysis of the law provided Cabinet with every excuse to do nothing.

When Martin Low testified before the Commission, he explained that the function of the inter-departmental committee was to canvass all legal options for dealing with alleged war criminals residing in Canada and to present these to Cabinet, so that it could assess each alternative and ultimately determine the appropriate course of action. "My instructions were to bring all of this together into a comprehensive document which could be considered by the Cabinet in due course and which could give them a sense of the prospects for action under the existing legal remedies which might be available." While styled as a discussion paper in form, the report was, in reality, a series of conclusions rather than, as Mr. Low claimed, a vetting of "prospects for action." Certain legal remedies were censored altogether or summarily dismissed, and by so presenting a limited range of legal and policy choices, the study curtailed Cabinet's decision-making powers on this highly sensitive and important issue.

Martin Low drew an analogy between the memorandum and a law review article. Yet the two are very different. The report, detailed and technical, resembled a law review article at face value. Unlike a law review article, though, it was extremely one-sided. The memorandum propounded the thesis that bringing Nazi war criminals in Canada to justice was a legal impossibility, either through existing law or new legislation. Unlike an article printed in a law digest, it argued this astounding proposition without reference to any opposing law, precedents, or arguments. Law review articles may postulate many shocking notions, but, if they are to be published, they cannot ignore all the relevant contrary law!

In his testimony, Low indicated that this discussion paper represented the views of all departments taking part in the committee he chaired. He described the committee's mandate as providing Cabinet with "a distillation, a synthesis and an expression of our best view as to what the administrative, factual and legal circumstances were as they applied to a possibility of developing a program of a comprehensive nature in relation to these allegations." The study, he said, served as "an abstract starting point for everyone's thinking." To the extent that it represents government thought up until the creation of the Deschênes Commission, the paper calls for a direct response.

The document is divided into four parts: background, present legislation, other considerations and policy options. A close survey of each of those sections points out the study's weaknesses. Of course, some of the specific legal statements contained in the memorandum were correct. The problem did not lie in the fact that each and every conclusion reached was wrong. Mr. Justice Deschênes accepted some of the paper's legal propositions, although he did not agree with most. The difficulty with the report was in its overall approach of raising obstacles for any means of recourse against Nazi war criminals in Canada, and suppressing every argument in support of bringing them to justice.

The report handed down by Mr. Justice Deschênes, on the other hand, presented arguments both for and against each issue, leaving the reader free to draw his or her own conclusions. Moreover, the Commission report contained several alternative ways that Nazi war criminals might be dealt with under Canadian law. He did not simply reject every option out of hand. The Deschênes Commission has unequivocally refuted not only the Low memorandum, but also the position held by the government for the past forty-two years.

In commenting in detail on the Low memorandum, it is necessary to go over some of the same material discussed in the previous chapter. However, this serves to highlight the thoroughly obstructionist nature of this document.

The background section of the inter-departmental memorandum briefly discussed Canada's efforts to screen out Nazis and acknowledged that certain suspected Nazis and Nazi collaborators may well have gained entry into the country. Yet nowhere did the paper analyze the immigration practices which led to this state of affairs. Nor was any reference made to the relationship between the ever-relaxing policies for Nazis and the unyielding restrictions imposed upon Jewish refugees. No mention was made of Canada's adherence to the 1948 secret British communique proposing an end to war crimes trials, nor to the episode in which Canadian leaders knowingly gave sanctuary to Count de Bernonville and other Vichy collaborators. All of these factors were significant omissions of highly relevant background.

While allowing that Nazi mass murderers were present in Canada, the Low committee refused to call them war criminals. Throughout the study, that term was carefully excluded. Such individuals were referred to as "a small number of persons now in Canada" who "could be shown to have committed offences of greater or lesser magnitude in Europe during the Second World War," or "persons who had co-operated with the various Nazi activities." In another passage, it discussed "ostensibly credible and serious charges against particular individuals," and later made reference to "specified persons...responsible for serious wrongdoing."

Yet, according to the memorandum, they could not be strictly termed "war criminals" because they did not necessarily fall within the definition of "belligerents," a term reserved for members of the Gestapo, SS, or Nazi military forces. The committee took the view that Nazi mass murderers in Canada were not, strictly speaking, "belligerents," but rather, "civilians." They were, explained Martin Low, "locally engaged personnel who were not part of the German military apparatus, but were people in the various occupied countries acting as police officers under the, I suppose, civilian administration of the occupying power."

The Low report was wrong. It has been well settled in law that perpetrators of war crimes, regardless of their official affiliation, are indeed war criminals. Abundant examples exist. Immediately after World War II, Canada conducted four war crimes trials of seven accused in Europe. Wilhelm Jung, one of the seven accused, was a civilian when he committed his crimes and at the time of his trial.[1] A civic official with a position in the Nazi party, Jung was charged with ordering a German soldier to shoot and kill a Royal Canadian Air Force prisoner of war. Jung was found guilty, sentenced to death and executed.

Britain also tried and convicted a number of civilians for war crimes under their War Crimes Regulations, after which Canada's own War Crimes Regulations were patterned. Both a doctor and a children's nurse were found guilty of war crimes in the *Ruhen Trial*.[2] In the *Essen* lynching case, civilians were among those convicted for involvement in the killings of three British prisoners of war. And in the *Velpke Children's Home Case*, a British court convicted two Nazi party officials—a nurse and a doctor—for killing, by willful neglect, a number of Polish children in Velpke, Germany.[3] In the forward to that case, international law scholar Hersh Lauterpacht emphasized that the laws of war bind individuals who are not members of the armed forces of the belligerent.[4] The writings of highly esteemed teachers of international law, such as Lauterpacht, are recognized as an important source of international law.

American Military Tribunals held civilians accountable for war crimes too. In the *Trial of Karl Brandt* and others, doctors were found guilty of war crimes. The *HadamarTrial* convicted the civilian personnel of a medical institution for unlawfully putting to death Russian and Polish nationals.

The laws and customs of war are addressed not only to combatants. They apply equally to anyone in a position to violate them. Any civilian who violates the laws and customs of war must be punished as a war criminal.[5] Yet, the inter-departmental memorandum did not mention the Canadian case of Wilhelm Jung or the British and American precedents. Nor did it refer to the opinion of Hersh Lauterpacht. The Low report passed over these authorities as if they did not exist.

So, the discussion paper concluded that the crimes perpetrated by persons who had slipped into Canada were not war crimes, but "crimes against humanity." This distinction fails to acknowledge that the categories overlap: most of the crimes committed were both war crimes and crimes against humanity. Having made this distinction, the study went on to suggest that crimes against humanity were not recognized offences under international law during World War II. This proposition ignored some very basic precedents. It was at odds with the judgment of the International Military Tribunal at Nuremberg, other war crimes trials, and the prevailing view among international legal experts. It also highlighted the committee's misguided notion of the principle of retroactivity.

Democratic societies are loath to punish individuals for acts which were not criminal at the time that they were committed. To apply that concern to crimes against humanity is unwarranted. Murder has always been criminal. The deeds perpetrated by suspects hiding in Canada have been recognized as criminal under international law since well before World War II. These principles were encoded by the historic Nuremberg Tribunal in the Charter under which it was established. That Charter expressly provided that tribunals would have jurisdiction over war crimes, crimes against humanity and crimes against peace. Nuremberg's judges accepted the Charter as a statement of pre-existing law: "The Charter is not an arbitrary exercise of power on the part of the victorious nations,...it is the expression of international law existing at the time of its creation."[6] The Tribunal convicted two of the sixteen accused, Steicher and von Schirach, of crimes against humanity alone.[7] When Nuremberg's defendants pleaded that the acts they committed during the Second World War were not illegal under the 1907 Hague Convention or the Law of Nations, their arguments were thrown out of court.

To raise the spectre of retroactivity is to miss the point. At the U.S. trial of John Demjanjuk, later extradited to Israel for his role at the Treblinka death camp, the court put it this way: "A defendant would have to state that at the time he operated gas chambers to exterminate unarmed men, women and children, he did not know he was doing anything wrong. He would have to plead that the burning, beating, gassing, shooting and torture that were the *modus operandi* of Treblinka were not criminal acts. These grotesque assertions were not made even by Adolf Eichmann."[8]

"If you were to say that these men were not guilty", said Mr. Justice Jackson in his summation of the case against Goering, Hess, Bormann, Von Ribbentrop and eighteen others at Nuremberg, "it would be as true to say that there has been no war; that there are no slain; that there has been no crime."[9]

The Low memorandum inexplicably failed to allude to the consensus within the international legal community affirming the principles of Nuremberg. Through a series of United Nations resolutions, which Canada has repeatedly supported since 1946, prosecution for war crimes and crimes against humanity has been recognized as a commitment for all countries of the world.

It is difficult to imagine an eighteen-page legal document on Nazi war crimes without a single reference to Nuremberg and its generally accepted principles of international law. But, for the purposes of the Low report, Nuremberg simply ceased to exist!

Martin Low's committee threw yet another terminological obstacle in the way of action by suggesting that war crimes and crimes against humanity covered a multitude of wrongs including "collaboration with occupying forces in greater or lesser degree." The committee, expressing concern with a "serious problem of definition," refused to distinguish between criminals and mere collaborators who committed no crimes. However, war crimes and crimes against humanity are precise, well-defined terms. A war crime is a violation of the laws and usages of war, a definition adopted by the Canadian War Crimes Act. It would include either the murder of an enemy civilian or murder of a civilian in enemy territory. A person could not become a war criminal if he simply co-operated with the occupying Nazi forces, resisted Soviet occupation during Hitler's battle against Stalin, or was taken as a prisoner of war by the Nazis. Nonetheless, the discussion paper raised the prospect that a mere resister, POW or collaborator who had not committed any crimes might be swept into the category of war criminals and unfairly subjected to punishment. Low based this concern on far-fetched Soviet allegations that have surfaced from time to time implicating opponents of the Communist regime in Nazi war crimes. But he took seriously claims that were obviously implausible and that no Canadian court would uphold.

During his testimony before the Deschênes Commission, Martin Low acknowledged that the mere act of collaboration with Nazi occupiers would not render an individual a Nazi war criminal. It would depend on the sort of collaboration. He agreed that under international law, an occupying power is not only at liberty, but has an obligation, to see to the administration of society. Normal police duties, such as monitoring traffic, arresting thieves and dealing with other routine matters of everyday life continued, even during the Second World War. Insofar as the Nazis complied with international law in seeing that these routine functions were carried out, local police units who co-operated with them were not guilty of any war crimes. On the other hand, if they co-operated with the Nazis in rounding up Jews and executing them, they were much more than mere collaborators. They were war criminals. There is a world of difference between a police issuing a traffic ticket and killing Jews. Martin Low's concession at the hearing differed from what was stated in the inter-departmental memorandum. Five years earlier, his report had suggested that all sorts of people might be punished as war criminals who did not deserve to be. This opinion could only have had a chilling effect on any initiative to bring Nazi war criminals to justice.

The Low committee was also critical of the allegations submitted to the government about suspected war criminals: "Many of these allegations have been lacking in detail and imprecise or

contained factual inconsistencies, and their accuracy and reliability is therefore often subject to serious question." This assertion ignores the normal onus on government to invoke its
investigative machinery to substantiate such an allegation and
gather the evidence necessary to either initiate legal proceedings or close the file. These resources and powers are available
only to government, not to private individuals or groups, who
generally submit complaints. Yet, as the memorandum noted,
the RCMP adhered to a strict policy of non-investigation concerning war criminals. "No investigation of any individual has
been conducted with a view to determining the veracity of an
allegation in the commission of war crimes. Under existing legislation, such an investigation would have no object, since it appears that no action can be taken." This was the kind of circular
reasoning that threaded its way throughout the study: On the
one hand, argued Low, the government could not investigate allegations because it had no legal basis on which to take action.
On the other hand, there was no legal basis on which to proceed
because of insufficient factual evidence.[10]

In the section entitled "Present Legislation", the Low report
canvassed the available remedies under current legislation—the
Extradition Act, the War Crimes Act, the Geneva Conventions
Act, the Immigration Act, the Citizenship Act and the Criminal
Code. Here, the committee's consideration of existing law was
marred by a seeming zeal to reject each and every viable avenue
of recourse. Available legal options were dismissed summarily,
selective arguments tended to omit competing views, legal obstacles were overblown and certain remedies were ignored altogether. While there can be no quarrel with the committee's
conclusion that the Criminal Code provided no basis for prosecution of war criminals in Canada, every other statute examined
was somehow misrepresented.

According to the memorandum, extradition "provides little
prospect for a solution to the problem" of Nazi war criminals in
Canada, because "primarily of the absence of extradition treaty
relations between Canada and most Eastern European countries."

It is true that Canada does not have operative extradition
treaties with most Eastern European countries, notably the
U.S.S.R. and Poland. The Low report did not contemplate the viability of Canada's treaties with Czechoslovakia, Romania, Yu-

goslavia, and Hungary. As previously mentioned, a Canadian court found no difficulty in extraditing a fugitive to Yugoslavia on the charge of rape.

No reference was made to the possibility of extradition to the Federal Republic of West Germany, which was judicially recognized in the 1982 *Rauca* case. Canada's extradition treaty with West Germany permits extradition of all Nazi war criminals to that country regardless of their nationality. Under the operative treaty, two separate provisions give Canada the right to extradite. The first basis for jurisdiction is the fact that all Nazi crimes were committed within what was then German territory, or at least under official German direction and command. The second basis is that Canada, itself, would have jurisdiction in a similar case involving one of its own nationals. For example, if a Canadian public official were to commit murder, Canada would be entitled to prosecute, no matter where the crime was committed.[11] By virtue of these provisions, Eastern European perpetrators of Nazi war crimes can be extradited today for trial in West Germany. The memorandum did not mention this viable legal remedy.

The War Crimes Act was enacted after World War II specifically for the purpose of prosecuting Nazi war criminals in Canada. Although that statute contains flaws which need to be addressed, none is fatal to its effectiveness. With comparatively minor improvements, the act could provide a mechanism for the prosecution of war criminals living in this country. The War Crimes legislation was tossed out by the discussion paper amid an avalanche of objections. In some cases, the triviality of objections raised only confirmed the government's longheld reluctance to prosecute Nazi war criminals in this country.

The committee was offended by the notion that an accused person would be prosecuted in a military trial under the act. What it failed to acknowledge was that military tribunals are expert on war crimes and are required by the War Crimes Regulations to be fully conversant in the laws and usages of war. To debate the relative merits of military trials is perfectly valid. To imply that they are somehow improper, as did the study, misrepresents the law.

The report also expressed concern that evidentiary standards under the statute did not measure up to normal rules of evidence. In fact, the rules set out in the War Crimes Act and its regulations are absolutely consistent with the standards applied in the Nuremberg Tribunal, British and American military courts and the Israeli court that tried Eichmann. As already mentioned, it is accepted that in war crimes trials any evidence may be admitted that can assist the court in ascertaining the truth. Again, one can argue about the worthiness of those rules, but any suggestion that they were abnormal for war crimes trials was a legal error.[12]

Another of the committee's misguided objections was its assertion that the War Crimes Act would "certainly" not provide for a fair trial in Canada within the meaning of the Bill of Rights. It failed to mention a ruling by the highest court in the country that military trials were not in violation of the Canadian Bill of Rights. In the case of *MacKay*, the Supreme Court of Canada upheld the conviction of a soldier tried by court martial for trafficking in a narcotic.([13])

Based on debates in Parliament at the time the War Crimes Act was passed in 1946, the inter-departmental study concluded that the statute had only been enacted as a temporary measure to prosecute war crimes committed against Canadians in the theatre of military operations. This conclusion was simply unsubstantiated by the wording of the law or the rules of statute interpretation. Statements made by politicians when legislation is passed must not be used to contradict the plain words of a statute to prevent their application.[14] Certainly, nothing in the act suggests its time has run out. Besides, even if parliamentarians had anticipated a limited purpose for the War Crimes Act, they either could not have foreseen that Nazi war criminals would be among us today or chose to ignore the fact that Nazis were slipping in.

Lastly, the Low report incorrectly stated that Canadian civilians could not be subject to military law. On the contrary, regulations under the War Crimes Act specifically provide that a person who appears to have committed a war crime is to be tried as if he were subject to military laws.[15] These provisions were never alluded to in the study.

With little more than a passing glance, the memorandum discarded the Geneva Conventions Act of 1965 as a means of recourse against Nazi war criminals. That statute is an enactment of the 1949 Geneva Conventions. As a signatory to the Conventions, Canada undertook a solemn obligation either to prosecute or to hand over to another signatory persons alleged to have committed grave breaches of the Conventions, such as the willful killing of enemy civilians. In its preoccupation with retroactivity, the committee jumped to the conclusion that the Geneva Conventions could not apply to offences committed during World War II. But the Geneva Conventions Act is, like the War Crimes Act and the Charter of Nuremberg, another codification of existing international law principles. War crimes were always criminal offences. War crimes were not created with the Conventions—what was created was a new procedure, or a forum for the prosecution of offences already recognized at law. As the court said in the *Einzatsgruppen* case, "No one can claim with the slightest pretense of reasoning that there is any taint of *ex post factoism* in the law of murder." A statute or treaty that is strictly procedural in nature is to be interpreted as having *bone fide* retroactive effect.[16]

No treatment was given to the ways in which a suspected war criminal might be deported under the Immigration Act. Rather, the memorandum focussed on impediments to deportation. Specifically, the report argued that Nazi war criminals who acquired domicile were protected from deportation by operation of the law's domicile clause. Under that provision, a person obtains domicile in Canada after five years residence, and, with domicile, a vested right to remain in this country.[17] But there is one factor that the study left out. In order to acquire domicile, a person's initial entry into the country must have been lawful. A Nazi war criminal who lied about his past upon admission to Canada did not enter the country lawfully and could never have acquired domicile.[18] The report argued that even a Nazi war criminal who went on to become a Canadian citizen, and subsequently lost his citizenship through denaturalization proceedings would retain his vested right of domicile. On the contrary, the Immigration Act specifically states that a person who is denaturalized is deprived of domicile when he ceases to be a citizen.[19]

In the process of rejecting deportation and denaturalization as feasible remedies, the Low report also pointed to the lack of evidence caused by the destruction of immigration documents. To establish grounds for deportation, it must be proved that a person entered the country on false pretenses. This requires evidence of the lies. Because of Canada's file destruction policies, argued the memorandum, no proof remained to establish falsehood on entry.

While many immigration records were destroyed in accord with a government policy in itself demonstrative of the government's apathy about Nazi war criminals, the memorandum failed to mention that certain documents had escaped the destruction process. As it has already been pointed out, ships' manifests and landing records, still in storage, might well establish fraud on entry. A landing record would, for example, reveal whether a person falsified his name on entry, a ground for deportation. The ship's manifest could be used to prove that a person had lied about his occupation before coming to Canada. If a person withheld information about a previous criminal conviction, his non-disclosure would show up on the landing record.

Even if no files existed, it would still be possible to establish false representations. Canadian officials posted throughout Europe after the war had a duty to ask pertinent questions of immigration candidates. There is a legal presumption that officials do their duty. Witnesses before the Deschênes Commission testified that officials indeed asked applicants about wartime activities. A Nazi war criminal could have come into Canada only by answering those questions untruthfully or by withholding information. Testimony at the Commission indicated that if a person passed the Stage B screening and adverse information subsequently turned up about his past, it would be fair to conclude that he had lied in his screening interview. Nowhere did the memorandum reflect upon this potential source of proof.

One other factor deserves comment. The committee based its conclusion that no files existed on its knowledge of the routine file destruction policy. However, as the testimony of Robert Kaplan showed, a large volume of immigration files dating back to World War II was in fact accumulating at headquarters in Ottawa. Their mass destruction, which so frustrated RCMP investigations at the time, did not occur until 1982, after the inter-departmental committee submitted its report. Had the committee cared to make a thorough check with Archives, it would have located files it wrongly concluded had disappeared.

Rather than attempt a positive evaluation of the mechanisms available for revoking citizenship, the Low report quickly brushed aside this remedy as an "abstract possibility." Both the

1946 Citizenship Act and its 1977 re-enactment provide for loss of citizenship, or denaturalization, where a person became a citizen through false pretenses or fraud. Under the 1977 Citizenship Act an individual is deemed to have acquired citizenship by fraud if he gained admission to Canada as a permanent resident on false pretenses by committing fraud, and later became a citizen on the basis of that permanent residence. This specific "deeming" provision did not appear in the text of the earlier, 1946 statute. Relying on an improper interpretation of the legislation, the memorandum argued that citizenship acquired before 1977 could not be revoked on the basis of fraud committed at the point of admission to Canada.[20]

In so doing, the report left out an important legal principle of statutory interpretation. Where a phrase in an updated version of an earlier statute is given a particular meaning, the newer meaning is deemed to apply to the phrase as it appeared in the former statute. The subsequent act is considered to be a statutory explanation of the former act.[20] In other words, the 1977 Citizenship Act adds fraud at the time of admission followed by citizenship to the grounds on which one might be denaturalized. This extended meaning must also be taken to apply to the 1946 statute, and so a person who obtained citizenship before 1977 after gaining admission to Canada on false pretenses could indeed be denaturalized today. Subsequent legal opinion within the Department of Justice has incorporated and accepted this view.[21]

The section of the Low memorandum entitled "Other Considerations" primarily examined the American experience, specifically the U.S. Office of Special Investigations set up in 1979 to initiate proceedings against Nazi war criminals residing in that country. The report focussed on doubts about the suitability of the U.S. model for Canada in terms of the costs, consumption of time and availability of evidence. In the committee's view, numerous problems with the American approach remained unresolved, especially at the end of the process. The Americans, reported Low, had reached no conclusions about how to deal with a person who might be deportable to an Eastern European country.

Granted that these reservations were stated during the infancy of the OSI. Since that time, though, the United States government has deported Treblinka camp guard Feodor Fedorenko to the U.S.S.R. for his role in persecuting Jews. (He was sentenced to death in June, 1986, in the Crimean city of Simferpol.) Valerian Trifa, a leader of the fascist Romanian Iron Guard and persecutor of Jews went, voluntarily, to Portugal, to avoid deportation to Romania. John Demjanjuk was extradited to Israel where he stood on trial for operating the gas chambers at Treblinka and for the abuse and persecution of Jewish prisoners there. While these occurred after the Low committee wrote its report, the Americans knew full well what the end of their process was when it was begun.

In highlighting the impracticability of the U.S. approach here, the Low report dwelled on the fact that Americans had access to immigration records unavailable to Canada. Because U.S. records had been preserved while our files were destroyed, the study concluded that the American government, unlike Canada's, could initiate deportation and denaturalization proceedings on the basis of fraud or false pretenses upon entry to that country.

Apparently unbeknownst to the committee, the Americans have never relied on this ground alone to denaturalize and deport Nazi war criminals. The American Displaced Persons Act also prohibited the entry of anyone who assisted the enemy in persecuting civilians.[22] In addition, the American Immigration and Nationality Act permits denaturalization if citizenship was "illegally procured."[23] Citizenship is considered to have been illegally procured by any person who fails to satisfy a statutory prerequisite to becoming a citizen.[24] In other words, a Nazi war criminal can be denaturalized simply because he is a Nazi war criminal. It is not necessary to prove that he entered the country on false pretenses and therefore not essential to review immigration records. Discussion of this law was omitted in the memorandum.

The Low study also paid scant attention to the "Holtzman amendment," which provided that a non-naturalized or denaturalized American resident could be deported strictly on the basis that he or she had participated in Nazi persecution. The memorandum stated only that this was still being tested in the courts and that U.S. policy had been not to rely on the new deportation law of 1978. Such a vague and incomplete description of American law seemed designed to create an impression that Canada was at a loss to take similar initiatives for want of immigration files. To acknowledge that the Americans did not actually need to rely on those records for either denaturalization or deportation would have undercut the singular goal of the Low report—to prove that the obstacles to Canadian action were insurmountable. The paper steadfastly refused to draw any positive lessons from the American model.

Having ruled out the possibility of proceeding under any existing laws, the final section of the Low memorandum, "Policy Options," considered legal reforms which might be made to permit action against war criminals. To some degree, the committee blurred the distinction between law and policy by dealing with legislative amendments under this heading. Nevertheless four areas of statutory reform were examined: extradition, prosecution in Canada, revocation of citizenship, and deportation. Once again, this examination was laced with negativity. Inevitably, the report overstated certain concerns, focussed on marginal issues and speculated on every imaginable hurdle.

After cursory analysis, extradition was rejected as a policy option on the basis that Canada should not enter into extradition treaties with Eastern European countries. Our existing treaties with four Eastern European states were ignored, as was the extradition treaty with West Germany. No reference was made to the possibility of amending Canada's current extradition treaty with Israel to allow the extradition to that country of persons accused of "universal crimes," including crimes against humanity.

While I do not personally advocate that Canada enter into an extradition treaty with the Soviet Union, I must point out a fallacy relied on by the Low committee to support its argument against such a treaty. The memorandum took the position that any Canada-Soviet treaty which extended to offences committed in the Baltic States would be incompatible with Canada's policy of non-recognition of Soviet occupation of these countries. This argument directly contradicts a fundamental principle of extradition law. For the purposes of extradition treaties, it is irrelevant whether territories are legally or illegally occupied. Countries do not enter into extradition agreements in order to recognize the occupation by one country of another's territory. They do so for the sole purpose of bringing international fugitives to justice.[25] For example, Canada extradited Albert Helmut Rauca to West Germany to stand trial for crimes he committed in Kaunas, Lithuania. Lithuania, at the time, was under Nazi German occupation. Canada has never acknowledged that Nazi Germany was entitled to occupy Lithuania, but conceded nonetheless that its extradition treaty with West Germany covered those crimes.

The committee identified three options for prosecuting war criminals in Canada: amendments to the Criminal Code, prosecution under the present War Crimes Act or under an amended War Crimes Act. Not surprisingly, it found many excuses for concluding that none of these was "a credible policy option for resolving the issue of war criminals."

A major factor militating against a new Criminal Code provision was Martin Low's insistence that prosecution under the Criminal Code would have to be by the provinces rather than the federal government. Provincial prosecution, he determined, would "entail difficulty in centralizing and coordinating the function of prosecuting war criminals."

Traditionally, the provinces have undertaken prosecutions under the Criminal Code. However, no binding constitutional principle gives them exclusive jurisdiction to do so, nor have the courts ever ruled that Ottawa is not permitted to launch prosecutions under the Code. In 1983, the Supreme Court of Canada specifically held that the federal government, like the provinces, may conduct prosecutions under the Criminal Code.[26]

The committee also expressed fear that the standards of proof for evidence under the Criminal Code could never be met in war crimes prosecution. Proof beyond a reasonable doubt, argued the report, would be difficult to muster and successful prosecution, even in the case of a genuine Nazi war criminal, was a "dubious proposition." Given the history of successful prosecutions in West Germany, this reservation was without substance. Surely a criminal such as Joseph Mengele, if he were alive and in Canada today, could be found guilty beyond a reasonable doubt.

Perhaps the most repugnant suggestion by the committee here and elsewhere in its report was that proceeding under an amended Criminal Code would "fly in face of some of the most fundamental of our legal traditions." How could these legal experts have overlooked one of our most fundamental legal traditions, if not the most fundamental—the right to life? Canadians believe that criminals should be brought to justice, that the crime of murder should not go unpunished. Any charge to the contrary turns this basic rule of law on its head.

These observations were made in the Low report in reference to the issue of retroactivity, with which the members of the inter-departmental committee appeared to be preoccupied for the wrong reasons. In this instance, it raised objections that new provisions in the Criminal Code to cover Nazi crimes would violate the Canadian Charter of Rights and Freedoms and the International Covenant on Civil and Political Rights, both of which prohibit retroactive criminal legislation.

In fact, both the Covenant and the Charter contain exceptions to this prohibition.[27] They permit the trial and punishment domestically for any act which, when it was committed, was already an offence at international law, or criminal according to the general principles of law recognized by the community of nations. War crimes and crimes against humanity were both crimes at international law and criminal according to the general principles of law recognized by the community of nations, both before and during World War II.

The history of Canada's Charter of Rights shows that criminal legislation of this type was anticipated. The Charter was being drafted and legislated as the inter-departmental committee carried on its deliberations. An earlier version of the Charter did not contain these exceptions to the prohibition against retroactive criminal law. However, a House of Commons committee adopted these exceptions on January 28, 1981. The Low memorandum was not delivered to Cabinet until February 11, 1981. And yet it failed to reflect these changes in the Charter, except to debate, in a roundabout way, the question of whether crimes against humanity were crimes at international law during World War II.

Discussion of the policy considerations of prosecution under the War Crimes Act gave the committee one last opportunity to raise a barrage of new objections it had not already raised in a previous section of the study. Here, the Low memorandum argued that even an amended War Crimes Act would be defective because it could only apply to offences intended to be tried by a military authority in an area of military command in or near a recent theater of war. On the contrary, the act does not contain this limitation, and the regulations allow for Canadian forces to convene a war crimes tribunal, "wherever such forces may be serving, whether in the field, or in occupation of enemy territory or otherwise."[28]

The discussion paper considered an amendment to the Citizenship Act to allow for revocation of citizenship of war criminals by a mechanism which involved the creation of an irrebuttable presumption that such persons entered Canada fraudulently. Having raised this possibility, the memorandum quickly shot it down, primarily on the ground that it would violate the Bill of Rights prohibition against arbitrary imprisonment, detention or exile of any person. According to the report, such legislation would be retroactive, leading to a potential, if not actual, conflict with the Bill of Rights.

Although this issue has not been litigated in Canada, the United States Supreme Court held, in 1912, that retroactive American legislation allowing denaturalization for citizenship obtained by fraud or other illegal conduct was not a violation of the American constitution.[29] The Court unanimously held that an alien has no moral or constitutional right to retain the privileges of citizenship if, by false evidence or other illegal conduct, an imposition has been practiced on the authorities, without which the certificate of citizenship could not have and would not have been issued. Here, in Canada, there is no doubt that a certificate of Canadian citizenship could not have and would not have been issued to a known Nazi war criminal.

After the report of the inter-departmental committee came out, this 1912 case was applied to revoke the citizenship of a Nazi war criminal. Between 1952 and 1961, a person in the U.S. could not be denaturalized simply because his citizenship had been illegally procured.[30] Fraud had to be proved. Bohdan Koziy, a Nazi collaborator who assisted in the persecution of civilians during World War II, became a U.S. citizen in 1956, when illegal procurement was not a ground for denaturalization. Yet, in 1982 his citizenship was revoked, on the ground (among others) that it had been illegally procured in 1956. There were other grounds of revocation as well. On appeal, Koziy argued that he could not lose his citizenship for an act that was not a ground for revocation at the time he obtained his citizenship. The court disagreed. It ruled that revocation did not violate Koziy's constitutional rights—it only deprived him of his ill-gotten gains.[31]

To these criticisms, the committee added the sweeping allegation that "revocation of citizenship runs counter to the spirit of the Citizenship Act." This proposition perverts the true intention of the statute. The Citizenship Act does in fact provide for revocation of citizenship in cases of fraud. Revocation of citizenship represents the spirit of the Act no less than the granting of citizenship.

The final objection raised by the Low committee was that loss of citizenship would lead to statelessness in violation of Canada's international obligations and general principles of international behaviour outlined in the Convention in the Reduction of Statelessness, the Universal Declaration of Human Rights, the Convention relating to the Status of Stateless Persons and the International Convention on the Elimination of All Forms of Racial Discrimination.

In reality, the likelihood of statelessness for a person whose citizenship has been revoked is very small. Nationals of many states, such as the Soviet Union, cannot lose their original citizenship when they subsequently become citizens of adoptive countries, unless their native homeland grants them permission to renounce. A person who has obtained Canadian citizenship, therefore, has not necessarily lost his former citizenship. In general, any person who loses his Canadian citizenship remains a citizen of his country of origin and does not become stateless. Only a natural-born Canadian could be rendered stateless through revocation of Canadian citizenship.

Moreover, none of the international instruments cited by the committee apply, nor did the report even attempt to explain their relevance. The Convention on the Reduction of Statelessness contains an exception, which the committee chose to ignore, for nationality obtained by misrepresentation or fraud.[32] If a person is rendered stateless because his citizenship was revoked on the grounds of fraud or false representations, such a revocation does not constitute a violation of the Convention.

As for the International Convention on the Elimination of All forms of Racial Discrimination, the committee referred to it as a relevant instrument without any explanation.

Pursuant to the Universal Declaration of Human Rights no person can be arbitrarily deprived of his nationality, but this provision is inapplicable here for the same reasons that the

Canadian Bill of Rights prohibition against arbitrary exile does not apply.

Nor does the Convention relating to the Status of Stateless Persons have anything to do with the conditions under which a person may and may not become stateless. That Convention was adopted to mitigate the consequences of statelessness. It does not apply to protect war criminals or criminals against humanity, who are specifically excluded from its ambit. Again, the committee cited this Convention without explaining its relevance. The entire group of instruments appeared to have been raised merely to create some illusion of injustice.

In considering deportation, the committee went through much the same exercise as with revocation of citizenship, setting up a policy proposal only to poke holes in it. The proposal discussed was a Holtzman-type amendment, permitting deportation upon proof that an individual was a war criminal without having to prove he entered the country on false pretenses or through fraud.

With this option, the inter-departmental committee foresaw the problem of a refugee claim by a war criminal which Canada might be bound to accept because of its obligations under the United Nations Convention relating to the Status of Refugees and the Protocol. The committee feared that an alleged war criminal might claim refugee status. If his claim were sustained, Canada might be powerless to remove him except to a country which is considered a haven for war criminals.

However, the report did not mention that the Refugee Convention explicitly excludes war criminals or criminals against humanity from its protection. Canada is under no obligation internationally to give these people refugee status. It is true that the exclusion of Nazi war criminals from protection is not reflected in Canadian legislation. Had the report stated only that fact, there need be no dispute with it. Instead, the paper suggested that Canada would be in violation of its international obligations by expelling war criminal "refugees," which is utterly wrong.

The Low study proceeded one step further, asserting that no suitable destination existed to receive deported Nazi war criminals. Eastern Europe was eliminated on the basis that war criminals would presumably be put on trial in accordance with dubious standards of due process. Sending them to a democratic country that would prosecute them under a fair legal system was out of the question, because that would amount to disguised extradition, without the protections of an actual extradition. And they could not be sent to a country which was not interested in bringing them to justice on the grounds that Canada would be conniving in the provision of a haven for war criminals.

This entire discussion suffered from a confusion between deportation and extradition. When Canada extradites an individual, he is sent out of the country because he has violated the laws of a foreign country. On the other hand, when Canada deports someone, he is expelled on the basis that he has violated domestic laws. With deportation, the primary concern is not which country the person goes to, but that he leaves Canadian soil. Rather than concerning itself with the mechanism of deportation proper, the Low report became side-tracked with the peripheral issue of which country was the preferable destination. While the Immigration Act sets out a list of potential recipient countries, its purpose is not, as the committee suggested, to establish the best location. The aftermath of deportation—whether or not a person is placed on trial, the fairness of the legal system in the country of arrival—is inconsequential to law of deportation. The only relevant consideration is the removal of an undesirable immigrant from Canada.

The Low report was filled with legal inaccuracies, stifling interpretations of the law and deliberate misrepresentations and omissions. Most disturbing is the report's fundamental thesis. Ultimately, the document is nothing short of an intricate rationalization for the government's historic policy of inaction.

The legal minds at work on the study seemed to exhaust every ounce of ingenuity and creativity not, as one might have expected, in identifying valid mechanisms for pursuing Nazi war criminals, but in searching for obstacles and problems. Having successfully put forward each and every defeatist argument, it is little wonder that Martin Low came to the conclusion that there were "grievous difficulties and very serious impediments." And yet, the committee did not consider itself to be blocking action—it was merely listing potential pitfalls. That sort of distinction becomes meaningless when the vast majority of objections raised were imaginary ones, and any means of removing those stumbling blocks were dismissed or not even mentioned.

Had the document been made public at the time it was written, its egregious errors undoubtedly would have been pointed out immediately. The work of the Canadian Jewish Congress legal committee on war crimes under my chairmanship was preparing a parallel report even as the inter-departmental committee carried out its deliberations. Although the Low memorandum remained undisclosed, we submitted our own findings and recommendations to Mr. Low and others in the government, in an attempt to canvass every concern which might be raised by the committee. Rather than release the Low study, in spite of our urgings and assurances by officials, the government chose secrecy. That decision forced Robert Kaplan and Cabinet into the embarrassing position of having to report that nothing could be done—and for no apparent reason.

Beyond that, the question remains: Why was the committee so determined that nothing be done about Nazi war criminals in Canada? Only one distressing answer can be found threading its way through the memorandum: bringing Nazi war criminals in Canada to justice was controversial. Ever reluctant to take action against persons "whose demeanour while in Canada over a lengthy period may have been exemplary," the committee suggested that subsequent good behaviour could somehow compensate for earlier obscenities. It was an approach that bespoke insularity, a willingness to forget crimes because they were committed outside of Canada, against non-Canadians. The Low memorandum lacked any sense of moral urgency, opting to ignore the repugnancy of allowing murderers to go unpunished.

Ironically, for all the controversies foreseen by Martin Low, the use of Soviet evidence in Canadian Nazi war crimes trials, which became the major point of contention during the Deschênes Commission, was not identified by his committee as an area of concern.

The report of the inter-departmental committee is now history—though not merely the history of 1980. Rather, it serves as a painful elaboration of just why the government failed to act for over forty years. The reasons enumerated in the report, or similar reasons, had always been at the root of government inaction. The publication of the Low report simply exposed the frailty of Canada's justification for doing nothing.

Chapter Eight

The Motives for Inaction

Governments are not motivated by legal considerations alone. The legal advice given to Canada's leaders over the years may well have identified many technical barriers to prosecuting Nazi war criminals, but had this country been serious about the issue, its law makers would have searched doggedly for other, better advice to come up with a mechanism for action. Instead, successive Canadian governments contented themselves with this legal counsel of inactivity and sought out no other opinions. While the detailed reasoning of documents such as the Low report sets out each rationale for inaction, it does not necessarily explain the actual motives behind Canada's desire to do nothing. Ottawa's failure to act for more than forty years has not been for lack of legal remedies, but because of an absence of political will.

Until the appointment of the Commission of Inquiry on War Criminals, Canada had taken virtually no measures against the perpetrators of the Holocaust. Official policy was to do no more than honour extradition requests from other states with which Canada shares extradition treaties. In reality, co-operation by the government with requesting countries was virtually non-existent, to the point where "official" policy came into practical effect only once, with the extradition of Rauca in 1982. A request from any state without an extradition treaty has always been denied, leaving the criminal free to remain in Canada, unpunished. That was the extent of Canada's efforts.

Why has Canada done so little—and so late?

Surely, it was not for lack of suspects. Throughout the years, concerned citizens and interest groups have submitted names and made allegations to the government. Simon Wiesenthal, who founded an organization in 1947 to track war criminals, has estimated that eight hundred to six thousand Nazi criminals have been in Canada. (Now seventy-eight, he has refused to visit this country for the past twelve years in protest against Ottawa's failure to act.) The Department of the Solicitor-General has opened dossiers on nearly three hundred suspects. In the course of its deliberations, the v made inquiries into hundreds of allegations.

While the horrors of the Nazi genocide do not dim with time, one cannot always hope for the kind of evidence needed to make a prosecution stick against every individual who has been named. In many instances, only sketchy details are readily available concerning suspects' identities, as well as dates and locations of crimes. Eye-witnesses may be dispersed around the world or may have died, documents are more likely than not stowed away in dusty archives or lost through the passage of forty years. Case files simply do not come filled with every graphic fact needed to take a criminal to court. That is the job of government and professional investigators—to verify and substantiate complaints. Canadian law enforcement agencies have declined to carry out this task.

But if many allegations are not so clear cut, even when faced with irrefutable evidence, Canada has chosen to look the other way. A number of specific examples come to mind.

The case of Rauca epitomizes the Canadian approach to Nazi war criminals. West Germany began searching for him in 1959. He had, in fact, been granted Canadian citizenship in 1956. Yet, his whereabouts remained unknown to the Canadian authorities until 1972 when the name R-A-U-K-A was discovered on a ship's manifest. By then he was living openly under his own name in suburban Toronto. Still, an inquiry made through the Canadian Embassy in Bonn brought no results in tracking him. The same year, Frankfurt's state prosecutor requested the RCMP to help locate Rauca, to no avail. Germany made further requests in 1973 and 1977, but Rauca could not be found. Throughout this period he continued to pay taxes, carry a Canadian passport that he had obtained in 1961, receive old-age benefits after 1974, hold an Ontario driver's licence and enjoy all other benefits of a Canadian citizen. Again, the RCMP attempted to trace Rauca, but failed to locate him. The slight change made to the spelling of his name seems to have thrown Canadian investigators off his trail time and time again. It was not until 1982 that Rauca was ultimately found as he prepared to make a hasty escape from the country. This undue delay is unfathomable in light of a complete set of landing records later entered into evidence at his extradition trial.

But Rauca was not the only war criminal in Canada who literally went unnoticed by the authorities. When Hermine Braunsteiner travelled to Canada in 1959 to marry her future husband, she was no ordinary visitor to this country. She was a convicted Nazi war criminal who had simply omitted to disclose her prior conviction and sordid record of war time activities. It was only years later, while she was living quietly as a housewife in Queens, New York, that her name leaped into the headlines for her roles as an overseer at the Ravensbruck concentration camp, and later as a guard at Majdanek death camp near Lublin, Poland. Along with Sobibor and Belzec, Majdenek was the killing centre for tens of thousands of Polish Jews and many from Germany and Holland.

Braunsteiner, called the "mare" of Majdanek by Jewish inmates there, was responsible for selecting inmates for the gas chamber. Described by survivors as tough and extremely cruel, she is said to have brandished a whip whose straps were filled with lead bullets. In the words of one survivor: "When mothers with small children were brought to the camp, Braunsteiner would tear the children away. She hated children. I've seen women prisoners scream and faint while she flogged them with her horrible whip. She enjoyed it; she was a sadist. I've seen cruel men and cruel women.... And Hermine Braunsteiner was one of the most vicious I ever met."[1]

In 1949 in Vienna, the People's court had convicted her for her work at Ravensbruck. She was charged with "mistreatment," based on evidence that she had kicked and trampled on Ravensbruck prisoners, including old women, until they bled and died. But no facts about her behaviour at Majdanek had come to light before that lower-level court, and so Braunsteiner had received a light sentence—three years' imprisonment. Released from prison shortly after her conviction, she was given an amnesty by the Austrian government and came to Canada in 1959. It was here that she married Russell Ryan of Brooklyn, New York. In April of that year, they left Canada and moved to the United States to live. She became a naturalized American citizen in 1963 and lived an uneventful life there until she was exposed in 1964.[2]

Her U.S. citizenship was finally revoked in 1971 after court proceedings that were drawn out for nearly seven years. Deportation proceedings followed. But, in the meantime, the Federal Republic of Germany had requested her extradition to stand trial there as part of a major trial against fourteen other Majdanek camp guards. The West German government supported its extradition request with three hundred pages of horrifying testimony of Braunsteiner's complicity in the deaths of thousands of Jewish Majdanek prisoners.

In February 1974, Braunsteiner was one of five women and nine men in Dusseldorf charged with the deaths of some 250,000 people at Majdanek. One of Germany's longest and costliest war crimes trials, the Majdanek trial finally came to a close after nearly six years. Braunsteiner was convicted in June 1981 of multiple murder and sentenced to life imprisonment—the highest possible sentence—which she is currently serving in a German prison.[3] When she entered Canada, the federal authorities made no attempt to keep this Nazi war criminal out of the country.

Haralds Puntulis was another known Nazi war criminal who had managed to find refuge in Canada. Puntulis was tried *in absentia* on a charge of treason by the Latvian Supreme Court in 1965, along with two co-accused named Boleslaus Maikovskis and Albert Eichelis. According to the evidence, the three played leading roles in the persecution and murder of hundreds of Jews and other innocent people in Latvia. Puntulis, a platoon commander in the semi-military Latvian rural police, was alleged to have offered his services to the Nazis when they marched into Latvia in 1941. He served as chief of police of the fourth precinct of the Rezekne district until the Russians retook Latvia. Puntulis is said to have ordered his men to round up the Jews in the village of Riebina and have them shot in a nearby forest in the summer of 1941. Later, he ordered the killings of the Jews in the town of Malta. He was also alleged to have assisted Maikovskis, chief of police of the neighbouring second precinct and his district commander, Eichelis, in a 1942 raid in which the village of Audrini was burned to the ground. Some two hundred men, women and children were murdered in that massacre.

As their trial unfolded in Latvia, the three men were far away. Eichelis had fled to Germany, Maikovskis had emigrated to the United States in 1951 and Puntulis had found haven in Canada. He landed at Quebec City in 1948, and eventually moved to the Toronto suburb of Willowdale. A successful building contractor, he became a Canadian citizen in 1962. When the Soviet Union requested his extradition to stand trial in 1965, Canada refused on the grounds that the countries did not share an extradition treaty and that the charges were not substantiated. Not a single effort was ever made by the Canadian authorities to investigate the allegations further. In fact, Puntulis spent the remainder of his years in tranquility in his comfortable suburban home. He died a natural death in 1982, undisturbed by a Canadian government that preferred to turn the other cheek to the allegations against him.

Meanwhile, just south of the border, the American government commenced long and drawn out deportation proceedings in 1977 against Maikovskis, who was also alleged to have led the execution squad responsible for the massacre of Riga's Jews. He was ordered deported in 1985. In West Germany, Eichelis was put on trial for war crimes. Canada's refusal to lift a finger to probe the rather serious charges against Pontulis was all the more repugnant when in other countries, justice was being invoked against his cohorts.[4]

As mentioned in a previous chapter, Count Jacques de Bernonville and his Vichy cohorts were prime suspects against whom action could have been taken. And there are at least two hundred more with dossiers containing serious allegations in Justice Department Archives. So Canada would be hard-pressed to attribute its perpetual inactivity on any shortage of suspected individuals.

Nor can the failure of our leaders to mobilize be blamed on the lack of public will. There is no popular constituency in this country that condones mass murder. Canadian society believes the crime of genocide calls for punishment, that Nazi war criminals among us deserve to be brought to justice. Vocal advocates have steadily cried out to government for action. The Canadian Bar Association, representing lawyers across the country, passed a resolution during its 1981 national meeting, calling for legislation "to allow for civilian trial of those accused of war crimes and crimes against humanity." At its 1982 convention, the membership of the Liberal Party of Canada voted in a priority resolution demanding legislative reform of the same type. Other interested groups have submitted concrete proposals for legal avenues of redress.

The will of the people, although muffled in the past, is now clear. But a government's commitment to justice really should not depend on or wait for pressure from its citizenry. Canadian prosecutors do not normally commission a Gallup opinion poll or hold a referendum before deciding whether to lay charges against a criminal and bring him to trial. When an offence has been committed, the Crown's prosecutors bring the accused person to court, without regard to public opinion.

If the general population kept quiet for too long on the issue of Nazi war criminals, the Canadian Jewish community has persistently lobbied the government to do something. It is true that in the early aftermath of World War II, many Jews in Canada and around the world were stunned into silence by the enormity of the crimes committed by Hitler. Some Holocaust survivors may have feared that the pursuit of Nazi mass murderers in Canada would mean the revival of their past nightmares. These were experiences better buried, to the extent that such horrors could ever cease to haunt the soul. The survivors looked around them and found no justice during the war, and likely, they expected little justice in Canada after war ended. In light of the Canadian record, who is to say they were mistaken? They were quite simply grateful to be alive, albeit permanently scarred. But as they gradually emerged from the trauma of their devastating tragedies, Jews began to raise their voices. Both of the major Jewish organizations and many smaller groups have actively pushed the government for a response to the problem of war criminals. The Canadian Jewish Congress set up its legal committee on war crimes to conduct an in-depth exploration of the legal avenues for redress. While I headed the committee, we sought and were granted status to intervene in the extradition case against Rauca, both at his bail hearing appeal and at his extradition appeal at the Federal Court of Appeal. In 1985, after serious study, the League for Human Rights of B'nai Brith Canada published a comprehensive report on the legal means to bring Nazi war criminals to justice.

The question arises, why should the Jewish community and Holocaust survivors carry the burden of seeing that Nazi perpetrators are dealt with? Surely the onus does not fall on the victim to ensure that justice is done—that is a responsibility for the state. Only during primitive times was the punishment of criminals of concern to no one but the injured party and his kin. Modern democratic systems require the law to be set in motion against a wrongdoer whether the injured party wishes it or not. Any state which has not adequate machinery to bring criminals to justice is regarded as extremely ill-regulated. The notion that a show of support from the Jewish community, or survivors, is a prerequisite to the punishment of Nazi war criminals in Canada is a regression to this early primitivism. It is the sign of a poorly regulated country.

Forty-two years have now passed since the end of World War II. Can the mere lapse of time account for inaction by the Canadian government? I don't think so. It doesn't explain why the government did nothing in the days, months and years after the war, while the wounds of the Holocaust were still raw.

The passage of years cannot lie at the root of this country's failure to take positive steps. Canada has no statute of limitations for murder. Indeed, when the West German Statute of Limitations was about to expire, Canada expressed its outrage that Nazi war criminals would soon be able to emerge from the shadows as free men. And while it is true that alleged war criminals have become old men, old age has not been a bar to other criminal prosecutions and is not a valid defence to the crime of

Canada's laws also do not provide a valid excuse. Canadian legislation contains legal mechanisms, and any technical difficulties in present laws—real or imagined—could easily be removed through legislative reform. Objections raised by the Low report and other legal opinions over the years were far-fetched, flimsy and fantastical. Each obstacle could have been overcome. Instead, however, the federal authorities have been perpetually stymied by perceived barriers in the law. Preferring to find impediments to action, they often employed outlandish reasoning which, if left unanswered, may have had a superficial plausibility. But specious arguments do not normally form the basis for government action. Rather, they are the rationale which justify already held views. The legal mind is capable of generating arguments to support any proposition, including the one that mass murder should go unpunished.

Why has the ingenuity of our law makers been channelled into a search for hindrances to prosecution? Several theories emerge. One is intelligence concerns. The Alti Rodal report is filled with abundant evidence to support this hypothesis. A glance south of the border reveals how active the Americans were in gathering intelligence with the aid of Nazis. Irrefutable proof now has surfaced that Nazis were used by U.S. intelligence agencies as informants about Soviet activities. A 1978 report by the General Accounting Office of the United States Congress stated that the CIA had sought payment for some twenty-two ex-Nazis living in the U.S. after the Second World War.

Gustav Hilger—Hitler's deputy foreign minister and liaison with the Special Task Force which murdered 1.4 million Soviet Jews on the Eastern Front—was brought to America after the War, where the CIA and the State Department paid him as a consultant on Soviet affairs.

Former OSI prosecutor John Loftus has said that the entire Nazi government of German-occupied Byelorussia was smuggled into the U.S. by American officials at war's end. The FBI, Army Intelligence and the State Department recruited them for intelligence purposes. Loftus estimated that as late as 1982 three hundred of these Nazis were still residing in the U.S.

Numbering among this group was Stanislau Stankevitch, recruited by U.S. intelligence and permitted to become a U.S. citizen. Stankevitch had been the one who implemented German orders to kill every Jew in Byelorussia, some three-quarters of a million people. He died a natural death in the United States.

Documentation also shows that Otto Von Bolschwing, a former Nazi SS captain who encouraged the 1941 massacre of the Jews in Romania by the Romanian Iron Guard, aided U.S. intelligence. He became a naturalized American citizen in 1959. When denaturalization proceedings were taken against him in 1981, he voluntarily surrendered citizenship on the understanding that he would not be deported because of ill-health. He died shortly after.

The Klaus Barbie affair is, perhaps, the best known example of U.S. reliance on Nazis for intelligence. Erhard Dabringhaus, a professor at Wayne State University in Michigan, has said that during his own stint as a U.S. intelligence agent in 1948, he paid Barbie $1700.00 a month.

The extent of Canada's involvement in intelligence schemes has at least partially surfaced with the Rodal report. Some of the hard facts may remain hidden under the cloak of secrecy because of the government's decision to censor significant portions of that study, but speculation has, nonetheless, been raised. Certainly we know that the U.S. harboured Barbie, and we know that Canada's leaders harboured Barbie's right hand man, Count Jacques de Bernonville. The report made it clear that the government brought a group of German scientists into the country as part of an American and British plan to keep them out of Soviet hands, and links between Canadian authorities and anti-Soviet spies were also alluded to. All of these circumstances may lead to an inference of Canadian participation in intelligence related activities. Moreover, the MacDonald Commission of Inquiry, which was set up in 1977, made a rather pointed observation in its report, one which would support this inference, indicating that there is "the danger of Canada's security intelligence agency adopting the outlook and opinions of a foreign agency, especially of an agency which has come to be depended upon heavily."[5] The prospect of such a peril is not likely to have been raised unless the fault had already been committed. By and large, Canada's outlook and opinions reflect those of U.S. in these matters. From witnesses at the Deschênes Commission, it is apparent that Canada did indeed depend heavily on the U.S. for security screening and intelligence. It would seem from all accounts that just as U.S. intelligence harboured Nazi war criminals for intelligence purposes, Canada, if only a bit player, did the same for parallel reasons.

Anti-Semitism may provide another explanation for Canada's past reluctance to prosecute war criminals. The government is today free from anti-Semitism, but unfortunately, that was not always so.

The determination of the Canadian government—under Mackenzie King, Vincent Massey and Fred Blair—to keep out Jewish Holocaust refugees, has been documented in chilling detail in *None is Too Many*. The diaries of Prime Minister Mackenzie King revealed his blatant anti-Semitic views. In one entry, he wrote, "I must say that the evidence is very strong, not against all Jews, which is quite wrong, as one cannot indict a race any more than one can a nation, but that in a large percentage of the race there are tendencies and trends which are dangerous indeed."

Prime Ministers Louis St. Laurent, and Lester Pearson, though not instigators of Canada's exclusion policies, enthusiastically carried them out. After the war, when St. Laurent was secretary of state for External Affairs, he disagreed with his own officials, who had proposed at least a limited immigration of Jewish refugees sponsored by private groups.

In Cabinet, St. Laurent led the fight for an even more modest program than his ministry had proposed. Even though immigration regulations had recently been amended to permit the admission of close relatives, St. Laurent suggested to Cabinet that, "until some estimate could be made of the total [number of Jews] involved, it would be difficult for the government to make any further commitment for the admission of others."

Lester Pearson became Canadian ambassador to Washington in the postwar years. Fiorello La Guardia, a former mayor of New York City, and, at that time, director general of the United Nations Relief and Rehabilitation Administration, wrote to Pearson asking what Canada was prepared to do to help Jewish refugees. Until that point, Canada had, in order to keep the number of Jewish refugees to a minimum, relied on the excuse that no ships were available to bring them into the country. Upon receipt of La Guardia's letter, Pearson advised the secretary of state for External Affairs, "I do not think we should mention the shipping difficulty to Mr. La Guardia, because I feel certain he will reply with an offer to get ships from the [American] Shipping Board." Hume Wrong, then acting undersecretary of state for External Affairs, replied to Pearson that, to be consistent with other Canadian statements, the shipping difficulty should be mentioned. If shipping were no longer the problem, another could be found.

Mackenzie King was Prime Minister of Canada until 1948. He was succeeded by St. Laurent, who held power until 1957. The Pearson government lasted from 1963 to 1968. Had these men felt a profound concern about the Holocaust, they would never have joined a systematic effort to exclude Holocaust refugees from Canada. Their failure to take measures against Nazi war criminals was consistent with their failure to provide asylum to Holocaust refugees.

In my view, the main reason for government inaction is insularity, the narrow-minded view that Nazi war crimes—perpetrated by non-Canadians against non-Canadians in foreign lands—have nothing to do with this country. In spite of Canada's duties at international law and the powers under Canadian law to prosecute those criminals, Canadian prosecutors have not been motivated.

This refusal to prosecute foreign offenders is not unique to war crimes. It characterizes a reluctance that has bedeviled all international criminal law, and which led to the development of extradition as a remedy.

In theory, extradition, or the surrender of a fugitive to the jurisdiction where the crime was committed, would not be necessary if the country in which the offender was found was prepared to bring him to trial. In practice, though, nations are hesitant to prosecute. This has been confirmed by international law academic I. A. Shearer in his book, *Extradition in International Law*: "Where no interests of the prosecuting State are affected by the crime, the prosecuting authorities may fail to display diligence or enthusiasm in their task."[6] Canada has fallen prey to this very problem. Our law enforcers have identified no Canadian interests affected by Nazi war crimes. As a result, they have shown neither diligence nor enthusiasm in their duty at international law to prosecute these criminals.

A word or two should be added about what Canada has done to date. While Robert Kaplan sat as a member of Parliament on the government back-benches, he introduced a private member's bill to denaturalize persons convicted under the Geneva Conventions Act. The proposed legislation was based on what has turned out to be the overly generous assumption that Nazi war criminals in Canada would indeed be prosecuted under the Geneva Conventions Act. While the government of the day did not pass the bill, it never actually defeated it. All parties agreed to refer the subject to a House of Commons committee on justice and legal affairs for discussion. Shortly after, Parliament was dissolved for the 1979 general election and the matter simply dropped out of sight.

In recent years, other initiatives have been taken. For one, the Canadian government consented to the extradition of Rauca and represented West Germany in our courts throughout the duration of the proceedings.

Following the Rauca affair, Robert Kaplan, as this country's solicitor-general, initiated investigations within the RCMP of over one hundred alleged Nazi war criminals with a view to possible extradition. By 1983, then Minister of Justice Mark MacGuigan indicated that he might be prepared to launch several denaturalization test cases against a few suspects on which there was an abundance of evidence. But the obstructionism throughout the government continued. It seemed that the evidence available was never sufficient to satisfy anyone that a case could go forward. In 1984, Prime Minister Trudeau stepped down from office, and John Turner took over the leadership and called a federal election. Still no cases were launched. Shortly after Brian Mulroney's Progressive Conservative government swept into power, newly appointed Minister of Justice John Crosbie said he would be willing to carry on where MacGuigan left off and go to court in appropriate cases. Again, nothing happened. In the meantime, Mulroney set up the Commission of Inquiry on War Criminals, which delayed further action in spite of Crosbie's assurances to the contrary. Finally, after the Deschênes report came out, Crosbie's successor as Minister of Justice, Ramon Hnatyshyn finally made a firm commitment to legislative reform.

So Canada has not done nothing. It has just done very little and begun the process very late. There is a saying that whatever happens in the United States occurs in Canada ten years later. The Holtzman amendment to deport Nazi war criminals from America became law in October, 1978. It is my hope that Canada will not have to wait until October, 1988 for legislative measures so urgently needed today. We have already waited over forty years since the war ended. That is long enough.

Chapter Nine

Why a Commission of Inquiry?

Realistically, the appointment of the Commission of Inquiry on War Criminals cannot be viewed as a triumph of the Jewish lobby. Jewish organizations had never requested government to appoint a Commission to study the matter. Quite to the contrary, they always believed that adequate legal mechanisms were in place to deal with Nazi war criminals. They felt that existing laws permitted action and for years had urged the government to initiate steps to pursue war criminals. Time was running out and the last thing they wanted was any further stalling. The previous government had already indicated its willingness to proceed on a number of cases, and the Commission's lengthy deliberations would only delay that prospect.

And yet, once it was appointed, the Jewish community hailed the Commission, hoping that the inquiry would at last mobilize a government long incapacitated by internal legal advice. As for the choice of Jules Deschênes to head the Commission, it was, in some ways, an ideal one. He was scholarly and judicious by temperament as well as by profession. As a judge of the Superior Court of Quebec and its former Chief Justice, he was immune from politics and imbued with the principles of justice. As a francophone who was equally fluent in English, he had the ability to engage the attention and interest of both Canadian linguistic communities. What is more, almost unique among the Canadian judiciary, he had a solid grounding in international human rights law. He had previously organized an international conference on the independence of the judiciary. While the Commission sat, he was a member of the United Nations Sub-Commission on Prevention of Discrimination and Protection of Minorities. Once the government decided to appoint a Commission, he became an obvious candidate to lead it.

No one factor can be identified as the springboard which launched the inquiry. Many elements contributed—mounting pressure by concerned citizens, a flood of allegations against suspected individuals pouring in over recent years, the threat of neo-Nazism as it was exposed in the trials of Holocaust deniers Ernst Zundel in Ontario and high school teacher Jim Keegstra in Alberta. Information suggesting Joseph Mengele may have attempted to enter Canada was also a factor. Another element was the election of a new government, willing to confront publicly an issue that preceding governments had preferred to keep buried in back files.

In spite of these very real influences, much speculation arose concerning the reasons behind the Commission's appointment. Most of it was false.

One unfortunate interpretation of events was typified by an article that appeared in a Ukrainian student newspaper.[1] The story attributed the creation of the inquiry to "clever manipulation" of the Progressive Conservative government by the Jewish "influence peddling machine," and to the Jewish community's great financial resources. Such assertions have reverberated through the ages, first to incite and then to justify discrimination, pogroms and genocide. They are words dripping with blood.

The author of the article was evidently impervious to the reality that the Deschênes Commission was anything but a success for the Jewish community. There are those who argue that the Jewish community's campaign over the past fifteen years or more to get the issue of Nazi war criminals onto the government agenda was, in fact, an abject failure. According to historian Harold Troper, the Deschênes Commission mandate was a regression to "ground zero" on issues that the Jewish community thought had already been decided. The Commission, rather than a culmination of years of Jewish activity, was in many respects a setback. Jewish lobbying had most certainly fertilized the ground for action, but it was nowhere near a key factor in the establishment of the inquiry. It was no victory that after more than forty years, Canada had done little more than appoint a Commission to look into the matter of war criminals. Had Jewish concerns had any importance, our government would have adopted a policy of action, not in 1985, but in 1945.

Speculation of this type also overlooks the fact that a policy of recourse against Nazi criminals benefits not only the Jewish community, but Canada as a whole. Prosecuting the perpetrators of war crimes will not bring back to life one person murdered in the Holocaust. All it can do is redeem a remnant of honour for a sullied justice system.

Some news reports incorrectly editorialized that the Deschênes Commission was sparked by lists of supposed war criminals released to Ottawa by the Soviet Union.[2] In fact, the genesis of the inquiry had nothing to do with these lists, which have been circulating for decades. Canada possesses much harder evidence on war criminals in its very own archives than anything of that nature.

The astounding volume of salient facts in existence was brought to the attention of Justice Minister John Crosbie in the early days of his time in that portfolio. A continuing flow of allegations submitted to the newly elected Mulroney government in the fall of 1984 led Crosbie's staff to look into the matter carefully. They requested a briefing from Justice Department officials on the status of war crimes matters. When the Justice files were shown to the minister and his staff, they were filled with graphic, horrifying descriptions of murder and destruction. Said a former aide to Crosbie, "It was worse than I imagined. They had identified a dozen or so in their files. It was clear from the records in the Department of Justice files that these people were the guys who were doing the shooting. There were details about Nazi mobile killing units. I found them chilling." The amount of available information was shocking. The records on one individual, he went on, "told quite enough about him to suggest that something pretty awful had gone on and that he was involved in it, assuming the records were accurate. I didn't realize that they knew his address, everything about him, and that they had his war records from the German archives. He had been involved in crimes in an Eastern European country now occupied by the U.S.S.R."[3] It was also clear that the bureaucrats in the Department of Justice had addressed this issue over and over with previous Cabinet ministers and that they considered the issue to be settled.

But, over the course of the next year, the government was mobilized. Only the minister of justice or Prime Minister Mulroney could say to what extent their decision to set up the

Commission was influenced by two other events in that time frame. The trial of Ernst Zundel for publishing Holocaust denial literature was one. The other was a claim indicating that Joseph Mengele may have tried to enter Canada in 1962.

In the fall of 1984, Ernst Zundel, a Toronto printer, was put on trial for his role in circulating pamphlets denying the occurrence of the Holocaust. His literature called the Holocaust a Jewish fabrication to win sympathy for the state of Israel. Zundel was convicted of spreading false news by the Supreme Court of Ontario on March 25, 1985. (On January 22, 1987, his conviction was overturned on a technicality and a new trial ordered to take place in January, 1988.) Most Canadians were shocked to find such hard core hate propaganda flourishing in their midst. Canada's leaders undoubtedly felt more than a little ill at ease with the appearance that they were dismissing the Holocaust with their continued inaction on Nazi war criminals in the country. Official silence when it came to the perpetrators of the Nazi genocide could only give comfort to those who denied it had ever happened. Combined with the outburst of public interest and the accumulation of allegations, this trial was bound to make Canada's leadership acutely aware of their responsibility to do something.

Soon after, in January, 1985, journalist Sol Littman held a press conference in Toronto where he released information alleging that Joseph Mengele had applied to immigrate here in 1962. Littman, a representative of a group called "Friends of the Simon Wiesenthal Centre for Holocaust Studies," had managed to obtain documents through the U.S. Freedom of Information Act that showed that the Canadian Visa Office in West Germany had made an inquiry to the American security authorities about Mengele. Less than one month later, Prime Minister Mulroney announced the creation of the Commission. If the Littman allegations set the timing for the Commission, it most certainly was not the reason for its creation. As Harold Troper explains, "It was not as much the cause as the excuse." Together with an acceleration of general interest and a growing disquiet, the Mengele claims may have been, in the words of Mr. Justice Deschênes, "the straw that broke the camel's back: the matter had to be clarified once and for all." The question of Mengele's effort to enter Canada became only one of the many matters that the government instructed Mr. Justice Deschênes to probe. By no means was it the primary focus of the inquiry's two years of investigations. Through its fact-finding process, the Commission ultimately determined that the available evidence did not reveal any attempt by Mengele to come here, and Littman's fears were laid to rest.

Because the Littman claim turned out to be wrong, some voiced skepticism about the Commission's appointment. Characteristic of this view was one letter to the editor of the *Winnipeg Sun*, accusing Sol Littman of perpetrating a hoax and calling for the dissolution of the Deschênes Commission altogether.[4]

More distressing, though, was the accusatory attitude adopted by the official federal government legal representative. Department of Justice lawyer Ivan Whitehall seemed to become caught up in the misguided logic that the dismissal of the Mengele charge deprived the inquiry of its entire raison d'être.

When Sol Littman took the stand during the Commissions hearings on December 4 and 5, 1985, Whitehall for no apparent reason became aggressive and abusive during cross-examination. He accused Littman of making unfounded allegations that no reasonable person would have made, calling him a vigilante and questioning his credibility. Such an attack was totally inappropriate for a government legal counsel whose role was intended not to be adversarial, but co-operative with the inquiry process. After all, nobody was on trial.

Testing Littman's credibility in an attempt to show him to be a liar, could not be constructive in furthering the work of the Commission. Littman did not appear before the inquiry as a witness to the events under investigation, but as a researcher and journalist who had drawn some conclusions from material he had supplied to the Commission. The Commission's mandate was to make detailed inquires and to draw its own conclusions.

While it was the duty of government representatives to defend the interests of the government, that duty did not go so far as to defend the inaction over Nazi war criminals in Canada that, until the appointment of the Deschênes Commission, and, except for the extradition of Rauca, characterized government behaviour over the past forty years. Whatever the intent of the attack on Mr. Littman, the impression it left was that it was an attack on the concerns that led to the creation of the Commission, and, as a result, an attack on the Commission itself.

Coming from a government that has done so little over the years about the issue of Nazi war criminals in Canada, such behaviour was an affrontery. Moreover, the Commission's worth did not rise or fall on the validity of a single journalist's allegations. It was justified by one key, undisputed fact: forty-two years of inactivity had made Canada a haven for war criminals. (In a letter to Minister of Justice John Crosbie, I conveyed my concerns on this point. He replied to my letter in January, 1986, but in a non-committal tone, writing, "It would be inappropriate for me as Minister of Justice and Attorney-General of Canada to comment on any specific matter which falls within the discretion of the Commission. I cannot agree that cross-examination of any witness can fairly be characterized as an attack on the Commission itself or on its mandate. I can assure you that the Commissioner continues to have the full support of the government in his important work.")

How many Nazis sought and found refuge in Canada? No one will ever know for sure. All efforts to arrive at an estimate amount to, at best, a numbers game. One statement, however, can be made with virtual certainty. The number of Nazi war criminals who obtained a safe haven here is by far greater than the sum total who will ever be brought to trial and convicted.

If one wanted to attempt a count, and many interested people have, there are essentially two methods that can be used. The first involves a calculation of the actual number of suspects or alleged criminals present in this country. The second would be to estimate how many suspected individuals can realistically be charged and found guilty of war crimes. The first figure will undoubtedly surpass the second. Neither is scientifically guaranteed to be accurate.

Any attempt to count alleged war criminals should begin with a look at the number of people involved in perpetrating the Holocaust—the camp guards who beat Jewish inmates to death, the local police units who marched Jews and other innocents into the forests and shot them, the gas chamber operators, and the many others who enthusiastically committed atrocities. Such a list does exist. A master list of some 160,000 names was compiled by the Central Agency of State Administrations of Justice for the Prosecution of Nationalist Socialist Crimes of Violence at Ludwigsberg, West Germany. The next step would be to look at immigration patterns after the war. How many citizens in each

European country committed war crimes? How many of those people made their way to Canada? In her study for the Deschênes Commission, Alti Rodal concludes that "significant numbers" of war criminals were among the 620,000 immigrants who came to Canada between 1946 and 1967 from twelve European countries where participation in war crimes was extensive. The countries identified are Bulgaria, Czechoslovakia, Estonia, France, West Germany, Hungary, Latvia, Lithuania, Poland, Romania, the Soviet Union and Yugoslavia. She also indicates that known war criminals were admitted to Canada as late as 1983. One would therefore have to consider, in any estimate, the potential number of war criminals who came to Canada in more recent years from countries other than their native lands. It would also be necessary to separate those who merely collaborated or passively co-operated with the Nazis from the true criminals. Demographic and life expectancy patterns would determine how many have survived until today. Using this technique, estimates numbering in the thousands would not be surprising.

The second estimate would focus on specific individuals and the evidence against them. Only those cases where sufficient proof had been uncovered to mount prosecutions could form part of this calculation. This would require extensive fact-finding investigations, digging through archives in foreign countries and identifying reliable witnesses who had not only seen the horrors committed but whose memories had survived the passage of time.

Unquestionably, a wide discrepancy in numbers is bound to arise between these different methodologies. Based on the first system, some people have estimated that as many as three thousand war criminals came to Canada after the war, with some two thousand still living here. In 1986, Simon Wiesenthal estimated that up to six thousand Nazi war criminals may have entered Canada, based on statistical calculations of this nature.[5] The Deschênes Commission, which relied on the second approach, concluded that only twenty cases should be launched and 218 files merited further investigations. Each of these estimates has its own validity.

Surprisingly though, Mr. Justice Deschênes charged that the higher figures were "grossly exaggerated" because not every suspect could be named, and because the evidence against many was sketchy. That sort of criticism is akin to the logic that fewer murders are committed in Canada than the number of victims murdered, because not every killer can be found or brought to trial. It is a fact of life that not every crime can be solved. To insist that an estimate of three thousand or even six thousand war criminals in this country was an exaggeration—unless each individual could be specifically identified—was unrealistic on the part of the Commissioner. His own findings were not conclusive on the number of war criminals here because, as Mr. Justice Deschênes himself conceded in his report, he was under pressure to carry out the mandate of the Commission "within a mercilessly short time frame." As a result, he and his staff were forced to close many files without completing exhaustive inquiries. A substantial body of evidence from Eastern European countries was never examined and the Commission left it up to the government to decide whether it would at some later date pursue those cases which involved foreign investigations and visits abroad. In short, due to the scarcity of both time and sources, the numbers issue was not determined by the Commission with any finality, nor will it ever be. There has been and continues to be a flood of allegations about Nazis in Canada. Thousands of complaints have come in over the years. As an advocate in this area, I am constantly approached with allegations about one individual or another. Although I have complete confidence in the dedication and skills of the Deschênes Commission, it is inevitable that, with the limitations imposed upon it, the Commission was unable to investigate each and every allegation with the thoroughness required to make a decisive pronouncement. All the Commission could have hoped to do was to act as a catalyst for the creation of some mechanism to examine all allegations and to begin systematic cross-

When it comes right down to the need for justice, it does not really matter how many Nazi war criminals are residing in our country. One is too many. For this reason, the position taken by counsel for the Ukrainian Canadian Committee during the inquiry came as quite a shock. Lawyer John Sopinka argued that if not more than a few Nazi war criminals could be positively found in Canada, the Commission should recommend that the government take no action against them. Only, he suggested, if numbers were "significant" should the government implement measures. This view flies in the face of justice. Even if not one war criminal could be found, Canada should have a functioning mechanism in place. The principle of justice should be reflected in this country's laws.

A specific offender cannot always be identified for every crime on the law books, but certain acts are made criminal just the same. Parliament recently passed legislation making theft of nuclear materials a criminal offence, for example. Enacted as an extraterritorial offence, the provision enables Canada to prosecute a nuclear thief found here no matter where he committed his crime. To date, no nuclear thieves have surfaced in Canada, but the government considered the matter serious enough to include it in the Criminal Code. The crime of mass murder is no different. It is illegal whether or not one can point to any of the wrongdoers within Canadian boundaries. Canada passes such laws because it believes the acts they forbid are criminal and wants to do its part in making sure that international criminals are brought to justice. A country cannot leave a gap in the system of legal protection until the fugitive has actually been located within its boundaries. Each state must be ready and able to deal with the criminal at all times. That logic applies equally to war crimes and crimes against humanity. If any gap exists in the law, it should be filled. We want to be prepared to deal with a Nazi war criminal in our midst, whenever he appears.

The numbers game is a red herring. Focussing on the question of "how many" is a strictly historical way of looking at the matter, and we cannot hermetically seal off Nazi crimes in the past. The past is a prologue to the present. Prosecuting crimes of the Holocaust is more than a means of dealing with past history—it is a statement of what we are as a society, and of what we want to become.

Canada's government should, admittedly, deal with major issues and put aside the minor ones. Yet, even one perpetrator at large threatens the integrity of Canadian justice. A single Nazi criminal symbolizes the atrocity of the Holocaust. By ignoring even one perpetrator Canada disregards the murder of millions of innocents.

It should not, then, be necessary to prove in advance that there are a large number of Nazi war criminals in Canada before we equip ourselves with a means of dealing with them. Suppose the government refused to establish a legal mechanism to bring them to justice because there weren't very many of them. Then suppose a war criminal who went undetected during the course of the Deschênes Commission surfaced here later, or subsequently came to Canada from another country. What would federal authorities do then? To cope with the future possibility that a criminal might enter our borders, we must have the legal capacity in the present. If a person such as Helmut Rauca managed to live openly in Canada without detection for thirty-two years, the odds are that others less notorious than Rauca who have concealed themselves carefully might still be well hidden. Canada ought to be prepared to deal with the possibility of such people now. We should not have to wait until they appear.

The Deschênes Commission did not have to establish, as a precondition of its works, the presence of any Nazi war criminals here. Its mandate was to examine the legal means of redress no matter what conclusion it could make about the findings against specific individuals. In the preamble to the order-in-council setting up the Commission, the Cabinet expressed its wish to "adopt all appropriate measures necessary to ensure that any such (Nazi) war criminals currently resident in Canada, or hereafter found in Canada, are brought to justice." By the phrase "hereafter found" the government instructed the Commission to look into legal remedies whether or not it could conclude Nazi war criminals were currently resident in this country.

Excerpts from the body of the mandate confirm that interpretation, calling for the Commission to "conduct such investigations regarding alleged war criminals in Canada, including whether any such person are now resident in Canada...in order to enable [the Commissioner] to report...his recommendations and advice relating to what further action might be taken in Canada to bring to justice such alleged war criminals who might be residing within Canada, including recommendations as to what legal means are now available...or whether and what legislation might be adopted."

The mandate refers to "alleged war criminals" who "might be residing" in the country. It specifically asks the Commission to make recommendations on the legal recourses available, regardless of whether criminals are found here. In essence, the mandate is to report on possibilities for action—any obligation to investigate individuals is auxiliary.

Had the Commission focussed on the evidence against individuals as a precondition, it would have been ignoring its mandate. Commissions of inquiry are inadequate vehicles for determining the guilt or innocence of individuals. That role belongs to courts of law. The Grange Commission of Inquiry, for example, was established to investigate the deaths of infants at the Toronto Hospital for Sick Children. In a case concerning its activities, the Ontario Court of Appeal accurately stated, "A Royal Commission is not for the purpose of trying a case or a charge against anyone, any person or any institution—but for the purpose of informing the people concerning the facts of the matter to be enquired into."

In other words, the Commission was not set up to determine the guilt or innocence of alleged war criminals. Had it taken on that role as its first logical task, and maybe its only task, it would have ceased to function as a commission and usurped the role of a court. Rather, the Commission was charged with providing the fullest possible accounting of both the facts and the law. To focus on the guilt or innocence of particular individuals as a precondition to the rest of its work would have been an abdication of its mandate.

Law makers ought to reflect upon the legal system and the evidence simultaneously and come to conclusions on both. If there be any sequence, it would be best to delve into the law before the facts. After all, it is impossible to identify what type of evidence and how much of it is needed against named suspects until the law is known.

The nature of evidence depends on what the law requires to be proved. Each offence has specific elements, each of which must be established. To extradite or prosecute, facts must be led to prove the commission of a war crime or a crime against humanity that must be proved. Under Canadian denaturalization and deportation laws, what must be proved is that a person gained admission to Canada or obtained citizenship by committing fraud or making false representations. The actual commission of a war crime need not be proved to deprive a person of his right to remain in this country.

Beyond this, the standard of proof depends on the legal mechanism employed. In extradition proceedings, *prima facie* proof of guilt—or enough evidence to warrant the launching of a criminal action—is sufficient. To denaturalize and deport a citizen, stricter requirements of proof are imposed on the authorities. The offending party must be proven on the balance of probabilities to have violated the Citizenship Act. In order to prosecute and convict a war criminal in Canada, his guilt must be established beyond a reasonable doubt. How can the authorities come to any conclusion on whether evidence against individuals exists or whether it is strong enough unless it also decides what legal remedies are applicable?

There is a danger of Canada continuing to be caught up in the vicious circle it has fallen prey to in the past. When evidence of Nazi war criminals has surfaced, government officials have raised questions about the law. When legal options were presented, problems about evidence have forestalled action.

The best way for government to avoid this vicious circle is to look at both law and evidence, as did the Deschênes Commission. Canadian law makers cannot impose upon themselves a requirement that certain evidentiary findings must exist before legal mechanisms can be put in place. Only by performing both tasks simultaneously can the government ensure justice is done.

Chapter Ten

Jewish-Ukrainian Relations

February 1986. During a demonstration by two thousand supporters of Croatian Solidarity in front of the U.S. Consulate in Toronto, sixty-three-year-old Marko Djukic, walked away from the crowd and, without warning, doused himself with gasoline. Yelling "Long live Croatia," he set himself ablaze. The burning man was saved only when nearby demonstrators rushed to smother the flames with a protest banner.

This extreme gesture was made at a rally to protest against the United States extradition of Andrija Artukovic, eighty-six, former minister of the Interior of the independent state of Croatia. He was accused of presiding over the deaths of 700,000 Jews, Gypsies and Serbs during World War II. It was also evidence of the highly charged emotions surrounding the entire question of prosecuting Nazi war criminals.

Many of the Croatians at the protest believed that Artukovic's case was directly related to the work of the Deschênes Commission, a feeling shared by Canada's Ukrainian, Lithuanian, Latvian, Slovenian and Estonian communities.

Upon the appointment of the Commission, the federal government came under immediate attack by Eastern European groups. Spearheaded by the Ukrainian Canadian Committee, a well-financed and sometimes turbulent campaign was set in motion, decrying the work of the Commission and branding its efforts to pursue Nazi war criminals as a witch-hunt. The Commission's legitimacy was assailed and its credibility thrown into question. Massive lobbying efforts were undertaken in the form of heated public forums and debates, meetings with federal politicians, full-page newspaper advertisements and thousands of letters to members of Parliament, Prime Minister Mulroney and even Commissioner Deschênes himself.

Publicity surrounding the Commission began to focus on historical enmities between Canada's Jewish and Eastern European communities, particularly Ukrainian Canadians, which worsened the tensions mounting during the inquiry. Spokesmen for the Ukrainian community expressed fears that the Commission was driving a wedge between the two communities. John Nowasad, president of the Winnipeg-based Ukrainian Canadian Committee said that, while he shared the belief in justice for war criminals, certain allegations reflected badly on people of Ukrainian descent. Orest Rudzik, that organization's past president, worried that many Canadians would be left with an impression that all Ukrainians had collaborated with the SS during the war. Suddenly Jewish-Ukrainian relations became the subject of much media coverage.

Originally, I was surprised that the issue of Jewish-Ukrainian relations, or for that matter Jewish-Eastern European relations arose in the context of the Deschênes Inquiry at all. Although I have been involved in the issue of war criminals for a few years, my perspective was always a legal one, rather than an ethnic one. Like many others, I viewed the Commission as a long-overdue process concerned with what legally could be done to bring to justice those perpetrators of Nazi horrors who have, for years, been left undisturbed.

That is not to say I was unaware of the difficult history of Jewish-Ukrainian relations—nor of the massive loss of life suffered by Jews from the Ukraine at the hands of the Nazis, with the help of the local population. In what is now the Ukrainian Soviet Socialist Republic, sixty percent of the Jewish community was exterminated, some 900,000 victims. Many of their fellow countrymen did risk their lives to shelter Jews. The efforts of the head of the Uniate Ukrainian Church, Metropolitan Andreas Sheptytsky deserve special praise. Sadly, these valiant efforts were overshadowed by the actions of collaborating officials and private citizens.

But this sorry record was not unique to the Ukraine or to the Baltic countries. Millions of Jewish victims died virtually everywhere the Nazis went. In Poland, only ten percent of that country's 3,300,000 Jews survived. Loss of life in Germany, the Netherlands and other Western European countries was equally devastating. Why did the controversy surrounding the Deschênes Commission become fixed on Jewish-Ukrainian relations and on Jewish-Balt relations, and not, say, on the relationship between Jews and Poles, the Dutch or indeed the Germans? What's more, why should whole communities have objected to the pursuit of individual wrongdoers? Bringing criminals to justice is a matter of individual innocence and guilt. In principle, it should not engage the interest of any group, except to the extent that they wish to see justice done.

Much of the conflict focussed less on the mandate of the Commission than on allegations made outside the inquiry. Shortly after the government announced its creation, Simon Wiesenthal said he believed 218 former Ukrainian officers of Hitler's elite SS guard, which ran death camps in Eastern Europe, were living in Canada. Sol Littman said that he had tracked down twenty-eight suspected criminals belonging to Ukrainian SS units through the Toronto telephone book.

By the time the first public hearings of the Commission began in April 1985, many in the Ukrainian community were convinced they had been libelled and slandered by the media and denounced the entire process as reminiscent of the McCarthy era. "They fear that the media have fallen victim to a campaign to identify Ukrainians as war criminals," said historian Harold Troper, who has conducted an in-depth study on postwar relations between Ukrainian and Jewish communities in Canada.[1]

Reflecting the concerns of their constituents, federal politicians began to raise the matter in Parliament. Alex Kindy, Conservative member of Parliament for Calgary East, urged that efforts to bring war criminals to justice not be allowed to reflect poorly on entire ethnic groups. Similar sentiments were expressed by Conservative MP Don Blenkarn, representative of the Toronto suburban riding of Mississauga South, in reference to Canadians of German descent. He charged that the government appeared to some to be castigating the German people in its effort to assure the world that Canada did not harbour war criminals. Justice, he said, is not advanced by the revival of memories of torture, injustice and old bitterness. He believed Canada had a duty to ensure that German Canadians would not be painted as war criminals.

These fears need not be realized. Certainly care must be taken that ethnic slurs are not resorted to in the pursuit of Nazi war criminals, but normally, when criminals are prosecuted, they are not identified by their ethnic origin. There is no valid reason that war criminals should be treated differently. We should not, however, be so hypersensitive to the possibility that a particular nationality might be named that we throw insurmountable hurdles in the way of prosecution. Seeking redress against a single war criminal is not an indictment of the people to which he belongs; it is simply the prosecution of one person. When criminals are put on trial for other crimes, it is not generally considered a slur or an attack on their community. The workings of the criminal justice system are the very antithesis of collective guilt, and it is the notion of collective guilt—and not the culpability of the individual—that lies at the root of hatred and prejudice.

Tragically, the Jewish community has learned that lesson throughout history. In urging action against Nazi war criminals, Jewish advocates would be the last to suggest that collective guilt be inflicted on others. As a group, Jews have been blamed since time immemorial for the death of Christ. It was only in 1961, less than thirty years ago, that the World Council of Churches resolved that Christians should repudiate the idea that Jews are accountable for the crucifixion of Jesus Christ. And not until 1965 did the Roman Catholic Church declare in the Second Vatican Council that the fate of Christ should "not be charged against all the Jews without distinction, then alive, nor against the Jews of today."

Indeed, the notion of collective guilt sparked the attempted extermination of the Jewish people and led to the Nazi murder of eleven million innocent victims, among them six million Jews. Unquestionably, Jews as a group were Hitler's intended victims. In the aftermath of the Holocaust, that same notion of collective guilt—or rather the paranoia of being linked to the evil of the Holocaust because of the deeds of fellow countrymen—has given rise, in its most extreme form, to modern-day Holocaust denial and historical revisionism. During the 1985 trial of Ernst Zundel, for instance, witnesses came forward in his defence to testify how much better they felt about their German heritage by believing Zundel's claims that the Holocaust never happened. One witness, named Armin Auerswald, is reported to have testified that "his feelings of guilt for being German were not rooted in reality." Another, by the name of Jurgen Neumann, is said to have told the court that he did not want his children "to grow up with an unjust stereotype of the Germans, to think badly of their father and grandfather."

An appropriate response to Holocaust denial is not merely to reassert that it happened. In addition, one must reject any notion that there is a link between the Holocaust and the perception of collective guilt on the part of any ethnic group. The matter of justice for war criminals should be approached, not as an ethnic issue, but as a Canadian concern that the innocent go free and that the guilty are punished—that Canada not be a haven for war criminals. With that attitude, there is little risk of smearing communities.

The idea that the Deschênes Commission represented a battle between Jews and Ukrainians may have been driven home by the fact that only Jewish and Ukrainian-based organizations were granted legal status to take part in the proceedings. The adversarial aspect was often played up by news coverage pitting one group against the other and making constant allusions to the re-opening of old wounds. To be sure, the occasional emotional outburst in the course of hearings tended to underline the tensions. One particularly dramatic scene flared up in May, 1985, when the Commission travelled to Winnipeg, Manitoba, the centre of Canada's largest Ukrainian community. In a jammed hearing room in that city's Convention Centre a shouting match involving Auschwitz survivor Phillip Weiss and former Ukrainian prisoner of war Dr. Michael Maranchak forced the Commissioner to call for order. Somewhat exasperated, Mr. Justice Deschênes stated in the clearest possible way that the inquiry had not been set up to indict any group of Canadians:

"Let me say bluntly that this Commission has not been set up in order to start the Second World War all over again. Therefore, the Commission is not sitting here, nor has it been sitting and will it be sitting elsewhere, to stir unkind feelings among various groups of people in this country. This Commission is not directed at any group of people of any ethnic origin whatsoever, and it is not, therefore, to be used a s a kind of platform where old wounds would be re-opened.

The purpose of this Commission, as you know from the Order in Council, is to find out if undesirable individuals, otherwise called war criminals, have slipped into this country, and, if so, to advise the government as to how they should be dealt with. There should be, therefore, no fear that, through the process of this Commission, any number of people, large or small, be smeared as a group. The Commission is geared otherwise and shall protect groups, as it has announced it would protect individuals."

In spite of the perceived conflict, the Jewish and Eastern European groups are not diametrically opposed on the issue of Nazi war criminals so much as they have diverging historical experiences and hence, different priorities.

For the Jewish community, it is repugnant that Canada has imposed an embargo on legal action against war criminals. Their attitude is that this embargo must be lifted and our justice system must be invoked to punish Holocaust murderers. The Ukrainian and Baltic communities, on the other hand, lost their homelands to the Soviet Union during World War II. Deprived of their national states, these people acknowledge in principle the need to bring Nazi war criminals to justice, but dismiss out of hand any evidence that might emanate from the Soviet Union as fundamentally tainted. They are convinced that the Soviets, as part of an ongoing program to repress Ukrainian and Balts in the U.S.S.R., are bound to falsify Soviet-held records and documents from the war and to intimidate witnesses into lying in order to disparage Canadians of Eastern European origin. For them, rejection of the Soviet Union is the first priority.

While the organized Jewish community does not have concerns about Soviet repression as its first priority, it is a concern to which the community is sympathetic. After all, the Soviet Union is even more repressive of the Hebrew language and culture than it is of the Ukrainian language and culture. The teaching of Hebrew is illegal, Hebrew works are confiscated, and Hebrew teachers are arrested.

Anti-Semitism and anti-Zionism are official Soviet policy. Jewish would-be emigrants are denied the right to leave, to be reunited with their families overseas. Jewish human rights activists, such as Anatoly Shcharansky, have been among the Soviet Union's best known political prisoners. It is a measure of the tragedies the Jewish community has suffered in the recent past and the dangers it faces elsewhere in the world that this bitter Soviet repression cannot be the Jewish community's only or even its main concern.

Nonetheless, it is Soviet oppression that the Ukrainian and Baltic communities have in common and which differentiates them from any other groups that might also have an interest in the Deschênes Commission proceedings. This factor, I believe, explains why these communities emerged as principals in the debates surrounding the inquiry. Their co-nationals in the U.S.S.R.. have been subject to repression, and not only from a military and political standpoint as is the case in other Communist states such as Poland or Hungary. Rather, Soviet domination of the Ukraine and Baltic states has been all-pervasive, extending to national, cultural and linguistic repression. Ukrainian and Baltic communities in Canada represent cultures and languages that have been subjected to forced russification. They represent peoples who have been denied the right to self-determination by the Soviets.

Similarly, Croatians and Slovenians feel they have been oppressed by the Serbs in Yugoslavia. They too claim they have been denied their national institutions. Their brethren in North America reflect their concerns through an out and out rejection of the oppressing regime. The fears of these groups surrounding the pursuit of war criminals stem from the very same cause as those of the Ukrainians and the Balts.

Because of their priorities, oppressed nationalities in both Canada and the United States have opposed certain aspects of the quest to bring Nazi war criminals to justice in North America. Whenever the pursuit of war criminals appears to collide or seems inconsistent with the overriding concerns of these communities, they have spoken out. The rejection of suppressor-supplied evidence—the focal point of their concern—has been a mammoth issue for the Deschênes Commission and will be examined fully in a later chapter. Eastern European groups have also fervently opposed any remedy which would involve the deportation or extradition of their compatriots back to the country of repression. Throughout the course of the inquiry, the consideration of these avenues for redress was hotly disputed by these groups, just as their American counterparts have consistently protested the deportation proceedings set in motion by the U.S. Office of Special Investigations.

The case of convicted war criminal Karl Linnas became a touchstone for the emigré activists. An Estonian national, the sixty-seven-year old Linnas was deported from the U.S. to the U.S.S.R., where a death sentence awaited him for his role as a death camp supervisor from August, 1941 until May, 1942. During that period twelve thousand people, including two thousand Jews, were executed. Charging that when he immigrated to the U.S. after the war, Linnas failed to mention this background, the Justice Department launched denaturalization proceedings against him in 1980. His deportation came after several years of appeals. He died of a heart failure following surgery in a Leningrad hospital in July, 1987.[2]

Neither the U.S. nor Canada recognizes the Soviet annexation of Estonia and the other Baltic captive nations, Latvia and Lithuania. U.S. emigré activists argued against the deportation of Linnas to the Soviet Union on the ground that it would contradict American policy of non-recognition. As a policy argument, this reasoning is without foundation. It is, however, indicative of the sorts of concerns these communities feel.

Similar arguments have been raised in relation to the case of John Demjanjuk. Before he was extradited to Israel, Demjanjuk went through deportation proceedings in the United States that might have ultimately led to his deportation back to the Soviet Union. The possibility that a Ukrainian national might be sent back to the Soviet Union outraged the Ukrainian community in North America.

The dramatic burning outside the U.S. Consulate to protest the extradition of Croatian Andrija Artukovic to Yugoslavia was based on the same principle—that no one should be sent back to the country of oppression. For months the Croatian Solidarity supporters picketed the Consulate, carrying placards and shouting, "Artukovic is innocent!"

During the course of the Deschênes Commission, the Ukrainian Canadian Committee ran an advertisement in ethnic Ukrainian newspapers alerting the community to the dangers of deportation back to the Soviet Union because of the creation of the Commission. The notices warned that Ukrainian-Canadians would be tarred as war criminals and deported to the U.S.S.R. on the request of the Soviet police force, the KGB, and charged that every postwar immigrant was at risk.

The campaign by oppressed nationalities or captive nations against aspects of the effort to bring Nazi perpetrators to justice is a particular manifestation of the general tendency to politicize human rights violations. Opponents of a regime are quick to note its human rights failings, but slow to acknowledge their own. A regime's supporters, on the other hand, constantly deny or excuse their own violations, while pointing a finger at their opponents. Human rights becomes a weapon in the battle for legitimacy. Supporters of a regime justify its legitimacy by labelling their opponents terrorists and criminals. Opponents justify their opposition by charging the regime with human rights violations.

Balts, Ukrainians, Slovenians and Croatians view the pursuit of Nazi war criminals in some respects as a taint on their nationalism. Certain aspects of the hunt are regarded as an attempt to delegitimize their claims to self-determination, and to sanction the oppressor's domination over their homelands.

That nationalism underlies the concerns of oppressed nations is also apparent from the sensitivity to ethnic designations. Whenever a suspected or convicted Nazi war criminal is identified as a Ukrainian or a Balt, these communities charge that there has been an ethnic slur. These complaints, in themselves, are totally justified. A criminal should not be identified by his cultural or ethnic origin. That problem is not so much a legal one as a journalistic one. The extreme sensitivity of repressed nationalities to these designations, greater than that of other groups, reveals a concern that goes beyond ethnic slander in a North American context. What they fear is that their nationalistic claims are being discredited. Many worry that their oppressors are trying to paint them as Nazis to put into doubt the validity of the claims to self-determination. In reaction, the concerned groups reject anything that might tar them with a Nazi brush.

Opposition to "selective prosecution" is another demonstration of this attitude. The mandate of the Deschênes Commission was restricted to the investigation of Nazi war criminals. But Nazi crimes are not the only war crimes or crimes against humanity committed during the war. Eastern European communities in Canada criticized the Commission for limiting the scope of the inquiry and lobbied the government to look into criminals on all sides in all wars. Romas Vastokas, in addressing members of Toronto's Lithuanian community in 1985 called for a reopening of the Nuremberg Tribunal to bring to light atrocities committed by Soviet war criminals. He urged other Eastern Europeans to join in the fight to bring these criminals to trial.

Complained Roman Serbyn, Chairman of the Ukrainian Information and Anti-Defamation Commission of Montreal, "War crimes were committed not only under the authority of Nazi Germany. Countless atrocities against the civilian population were also committed by Communists and by criminal collaborators in the service of the Soviet Union. Limiting the work of the Deschênes Commission only to Nazi criminals is selective and incomplete justice."

The Ukrainians, Balts and Slovenians ran a full page ad in the Toronto *Globe and Mail* and in Montreal's *La Presse* in September 1985, asking why the Commission of Inquiry was focussing on political enemies of the Soviet Bloc. The ad asked, "Does Moscow have a vested interest in discrediting refugees who were forced to flee from Eastern Europe?" These communities spoke out, urging that all war crimes be punished. On occasion, vocal activists were heard to argue that unless Soviet war criminals were punished, neither should Nazi war criminals be brought to trial.

While failure to prosecute one criminal does not justify acquitting another, in terms of law reform, the argument against selective prosecution is a valid one. Any reform of the law should be general in nature in order to give credibility and balance to the prosecution of Nazi war criminals.

However, there was every reason for the Commission to confine itself to Nazi war crimes. Given the size of the task—a comprehensive historical and legal review of the past forty years—specialization was the only practical approach in the limited time available to the Commission. One government inquiry could not look at all war crimes without diminishing its effectiveness. For much the same reason that Canada needs a special department to investigate and prosecute Nazi war criminals, Canada needed a specialized commission. Nonetheless, any government action and legislative reforms based on the Deschênes report can and should be comprehensive in scope. All war criminals deserve to be brought to justice.

What is noteworthy about the hostility to this perceived selective prosecution is the context in which it has arisen. It did not issue forth from individuals complaining that others guilty of the same crimes were escaping punishment. Rather, it came from oppressed nationalities, protesting that the oppressors were not being taken to task for their wrongs. Oppressed groups believe that the prosecutions discredit them and they want their oppressors to be equally discredited.

Eastern Europe's repressed cultures have rallied around their national institutions—for Ukrainians that has meant the Galicia Division of the Waffen SS, otherwise known as the 1st Division of the Ukrainian National Army; for the Croatian community, the Nazi puppet government of Pavelic.

The Galicia Division of the Waffen SS was founded by the Nazis on April 28, 1943. The Ukrainian Central Committee, which represented the local Ukrainian population in dealings with the Nazi occupation authorities, appealed to Galician Ukrainians to join the division. Eighty-two thousand volunteers from Galician towns offered their services. Of those, twenty-seven thousand were accepted. On April 25, 1945, thirteen days before it withdrew in the face of the advancing Soviet forces, the division changed its name to the Ukrainian National Army. As many as two thousand members of the division came to Canada in the early 1950s after being detained for three years in Italy and England. As mentioned earlier, Simon Wiesenthal charged that since Canada was the most favoured immigrant country of Ukrainians, at least some of the 218 former SS officers of the Division had immigrated here. Later, Sol Littman said that twenty-eight suspected Nazi war criminals in Canada belonged to Ukrainian SS units. These allegations caused a furor within the Ukrainian community, and the Galicia Division sought and obtained standing before the Deschênes Commission. The division's lawyers exercised their right to examine witnesses in an attempt to elicit answers that would exonerate the six hundred former members of the Ukrainian National Army still in Canada.

One line of argument raised to vindicate the Galicia Division was that its members acted under duress, forced to comply with Nazi commands. In reaction to Simon Wiesenthal's claims, one irate citizen made his point in a letter to the editor of the *Winnipeg Free Press*: "Mr. Wiesenthal's statement about Ukrainian officers who allegedly participated in running death camps is false and unfounded. In some cases, the Gestapo used some individuals from the local police forces to patrol barracks from the outside and to assist in transportation of prisoners, but all of them served as ordinary robots in such situations. Their services were similar to services of the Jewish police in Jewish ghettos."

While duress is a valid defence under the Canadian Criminal Code and applies to the offence of aiding and abetting murder, it does not apply to the crime of murder or attempted murder. (The actual Criminal Code provision reads, in part: "A person who commits an offence under compulsion by threats of immediate death or grievous bodily harm from a person who is present when the offence is committed is excused for committing the offence, if he believes that the threat will be carried out, and if he is not a party to a conspiracy or association whereby he is subject to compulsion.") The defence of duress must be distinguished from the defence of acting under superior orders. Under both Canadian and international law, superior orders does not constitute a defence.

The defence of duress cannot be raised across the board by any person accused of a Nazi war crime. Its validity depends on the facts of a given case. In some trials, evidence has shown that where a person refused to work in the death camps, while he might still have been forced to work for the Nazis, he was likely transferred to another task. The facts in still other cases have revealed that the accused party supported the genocidal acts of the Nazis and participated enthusiastically.

Croatians have rallied around their own national institutions in the same vein. In coming before the Deschênes inquiry, the Croatian Committee for Human Rights presented a submission, the thrust of which staunchly denied any wrongdoing on the part of their countrymen. For Croatians, support for the Pavelic government has focussed on the case of Artukovic. Not merely an average Croatian citizen, Artukovic held offices in the Pavelic government, first as the minister of the Interior and later as minister of Justice and Religion. All accusations against him concern crimes he perpetrated in his capacity as a Croatian government minister. The fact that he was an official of the Croatian regime has generated more support for him in the Croatian community than he would have received had he been an ordinary Croatian national. Demonstrators in the lengthy U.S. Consulate protest in Toronto even went so far as to rally support for Austrian President Kurt Waldheim when allegations about his

Nazi past surfaced. Decorated in 1942 by the Nazi puppet government of Croatia, Waldheim is still regarded by the Croatian community as a hero.

In attempting to exonerate themselves and accuse their oppressors, captive nations are not motivated by tactical considerations alone. They honestly believe they are on the side of right and those who subjugate them are on the side of evil. Whether or not Soviet-supplied evidence is in fact fabricated, they are convinced it will be nothing but lies. Regardless of whether a Yugoslav trial will be fair or not, they really believe it will be biased. This is not to suggest that the debate should lapse into a false symmetry. When both oppressors and oppressed attempt to discredit each other, the rest of the world should not stand back and be neutral. I, for one, support the continued Canadian and American refusal to recognize the Soviet occupation of the Baltic states. I would like to see an independent democratic Ukraine. I support the right to self-determination of all peoples in Yugoslavia.

But all of these issues are irrelevant to the pursuit of war criminals. Here, as elsewhere, we must depoliticize human rights issues. Bringing Nazi mass murderers to justice has nothing whatsoever to do with condoning Communist repression and discrediting oppressed nationalities. The two are absolutely unrelated. Put another way, the right to self-determination of peoples must not be viewed in isolation. We cannot ignore the basic right to life. Without respect for that right, all other privileges become meaningless. The greatest threat to self-determination is genocide, the extermination of peoples. Even those whose primary goal is freedom from repression must be concerned with the punishment of criminals who took part in Hitler's plan to wipe out a race. Human rights values are universal values, and must not be treated as secondary to political, nationalistic or ethnic concerns. They are the prerogative of no one political, national or ethnic group. When human rights values are subordinated to others, not only human rights are weakened, but also the national groups that push them aside.

Shortly before she was dragged off to her death at Bergen-Belsen concentration camp, Anne Frank wrote in her now famous diary, "It's really a wonder that I haven't dropped all my ideals because they seem so absurd and impossible to carry out. Yet, I keep them, because in spite of everything, I still believe that people are really good at heart." Today, we have even more cause for optimism and idealism than Anne Frank did. We live in an era of human rights commissions, the Bill of Rights, the Canadian Charter of Rights and Freedoms. It is this enhanced respect for human rights that led, above all, to the appointment of the Deschênes Commission. We could not, in good conscience, show punctilious concern for all other rights, and ignore the most basic right of all, the right to life.

Oppressed nationalities do not have to condone persecution in order to accept the notion that war criminals should be brought to justice. All they need do is break the linkage in their own minds between the two issues. Freedom for Croatia does not hang upon the innocence of Andrija Artukovic, just as the independence of the Ukraine does not depend on the categorical rejection of evidence in Soviet archives. Continued recognition by Canada and the United States of the Baltic states is not contingent upon Canadian or American refusal to deport Baltic nationals to the U.S.S.R. where warranted. If that lesson is learned, all the other debates will properly recede into the background. To be sure, the guilt or innocence of Artukovic or Demjanjuk must still be determined according to the principles of law and evidence in Soviet hands must continue to be tested for reliability. But these questions can be examined in a calm atmosphere where the issues are legal rather than political, and where the primary concern is whether the result is right, not who gains.

Nonetheless, in an emotion-charged debate which is wrapped up in so much history, it is neither surprising nor inherently destructive that the perspectives of the Jewish and the Eastern European communities are divergent. The differing vantage points of Ukrainians and Jews were made clear from the types of issues raised by each group during the hearings of the Deschênes Commission and the varying court actions launched. While I was in court on behalf of the League for Human Rights, seeking an order for the release of confidential legal opinions on the available remedies (my client feared arguments in the opinions that opposed action would, if kept secret, go unanswered), the Ukrainian Canadian Committee, joined by the Baltic Federation of Canada, the Estonian Central Council, the Latvian National Federation in Canada and the Lithuanian Canadian Community, launched its own court action requesting the court to forbid the Commission to travel to the Soviet Union to collect evidence, unless it went with lawyers representing the suspects under investigation. (Because Mr. Justice Deschênes eventually decided not to go, the case was never heard.)

Contrasting perspectives are inevitable. They are differences which are neither regrettable nor harmful to the Canadian national fabric. On the contrary, the entire debate about Nazi war criminals can be handled in such a way as to contribute to Canada's national unity. The social fabric of this country is in much greater danger of falling to shreds if the murderers of one community were left unpunished due to perceived pressure by another. There is no community in Canada that takes the position that Nazi war criminals in this country should be allowed to go free.

A systematic policy to assess allegations about Nazis in Canada can dispel the rumours and suspicions. Instead of widely fluctuating guesses about the number of murderers, we would gain knowledge of how many there were and who they were. Until a working policy is put in place, all we have are the fears and doubts. When the guilty go free, there is nothing to distinguish them from the innocent, and the innocent are swept into the net of suspicion. It must be remembered that no person is guilty of a war crime simply because of his nationality or ethnic origin. Neither is he necessarily innocent of all war crimes on that basis. Only a functioning legal system, where the facts are properly canvassed, can sort out the innocent from the guilty.

A parallel exists between Ukrainian-Jewish relations and the history of relations between the English and the French in this country. Recently in Canada, we have undergone a trying period in that context. The anglophone and francophone communities began as two solitudes, with little understanding of each other. There evolved the Bilingualism and Biculturalism Commission, the Official Languages Act, the Quebec referendum and finally repatriation, with the historic signing of the Canadian Constitution by the province of Quebec in the spring of 1987. They were difficult times, often punctuated with a good deal of heated debate. The result, though, was positive, leaving each linguistic community with a greater understanding of the other, and Canada a much more united country.

The Eastern European and Jewish communities, too, at least at the organizational level, have been functioning as two solitudes. There has been virtually no co-ordinated liaison between their respective leaders. Like the French and English, these communities have been through difficult times and many heated exchanges as the result of their initial contacts over the war criminal issue. But periodic meetings by group representatives throughout the past two years have broadened each community's appreciation of the other's concerns. Personally speaking, I have learned much from this dialogue. The concerns expressed by Ukrainian and Baltic Canadians at the Deschênes hearings have shed light on the Soviet-imposed forced famine in the Ukraine during the 1930s. I have been made aware of the forced repatriation of Ukrainians and Balts from Western Europe to the Soviet Union and the Gulag Archipelago following World War II as a result of the Yalta Accord. My knowledge of the national, linguistic and cultural repression of the Baltic states and the Ukraine by the U.S.S.R. has been radically expanded.

So the exchange can be a positive one. I am optimistic that Ukrainian-Jewish relations will improve and not deteriorate because of the Deschênes Commission, and that Canada will be a stronger and more united country in the end. This calls for a balanced and level-headed approach. If we are not careful, though, the debate can become antagonistic, sinking into a morass of name-calling, disinformation and mistrust, which could only taint an otherwise important process.

• • •

Three months into the public hearings of the Deschênes Commission, in June 1985, a distressing report issued out of the United States from the Anti-Defamation League of B'nai Brith. Entitled *The Campaign Against the U.S. Justice Department's Prosecution of Suspected Nazi War Criminals*, the forty-page release documented the escalating "smokescreen campaign" by some Ukrainian and Baltic emigré activists over the past five years to undermine the American government's efforts to bring Nazi war criminals to justice. "At times," the report concluded, "this campaign has been marked by ill-concealed anti-Semitic propaganda themes. Another element is an effort to rewrite the history of the World War II era and to distort essential facts about the Holocaust." By December 1985 the World Jewish Congress warned that the situation was deteriorating. Militants were continuing to utter unabashedly anti-Semitic statements and to tighten their ties with Holocaust-denying hate groups.

Canada was not immune from these inflammatory actions. During the summer of 1985, Sol Littman accused influential members of the Ukrainian and Baltic communities of sending up a similar cloud of smoke to sidetrack the Deschênes Commission. He criticized the representatives of these groups for expending a great deal of time and funds in an attempt to derail the Canadian Nazi hunt. In some instances, certainly, anti-Semitism marred the sometimes raucous campaign to convince the Commission that there were not enough Nazi war criminals here to merit the government's attention.

One tactic taken in the two million dollar lobby effort was a series of advertisements in the ethnic press and in Canada's nationally distributed newspaper, the *Globe and Mail,* implying that the work of the inquiry threatened the good name of the Eastern European community and was tainted by Soviet motives. On September 28, 1985, a large drawing of a young girl dressed in folk-dancing garb with the caption "Why discriminate?" appeared as a full-page advertisement in the paper. Said the ad, "It is a tragedy for all Canadians of Eastern European descent that the memory and the history of our homelands are being defiled by Soviet allegations of war criminals in Eastern Europe more than a generation ago."

In February, 1987, shortly before the Deschênes report was slated for public release, the World Congress of Free Ukrainians sponsored another advertisement, this time denouncing the Israeli trial of John Demjanjuk, who has consistently claimed he is a victim of mistaken identity. The ad was part of a continent-wide "Free Demjanjuk" campaign launched by his son-in-law in the U.S. and spilling over into Canada, which was mounted to help offset the costs of his defence. The advertisement, in asking the question "Will justice be seen to be done?" cast aspersions on the partiality of the trial and charged Israel with serious violations of the defendant's fundamental rights. Raising the spectre of Jewish vengeance, the ad stated, "Justice ordinarily does not flourish when an alleged wrongdoer is turned over to his victims." It continued, "There is reason to be concerned that Israel would consider an acquittal a serious setback to

Holocaust remembrance....Thus, the issues of fact in this case will become overshadowed by the interests of the State of Israel. This combined with the general prejudicial atmosphere surrounding the trial will create a propitious climate for a conviction at any cost." The cornerstone of the case against Demjanjuk, it alleged, was a forged piece of evidence from the Soviet Union. No mention was made of the fact that the evidence against Demjanjuk—quite apart from an identity card supplied by the Russians placing him in the SS training camp at Trawnicki—was significant. Nor that Demjanjuk exhausted the entire appeal process, going through every level of court available to him in the United States in the denaturalization, deportation and extradition proceedings—without one dissent. At each stage, the prosecution established a clear, convincing and unequivocal case against him. A person accused of a war crime does not become innocent simply because additional supporting evidence is found in Soviet archives. But that is what the John Demjanjuk campaign of the World Congress of Free Ukrainians amounted to. By clear implication, their message is an attack on the entire process of bringing Nazi war criminals to justice and a part of the effort to halt the workings of the Deschênes Commission.

At the same time, as speculation grew about the anticipated recommendations of Mr. Justice Deschênes, a final full-page advertisement appeared in the *Globe and Mail*. Under the huge banner "Protect the Innocent," and featuring a sketch of children of different nationalities, was the notice presented by a group calling itself the Civil Liberties Commission and sponsored by eleven ethnic organizations. A strident assault on the U.S. Office of Special Investigations, its real purpose was painfully obvious: to undercut the Deschênes report by condemning legitimate American efforts to track down Nazi war criminals. "Your civil liberties are threatened," warned the ad. "Millions of Canadians are outraged by the recent suggestion that a special agency be created to investigate Canadian citizens alleged to have committed war crimes in Europe during the Second World War."

As it turned out, the ad was, in fact, placed by the Ukrainian Canadian Committee, a feature which was nowhere mentioned. It was signed by ten other bodies representing Afghans, Croatians, Estonians, Germans, Latvians, Lithuaninans, Italians, and

Slovenians. The Canadian Civil Liberties Association, a legitimate national human rights body, felt compelled to write to the *Globe and Mail* to dissociate itself from the message.

The advertisement was riddled with glaring inaccuracies and omissions, and played up the "witch-hunt" theme. In so doing, it fell prey to that subtle form of Holocaust denial which hints that the pursuit of war criminals is the search for something that does not exist. "Protect the innocent" suggests that all Nazi criminals who have been denaturalized, deported and extradited are innocent, despite the findings of independent American courts on the basis of clear, convincing and unequivocal evidence.

Claiming that the American's war crime agency was set up with disastrous results, it charged that "In the U.S., investigations are launched based on evidence supplied by the secret police of the Soviet Union, which refuses to respect human rights. *It could happen here!* " This assertion is absolutely false. No case has ever been mounted by the OSI without an independent investigation of all the evidence lasting at least one year. Recently, the majority of files have been opened as a result of cross-checking the extensive lists prepared by the United Nations War Crimes Commission and CROWCASS against American lists of immigrants, citizens, tax payers, drivers licences, and so on. No allegations, tips or denunciations from the Soviet Union or any other source have instigated any proceeding. To name a few, Auschwitz guard Hans Lipschis, deported to West Germany in 1983, Conrad Heinrich Schellong, a supervisor at the Dachau concentration camps who was ordered deported in 1984 and three Mauthasen camp guards recently put on trial were all identified solely through cross-checking. To suggest, as the ad did, that the American pursuit of Nazi murderers is intended to satisfy the political interests of the U.S.S.R. is to ignore reality. Why would the U.S. undertake any action to indulge the Soviets? If anything, OSI proceedings counter Communist propaganda which accuses the West of tolerating

The ad also claimed that "instead of proving that the accused persons committed war crimes, the special agency uses the courts to strip away citizenship and deport the defendants to the Soviet Union for breaking immigration laws. *It could happen here!* " Again, not true. In the United States, unlike in Canada, a person can be denaturalized and deported specifically for having participated in Nazi persecution. To mount a case against an individual successfully on this ground, the OSI must also prove that the suspect actually took part in Nazi crimes. According to Allan Ryan, who has headed up more than forty proceedings, the OSI prosecutions have only succeeded upon the presentation of clear, convincing and unequivocal evidence. American courts have ordered nineteen residents deported and twenty-three others denaturalized—but only after establishing on clear, convincing and unequivocal evidence that they entered the country illegally by concealing their participation in war

"Because the American agency has singled out and prosecuted Eastern Europeans," charged the advertisement, "whole ethnic communities have been slandered by the process. *It could happen here!* " The record speaks for itself: the OSI has probed allegations surrounding Josef Mengele and Klaus Barbie, both. It extradited German national Hermine Braunsteiner Ryan for trial in West Germany. Cases have also been launched against Germans Otto Von Bolschwing and Conrad Schellong. And the OSI has recommended that Austrian head of state Kurt Waldheim be barred entry from the United States because of his shady Nazi past. Eastern Europeans have never been unfairly targeted. In fact, the Polish and Serbian communities, devastated by Nazi atrocities in their homelands, have never felt stigmatized by the agency. Responding to the unwarranted attacks on the OSI, the Polish American Congress wrote a strongly supportive letter in January, 1985 to the director of the OSI, which stated, "the efforts of OSI are in accord with the belief we share that America exists as a haven for the victims of persecution and not the perpetrators of it."

The ad claimed that "individuals investigated by the agency have been attacked and terrorized in their own homes by vigilantes....*It could happen here!* " Just the opposite is true. A functioning justice system, with the legal apparatus to track down and prosecute war criminals is much more likely to guard against vigilantism than foment it. It is when the guilty are allowed to go free and there is neither prosecutor nor courts, that those who are accused—fairly or unfairly—are at risk. "South of the border," said one angry editorial, "justice is in belated pursuit of Nazi war criminals. It could happen here. It *should* happen here."[3]

"All legitimate war criminals *must* be brought to justice," conceded the advertisement's writers, "But not at the cost of our civil liberties." In reality, the OSI is no more frightening or threatening than a special unit set up to deal with drug crimes or commercial fraud. There is every reason in Canada to have a unit that specializes in Nazi war crimes in order to develop an expertise and continuity needed to prosecute such cases. The Deschênes Commission functioned as an office of special investigations with no harm to civil liberties in this country. I fail to see how a unit of skilled prosecutors can pose a menace to the rights and freedoms of any Canadian. Protection of civil liberties means penalizing the guilty as well as ensuring that the blameless go free. In prosecution, as in every other endeavour, if it is worth doing, it is worth doing properly. An amateurish, uninformed, disorganized legal process is of benefit only to the guilty. To suggest, on the one hand, that legitimate criminals must be brought to justice, but on the other, that the necessary legal machinery not be set up, is self-contradictory. One cannot deny the means without devaluing the goal.

While the message spoke of civil liberties, its concerns lay elsewhere. Its hidden agenda was purely political, underscoring the battle over Communist-controlled territories around the world. Except for the Italian community, virtually every signatory to the ad protests the domination of their homelands by Communist regimes. The Afghans, Balts and Ukrainian contest Soviet subjugation of their nations. Croatians and Slovenians reject the current Yugoslav regime. West Germans want a united country with an end to Communist rule on the eastern side of the Berlin Wall. I share these legitimate political aspirations and would like to see the domination cease. But blind anti-Communism ignores the validity of bringing Nazi war criminals to justice.

This political battle, particularly on the Soviet side, is rife with name-calling. Although evidence used in Western war crimes trials has never been proven false, accusations made by the Kremlin outside of court are often wild and outlandish. Communists do not hesitate to brand as war criminals their most inoffensive opponents. For instance, Moscow is blocking several citizens from joining their families in Canada for no apparent good reason. A top Soviet official said in September 1986 that many Canadian residents seeking the release of their relatives are war criminals who themselves fled the U.S.S.R. The Canadian government has no reason to believe these allegations—they seem to be empty propaganda designed to justify Soviet recalcitrance and discredit Canadian efforts. With so many claims of this type floating around, a reading of enough Communist literature makes one wonder whether it is an ideology or a form of abuse. The knee-jerk reaction by oppressed nationalities to this name-calling is all out denial of any wrongdoing by their compatriots. As a result we become caught in a vortex of charges and counter-charges, denunciations and allegations that have nothing to do with justice and everything to do with politics.

There is a logic at play here that came up over and over again during the Second World War, when many people, their sights set only on the defeat of the Communists, collaborated with the Nazis. Taras Hunczak, Professor of History at Rutgers University in New Jersey, wrote that the peoples of the non-Russian Soviet republics viewed the Soviet government as the enemy and looked to foreign powers, including Nazi Germany, for national deliverance. In urging Galician Ukrainians to join the Nazi-formed Galicia Division of the Waffen SS, the Ukrainian Central Committee believed, in the words of Metropolitan Sheptytsky, "there is virtually no price that should not be paid for the creation of a Ukrainian army." For many, collaboration with the Nazis in Central and Eastern Europe became the lesser of two evils—a way of combatting Soviet tyranny. The choice of free and democratic institutions, in the minds of these people, was simply not available. The U.S.S.R., in its propaganda, often blurs the act of collaboration with the actual commission of Nazi war crimes. But the West has maintained the distinction between the two, and in Canada, the choice of democratic institutions is available. In this country as in the U.S., we are not forced to choose between crediting the wildest Soviet accusations and allowing Nazi criminals to remain at large—we are able to opt for justice and democracy. Somehow the authors of the advertisement wrote as if they were faced with the same dilemma as their predecessors in World War II—to give credence to the most outrageous charges of the Kremlin or to take no effective legal recourse against the real Nazi perpetrators. The notion that a system for prosecuting war criminals can exist independent of the Soviet menace is not contemplated.

I do not accuse the writers of the advertisement of contemporary collaboration with the Nazis. But I do charge them with a lack of confidence in the democratic process of justice. In their demonology, the courts are "used" by the OSI, which, in their minds is an agent of the KGB. This not only debases the American system, but our own as well. Nor do I accuse the authors of anti-Communist paranoia. Any fear on the part of Ukrainians is more than justified by the Soviet forced famine in the Ukraine that killed millions. The genocide in Afghanistan inflicted by Moscow has given Afghans every reason to regard the U.S.S.R. with suspicion. But the Soviet threat does not justify the vilification of our own legitimate efforts at justice for barbarous criminals.

Reaction to the ad was swift and furious. In the House of Commons, politicians registered their dismay. Sheila Finestone, member of Parliament for the Montreal constituency of Mount Royal condemned the tactics used. In a prepared statement, she said it was totally reprehensible to suggest that individuals who should not have been admitted to this country in the first place because of heinous crimes, be allowed to enjoy the privilege of Canadian citizenship due to lapse of time. "At a time when neo-Nazism is rearing its ugly head and when some pretend the Holocaust never occurred", she went on, "failing to bring war criminals to justice vindicates old Nazis and encourages new ones. To do anything less would betray what the victims of World War II died for, and what this country and its soldiers bravely fought for. It is a moral stain on the fabric of Canadian society to allow such persons to use this country as a safe haven. *That* is what outrages millions of Canadians."

A scathing editorial which appeared in the *Globe and Mail* on February 4, 1987 lashed out at the "self-styled 'civil libertarians'" for confusing a "legitimate and overdue manhunt for individual war criminals with a witch-hunt aimed at their communities" and for "grossly distorting the role of the OSI." Challenging each of the assertions raised by the ad, the newspaper noted that "the advertisers are themselves culpable of disinformation." The Metropolitan Toronto Mayor's Committee on Community and Race Relations expressed its shock and dismay. Its vice-chairman, Martin I. Applebaum, wrote in a letter to the *Canadian Jewish News* on February 11, 1987, that the committee was "most distressed by the contents and implications of this advertisement; it was clearly in anticipation of a possible recommendation of the Deschênes Commission, and a slanted approach as to what that recommendation might lead to." Applebaum also indicated that he had received assurances from a Ukrainian spokesman that the "mainstream, middle-of-the-road Ukrainian community was upset by the advertisement," and that it did not represent their views. Nor did the Canadian Coalition for Vietnamese Human Rights speak for any of the conventional Vietnamese-Canadian groups. Only two members of that organization were, in fact, Vietnamese.

The involvement by the Italian community—the only signatory to the ad whose home territory is completely free of Communist domination—was an anomaly in both contemporary and historical terms. During the war, the Fascist Italian government remained unresponsive to German demands to deport Jews. In Fascist Italy proper and in all areas occupied by the Mussolini regime, the Jewish community was protected. The Italian Resistance movement was not by and large Communist. Unlike the Croatians, Balts and Ukrainians, the population of Italy never felt forced to elect between Nazism and Communism. To join in such an intemperate attack on American legal institutions seemed to be a violation of the Italian historical tradition.

I travelled to Montreal to talk with the Executive of the National Congress of Italian Canadians, to ask that they not join in any future campaigns of this type. As it turned out, the Italian organization had lent its name to the notice in good faith, without verifying the substance of the accusations against the OSI. Its president, Antonio Sciascia, assured me that his group was in favour of a Canadian agency to prosecute war criminals, so long as it respected civil liberties and followed the due process of law. He also showed me a letter he had just sent to the press which made that very point.

"Protect the innocent" cried out the message. We must not forget the victims of the Holocaust. They were innocent, all of them, and their murders were for no reason. Unless the killers are brought to justice, how can the innocent be protected?

Chapter Eleven

Evidence from Eastern Europe

When Mr. Justice Deschênes announced that officials of the inquiry were contemplating a visit to the Soviet Union to collect evidence against several suspected Nazi war criminals, he sparked an outpouring of emotion and heated debate that spilled over into the general public.

In a letter to the lawyers for parties with standing before the Commission he wrote, on September 13, 1985, "The Commission is currently considering, out of its list of suspects, the cases of eight persons who are residing in Canada and against whom serious allegations of war crimes have been made. It appears that evidence concerning those persons is available in the Netherlands, the United Kingdom, the U.S.A., Poland and the U.S.S.R. Before reaching a decision, the Commission wishes to hear your views as to the legality and advisability of collecting such evidence abroad."

For the Ukrainian and Baltic communities, this was, and remains an explosive question. The Canadian League for the Liberation of the Ukraine, the Ukrainian Federation of Canada, the Ukrainian Youth Associations of Canada, the Committee of Ukrainian Canadian Prisoners, the *Commission d'information et contre le diffamation de Communauté Ukrainien du Canada* and the Ukrainian Canadian Committee all stood before Mr. Justice Deschênes and implored him not to look at any document or examine a single witness from the Soviet Union. This plea was echoed by the Baltic Federation of Canada, the Estonian Central Council of Canada and the Latvian Foundation of Canada.

As the parties to the inquiry battled out the legalities of the issue before the Commissioner, across the country Canadians became polarized on the question of whether or not this evidence ought to be examined. Federal politicians lamented that they had never received so much protest mail. Impassioned letters, for and against, appeared in newspapers from coast to coast. Many arguments have been advanced both in support of and vehemently opposed to the use of evidence from Soviet sources. In my view, none of the objections has been terribly convincing. Each and every ground of opposition can be rebutted, and as an advocate, I have had occasion to respond to them all in one forum or another. Given the intensity of the debate, however, I believe that they deserve to be addressed and refuted here.

One ground of opposition is that the Soviets, who seem so eager to jump on the bandwagon to incriminate Nazi war criminals, have done absolutely nothing to prosecute their own. One question I have heard asked is, "Should we not object to Russian interference in Canadian affairs when Russia supplies Canada with lists of witnesses to war crimes committed by Ukrainians, while closing their eyes to Soviet crimes?"

The outlook betrayed by that question is troublesome. One of the great achievements of the international human rights movement is acceptance of the principle that violations of human rights are not merely of internal domestic concern. They are matters of concern to the international community. No government is free to brutalize, to imprison arbitrarily, to terrorize, to torture, or to murder its own population without reproach from the rest of the world. The Soviets are quick to charge the West with intruding into domestic affairs whenever democratic nations point out human rights violations within the U.S.S.R. A similar Canadian response to Soviet lists of criminals and witnesses, would only reinforce their demands for non-interference in other human rights matters.

Rather than reject the lists, Canadian authorities should examine seriously all information and allegations supplied. Canada could then use this seriousness to set an example when raising our own concerns about Soviet human rights violations. By the same token, witnesses should be examined and cross-examined. It is for Canada to make its own assessments in accordance with Canadian standards of justice. We should not sit back and fold our arms, doing nothing about Nazi war criminals, just because the Soviets do nothing. Rather, our actions should be held up as an example for the U.S.S.R. to follow in dealing with its own offenders.

Another argument against using Soviet evidence was raised by American attorney Paul Zumbakis, who defended Hans Lipschis, a former member of the SS Death's Head Battalion at Auschwitz who was accused of taking part in the persecution of Jews there. Lipschis was deported to the Federal Republic of Germany in 1983. In that case, as in numerous other proceedings brought by the U.S. Office of Special Investigations, officials have examined archival documents and oral testimony from the U.S.S.R. Zumbakis has accused the West of being morally inconsistent when it brings Soviet evidence into Nazi war crimes proceedings. In Nazi trials, people are brought to court for collaborating with the Gestapo, the Nazi secret police, the argument goes. But reliance on Soviet evidence is, in effect, a form of collaboration with the KGB, the Soviet secret police. Historically, the KGB has committed crimes against humanity that compare in enormity with the deeds of the Gestapo. How can we justify collaboration with the KGB?

This reasoning has fatal flaws. For one, when an alleged Nazi war criminal is put on trial, it is not for mere collaboration. Whether he is prosecuted in Canada or extradited for trial overseas, the charge is not collaboration. It is murder. If an accused person is being deported, the ground is not collaboration. It is because he entered the country under false pretenses. Any collaboration involved in collecting evidence from the Soviet Union is not collaboration in murder, but rather, in bringing a Nazi killer to justice. In other arenas, the West is in constant negotiation with the East. The issue of nuclear disarmament is a prime example. Is there anyone who would argue that we should halt those talks on the basis that it amounts to collaboration with the Soviets? One must look beyond the act of collaboration to the purpose and content.

Charges have also been made that the Soviets are only too willing to supply names and evidence in order to sow discord among their most vocal dissident communities, the Ukrainians and the Jews. By fomenting allegations against Ukrainians in North America, the U.S.S.R. hopes to pit the two communities against one another at home, and thereby weaken the dissident movement. It is a classic case of divide and conquer.

Evidence emanating from the Soviet Union has led to ethnic friction. No case more sharply demonstrates the potential for strife than that of John Demjanjuk, a retired autoworker living in

Cleveland, Ohio and born in Dub Macharenzi, Ukraine. In the U.S. deportation case that preceded his extradition to Israel, a key piece of evidence casting him as the sadistic "Ivan the Terrible" was a Nazi SS identification card with Demjanjuk's picture on it. The card, supplied by Soviet archives, originated from the SS training camp at Trawnicki. Demjanjuk was also identified by a series of eyewitnesses. U.S. courts accepted the card as authentic and ordered his deportation in 1984. The judges held that even without reference to the card, the testimony of eyewitnesses left no doubt that he was the cruel "Ivan," who distinguished himself by allegedly standing at the entrance to the gas chambers armed with a sword and tearing off bits of flesh of naked Jews as they arrived.

The American court proceedings and the Israeli trial that began in the spring of 1987 incensed the Ukrainian community. Activists decried the Trawnicki ID card as a Soviet fake. Demonstrations by Ukrainians in the United States protesting the use of Soviet-supplied evidence and counter-demonstrations by Jews denouncing Demjanjuk as a Nazi heightened tensions between the communities and dramatized the disharmony.

Despite these battles, the outright rejection of Soviet evidence will not eliminate ethnic friction. It may satisfy the communities targeted by the Soviets, but it will not satisfy everyone. Only a process that scrutinizes the evidence and throws out the false while accepting what is true, is completely acceptable. A far better response is to avoid treating Nazi war crimes trials as ethnic matters. We should approach them, not as Ukrainians or Jews or Germans, but as Canadians, concerned with justice.

The belief that the Soviets may be using the evidence to sow ethnic discord really forms part of a more general suspicion about Soviet motives in producing names or witnesses. Another motive attributed to them in this regard is that of attempting to discredit Western institutions for which alleged criminals work. For instance, the Soviets may produce an allegation against someone who works in the American media to undermine its credibility. While I hold no brief for the Soviet justice system, or Soviet motives, it is not necessary to go to the same extreme as Ronald Reagan, who has called the Soviet Union an evil empire. (One can, all the same, acknowledge that the Soviet system is less than pure. Trials of dissidents such as Anatoly Shcharnasky and the Soviet campaign equating Zionism with racism are but two graphic illustrations.)

Still, even those with the most deplorable motives can produce solid, usable facts. In ordinary criminal trials, it is common practice to take sworn testimony from accomplices who have plea bargained for lesser sentences in exchange for incriminating evidence against the defendant. A prison cell mate may come into court and testify about the confession made by the accused in his cell. The cell mate himself may stand to gain by testifying. Courts often hear testimony from underworld informers who may be "spilling the beans" simply to get revenge on a rival. In every one of these situations, the evidence is admissible. Certainly, the ulterior motives will cast a cloud over the statements of these witnesses and diminish the weight allotted to them by a judge, but the court will, at the very least, consider what they have to say.

Some critics argue that it is a complete waste of time to look at Soviet-supplied evidence because the more we scrutinize it, the more it will prove to be unreliable. Close examination will inevitably lead to its rejection, so why not short circuit the process altogether. Why squander valuable time and effort? Two very good reasons come to mind. First, rejection is not inevitable. In the Rauca extradition proceedings, for example, Canadian courts accepted a critical piece of evidence supplied by the U.S.S.R. The Jaeger report, prepared by Rauca's Nazi superior, was an account of the killings that Rauca presided over. The original of the report remained in Soviet archives during the case, but a copy filed in court by the Crown was accepted. It would have been a travesty of justice to overlook that document simply because it came from Soviet archives.

Secondly, even if we ultimately throw out Soviet evidence, it is better to do so after full scrutiny than without so much as a passing glance. There is an important element of imitation involved in East-West relations, and an outright rejection of the Soviet legal system will result in an outright rejection by the U.S.S.R. of the Canadian legal system. A thorough examination of the evidence—case by case, witness by witness, document by document—does not only provide the best justice, but also an example we would want the Soviet Union to follow.

The fact that Canada has refused to sign an extradition treaty with the Soviet Union in protest against its unfair justice system may appear inconsistent with our willingness to look at Soviet-supplied evidence in war crimes proceedings. However, when a person is brought before a Canadian court for violating a domestic law, he is not being subjected to a foreign legal process we may believe to be unfair. Soviet evidence used here is carefully evaluated according to Canadian standards. That is a far cry from being forced to submit to the Soviet legal system.

While the danger of fabricated evidence from the Soviet Union may loom large, there is a converse danger that any truthful information emanating from Soviet sources will not be believed. Just like the boy who cried wolf, the U.S.S.R. faces the prospect of being doubted even when it tells the truth. Such is the inevitable punishment suffered by liars. Generally, the manner in which Soviets collect evidence makes it untrustworthy. As a result, we may be inclined to reject it even though it may be accurate. A method of collection is needed so that we can sort out fact from fiction.

There has been a tiny percentage of American cases where evidence was rejected because of the potential for abuse. These cases make it abundantly clear how important it is to put safeguards into effect when gathering information on Soviet soil. The U.S. has made painstaking efforts to ensure that its guidelines are honoured by the Soviets. During the course of the Deschênes Commission, a list of precautions was developed by the Commissioner after considering the submissions of all parties to the hearings. One must, however, avoid the kind of paranoia that replaces reason with fear.

Having said that, why should we examine evidence from the Soviet Union and what can we gain from the effort?

An abundance of evidence about Nazi war crimes is available in the East bloc that does not exist anywhere else. Soviet archives contain mountains of captured German documents. The U.S.S.R. is the repository of virtually all of the records on SS-related activity throughout Eastern Europe. These documents, captured by Soviet forces at the end of the war, consist of exchanges, letters, telegrams and communiqués between the Gestapo and SS units, and correspondence between the German administration and local authorities in Communist countries. In addition, the Soviet Union took over a huge quantity of records from the Berlin Documentation Centre following the war, leaving a serious gap in the Nazi German records available to the

West. Without looking at Soviet-held Nazi documents, it is impossible to judge the extent of the gap.

Then there are the crucial eyewitness accounts of people who lived in the villages of Eastern Europe when the Nazis carried out their program of extermination. There are few Jews among them, since most were executed, but there are still many survivors, bystanders and even people who took part in the crimes and later served jail terms after the war for their collaboration with the Nazis. Soviet authorities interviewed local populations as soon as they marched into Eastern Europe, and carefully documented the devastation. Many of these people are alive today, and can still recount the horrors they witnessed, suffered and in some cases perpetrated. Their original testimonials, recorded after the war, are available today. So is evidence accumulated in various Soviet war crimes trials, as well as the transcripts and judgments of those cases.

Since every Nazi extermination camp was located on what is now Soviet-controlled territory, it is hardly surprising that the witnesses and documents shedding light on the death camps are behind the Iron Curtain. In fact, it is really a misnomer to refer to all of this evidence as "Soviet evidence." The evidence does not emanate from the Soviet government, but from Nazi German records and people who saw the crimes being perpetrated. Perhaps "Canadian evidence" would be a more accurate term: once it has been assessed by our courts according to Canadian standards for trials in this country, it truly is Canadian evidence.

Canadian authorities have never examined the evidence in Eastern bloc countries. Canada did not conduct its own immigration security screening investigations of postwar immigrants, relying instead on friendly foreign government sources. None of them examined Eastern European documents or witnesses. This was made abundantly clear in the testimony that surfaced in the Deschênes Commission. The argument is sometimes raised that every person who has entered Canada has been cleared by security, so that there is no need to investigate further today. But, as the witnesses before the Deschênes inquiry revealed, clearance was more often than not a negative clearance—no evidence was examined.

Not a single piece of evidence from Eastern Europe supplied for Western Nazi war crime trials has ever been judged to be false. No document has ever been found to be a forgery and no eyewitness has been found to have committed perjury or to have been subjected to improper pressure or any other influence. The West has had considerable experience with this evidence both in European and American trials. Originals of documents are invariably made available for inspection and examination by Western forensic experts, including experts brought in by the defendant. When John Demjanjuk complained that the Trawnicki identity card with his picture on it was a Soviet forgery, the U.S. court made the original available to him for expert document analysis, but he chose not to present any analysis in court. His bald assertion of falsification was never substantiated.

Eyewitnesses in these cases are examined by Western prosecution lawyers and cross-examined by lawyers for the defence. Because the witnesses cannot travel abroad, their evidence is taken in the form of depositions. A deposition is a method of taking the testimony of a witness who is unable to appear at a trial. Although the presence of a judge is not required, witnesses are thoroughly examined and the questions and answers form part of the record of the trial. Most recently, depositions taken for trials in the United States have been recorded on videotape to afford the judge the opportunity, not simply to read the evidence on transcripts, but to observe witnesses' demeanour—reactions to questioning, hesitation or discomfort—in order to form impressions about their credibility. Quite often, their testimony is corroborated by Western sources. In many instances, the defendants themselves acknowledge the authenticity of documents and eyewitness accounts or make their own admissions. At the U.S. proceedings against Karl Linnas, for example, it was revealed that twenty years earlier he had admitted the fact of his service at the Nazi concentration camp in Estonia to a co-worker in his home on Long Island, New York. Ignoring his extraordinary admission, Eastern European activists have persisted in charging that he faces deportation solely because of "Soviet evidence".[1]

People who testify from Eastern Europe are like witnesses everywhere. Some have excellent memories. Some are confused and forgetful. Some people are honest, others are deceitful. Here is what Allan Ryan, former head of the OSI had to say in his book *Quiet Neighbors*, about his experience with people who testified in the numerous American war crimes trials: "My conclusion, after seeing scores of such depositions, was that Soviet witnesses, on the whole, were about as truthful and reliable as American witnesses; that is to say, most of them told the truth to the best of their recollection; some were vague and not helpful one way or the other; a few were probably liars. I became firmly convinced that the witnesses had not been 'programmed' or rehearsed by the Soviets. An attempt to show the contrary was a common tactic in cross-examination, which is fair enough, but it never succeeded. More importantly, the judges who saw the videotapes at trial were impressed with the truthfulness and candor of the witness and often cited their testimony in the course of explaining the verdicts."

In a very few cases, American investigators have believed that certain witnesses were being dishonest. But, said Allan Ryan, "There was no pattern to these, as there would have been if the witnesses had been rehearsed by Soviet officials beforehand. I think personal animosity of the witness toward the erstwhile collaborator was the motivating force in such instances." In cases such as these, the testimony has not been put forward as evidence in trials.

Only rarely have American courts decided against relying on Soviet evidence heard at trial. Where it was weak because of fuzzy memories or insufficient safeguards, courts have ruled evidence inadmissible. But no court has judged any of it to be false. This very problem arose in the United States denaturalization case against Juozas Kungys, a Baltic emigré accused of taking part in the killing of innocent people in Lithuania and the confiscation of property from Jews in the ghetto of Kedainiai. The court of first instance held that depositions of Lithuanians taken in the U.S.S.R. by an American investigatory delegation were not admissible in court as evidence that the defendant had participated in Nazi killings. They were ruled out on the basis that the Soviet Union's state interest in discrediting Baltics may have led to the fabrication of evidence. In this case, a Soviet procurator, part of the state prosecution team, had presided over the depositions of witnesses. The translator, too, was a Soviet state employee and a suggestion of bias showed up in the translation. In addition, the procurator imposed restrictions on the cross-examination by the Americans into witnesses' previous statements and dealings with Soviet authorities, so that it would be impossible to judge whether they had been coerced into making their statements. The contents of the depositions gave the impression that portions of earlier protocols (statements), signed by the witnesses, had been invented by the Soviets. Finally, protocols and transcripts of witnesses' testimony that had been taken immediately after the war were not made available to the court, despite its request. So, that evidence was held to be inadmissible. Based on the rest of the evidence that was ruled admissible, the court could not establish Kungys' participation in the Nazi murders and the denaturalization proceedings failed. The decision was, however, reversed on appeal and Kungys lost his U.S. citizenship. Even though the trial judge was highly critical of the evidence and refused to admit it, he specifically ruled that the defence had failed to establish "that any document supplied by the Soviet Union in any denaturalization case was false or that an eyewitness whose testimony was taken in the Soviet Union was subjected to improper pressure or other influence." This case was an aberration, and the bulk of U.S. cases have found Soviet evidence to be true and trustworthy.

Evidence supplied for Western Nazi war crime trials must be distinguished from Soviet propaganda, which is frequently false. But the Soviets have not offered, and the West has never relied on this propaganda.

It is in the Soviet state interest that the evidence be true. The Soviets have made much political mileage from allegations that the West harbours Nazi war criminals, and they have propagandized about the failure of Western nations to punish Nazi murderers. Certainly, as far as Canada is concerned, there is weight to the charges of inaction. But if even one document from Soviet archives is found to be a forgery, or if one witness is shown to have lied, the Communist propaganda advantage will disappear. The entire campaign to portray the West as a haven for Nazis will collapse, and the Soviet Union has nothing to gain by that.

Nonetheless, one often hears the opposite theory—that Soviet state interest is well served by concocting evidence about Nazi war crimes to discredit and defame staunch anti-Communist activists from the Eastern bloc and their leadership. The claim that Soviet co-operation is really a KGB plot to subvert emigré groups in the West holds no water. For one, the people charged with Nazi war crimes and brought to trial are usually of little prominence in the West. A typical accused is hardly the head of a vocal emigré lobby. As a fugitive from justice, he or she has more likely sought anonymity to avoid being found out—the "quiet neighbour" Allan Ryan so aptly describes in his book. Besides, suspects who are put on trial are not identified by the Soviet authorities but by Western law enforcers. The Soviets do not know in advance whom the Americans or West Europeans are going to investigate. The several hundred suspects investigated by the Deschênes Commission were not identified by the Soviets, but by the Commission itself.

One further point. The Soviets do not only provide incriminating evidence. Exculpatory information has also issued from the U.S.S.R. In the United States, the Office of Special Investigations launched cases against two Kowalchuk brothers, both former members of the Ukrainian police in Luboml, Poland. One, accused of taking part in the persecution of Jewish civilians, was denaturalized. In the case against the second brother, the Soviet authorities found a witness who could provide exculpatory testimony. The OSI dropped the charges.

Of course, it is in the interest of the accused to denounce evidence from Eastern European sources as false. Throughout the long history of Western Nazi war crimes trials it is unheard of for an accused person to admit to the deeds he is charged with and beg forgiveness. More typical reactions are either to claim that the crimes were justified or to flatly deny them. Some defendants have even raised both defences at once. The campaign to discredit Soviet-supplied evidence is not a deliberate one mounted by Nazi war criminals and their supporters, but, that they reap the benefits cannot be ignored. And there is most definitely a concerted effort, particularly in the United States, to halt any effort to bring Nazi war criminals to justice and to disband the OSI. For those who believe the Holocaust was justified, any argument—including anti-Communism—will serve their purpose. Neither must we forget the standard criminal response to the prosecutor. When the facts are against him, the accused will assail the law. When the law is against him, he attacks the facts. When both are against him, the criminal lashes out against the prosecutor. Criticism of evidence supplied by the Soviet Union for no other reason than where it comes from is another way of impugning the prosecution.

The attack on Soviet evidence is a prime example of the *ad hominem* fallacy (i.e., because the person is evil, what he says is false). Actually, in this case one might want to call it the *ad imperium* fallacy (since the Soviet empire is evil, what its authorities say is false) fallacy. Since the Soviet regime is evil, its witnesses must be liars and its documents false. The notion that only the good can speak the truth and that the wicked always speak deceit is illusory. If Canadian courts required all witnesses to be angelic before putting them on the stand, it would cease to function. The strength of our court system does not guarantee the truth of our witnesses, nor does the weakness of the Soviet system mean everyone there will be dishonest. Granted, most of us would like to see a democratic government in the Soviet Union. But if we have to wait for that to happen before we can consider all relevant evidence from Eastern Europe, the opportunity to bring Nazi war criminals to justice will have long passed. Time is short enough as it is.

I am sometimes asked whether I would be prepared to accept evidence emanating from Nazi sources in Canadian court cases. The answer to that is, yes. If, during the Nazi years, Canada were conducting trials of Soviet war crimes, it would have been perfectly appropriate to examine documents from Nazi archives and to hear testimony from those who were eyewitnesses to the events. Again, all facts and figures would be put through the admissibility tests imposed by the Canadian trial system. An example for this, in fact, exists. The Swiss Red Cross conducted an inquiry into the Russian massacre of Polish officers at Katyn in Poland, at the behest of and with the assistance of, the German Army.

Use of evidence from Eastern Europe does not legitimize the Soviet system. An examination of documents and witnesses that come out of the Soviet Union is not a seal of approval for Communist regimes. It does not legitimize Soviet domination of the Ukraine or its claims to Latvia, Lithuania and Estonia, and Canada's non-recognition policy is not offended in any way.

The attack on evidence from the U.S.S.R. is, in reality, a denunciation of Canadian courts. The suggestion has never been made that every ounce of information offered by Eastern Europe ought to be accepted on blind faith. Rather, it must be scrutinized like all other evidence and admitted only if it meets Canadian standards. To say Canada should not even look at what the Soviets have to show us is to insinuate that our courts are incapable of sorting good evidence from bad—it bespeaks a lack of confidence in our judicial system. It reflects an undemocratic mistrust in Canadian institutions.

Some people ask, however, how can we accept evidence from the Soviet Union on the one hand and, on the other, denounce the trials of Anatoly Shcharansky and other dissidents from the U.S.S.R.? The difference is strikingly clear. Shcharansky and others like him were tried in Soviet courts, according to Soviet standards, for Soviet offences. War crimes trials in Canada would not be Soviet trials. The Soviet Union has political crimes. Its judiciary is state-controlled. Canadian law is free from political crimes and its judges are completely independent.

The Canadian justice system is fair. This point, I would like to think, need not be made. While there is always room for improvement in our legal system, all judicial proceedings— whether they be criminal, extradition, revocation of citizenship or deportation—are equitable. The system is fair both to the innocent and the guilty. The fact that a person might be accused of a Nazi war crime and be acquitted is no justification for failing to invoke the justice system. It is a strength of our legal system that some people are convicted and others are acquitted. Any perceived imbalance between the accused and the state is more than compensated for by the onus on the prosecution to prove the guilt of the person charged. The protections built into our legal system mean fair trials for any defendant, including accused Nazi war criminals.

It is an affront to survivors to deny them the opportunity to testify against the perpetrators of the Holocaust. Not all Holocaust survivors departed for the West and Israel after the war. Many stayed behind in Eastern Europe. The stories they have to tell against the murderers of their parents, children, brothers and sisters deserve to be heard. To deprive them of the chance to give their testimony is to victimize the survivors twice over. The living owe it to the dead to bring these killers to justice.

I haven't the slightest doubt that the abundance of testimony and archival records in the Soviet Union has proven to be invaluable in fleshing out all the facts about Nazi war criminals in the West. The unrelenting campaign to undermine the use of Soviet-supplied evidence—the denunciations, the petitions, the demonstrations, the letters—is based on irrational fears about a Soviet conspiracy and ignorance of the protections built into the process of weighing the evidence. Those who protest any form of co-operation with a state which has oppressed their brethren are unlikely to be convinced about the validity of the effort.

Against this backdrop of bitter controversy and emotionalism, the Deschênes Commission of Inquiry and the lawyers who appeared before it, applied themselves to the more dispassionate task of sifting through the legal and logistical issues facing Canada as it contemplated its first ever fact-finding mission in the Soviet Union.

Presentation of the arguments before the inquiry consumed three full days of hearings on September 23, October 3 and October 10, 1985. As representatives of the parties with standing, we were asked to address ourselves to two distinct issues: first, whether the Commission was legally empowered to go to look at the evidence and second, whether it was advisable.

On the question of the legality of sending an investigative team to the Soviet Union, four of the five counsel were in accord that Mr. Justice Deschênes was entitled to do so—I on behalf of the League for Human Rights, Irwin Cotler for the Canadian Jewish Congress, Yuri Botiuk, who now represented the Ukrainian National Army and Department of Justice lawyer Ian Binnie for the Government of Canada. Not surprisingly, John Sopinka, on behalf of the Ukrainian Canadian Committee, was absolutely and utterly opposed. The collection of evidence would be so defective, he argued, that it would bring the administration of Canadian justice into disrepute and as a result violate our Charter of Rights and Freedoms. Mr. Justice Deschênes, therefore, had no legal authority to conduct his investigations in Eastern Europe.

As to the advisability of going, both Irwin Cotler and I submitted that it was perfectly acceptable, so long as certain safeguards were agreed to by the Soviet Union. Between us, we recommended a list of ten precautions based on the model of the American OSI:

1. Any Deschênes Commission hearings in Eastern Europe should be held *in camera*, to protect the reputation of individuals under investigation. In the experience of the OSI, the Soviets had never publicized the name of any person who had been investigated but not brought trial.

2. The testimony of all witnesses should be videotaped.

3. An independent interpreter, not a Soviet employee, should be used for translations.

4. All examinations of witnesses should be supervised by the Honourable Jules Deschênes or an official of the Commission.

5. Where the authenticity of any document is in question, the Commission should examine the original.

6. Forensic experts should examine any documents whose authenticity is doubted.

7. The Commission should avoid, and insist that any Eastern European officials involved in the examination of witnesses avoid, prejudicial statements.

8. Witnesses should be asked about the manner in which they were prepared for their testimony, where feasible.

9. The Commission should ask witnesses about their own involvement in the crimes under investigation, in appropriate circumstances.

10. All relevant documents, including earlier protocols signed by witnesses, and transcripts of testimony in other war crimes trials, should be examined.

Besides these, I recommended two other precautions which should be implemented in the event that any cases went to trial. First, the Canadian government should offer to pay the expenses of defence lawyers who travelled to Eastern Europe to cross-examine witnesses in appropriate cases. In addition, defence counsel should be given access to any exculpatory documents or witnesses known to the Soviet authorities.

In spite of these suggested guidelines, both John Sopinka and Yuri Botiuk argued adamantly against the advisability of any fact-finding in the U.S.S.R.

After weighing the submissions of all counsel and deliberating on the matter for one month, Mr. Justice Deschênes came down with a lengthy written judgment in which he concluded that he was both permitted by law to proceed with the gathering of Soviet-held evidence and that it was wise and fitting for the Commission to do so.

Responding to Sopinka's argument against the legality of going, Deschênes reasoned, "The whole argument is of course predicated on the existence of the defects which have been alleged. That is the Achilles' heel of the argument: the defects cannot be shown to affect the evidence before the evidence has actually been taken. Assuming respect for the Canadian rules, such defects would *never* arise; assuming their disregard, they *may* arise. Either way the argument is *now* premature." The Commissioner was equally firm in his resolve that the visit was advisable:

> "It is worth recalling that this Commission is not trying anybody. It is inquiring into allegations of war crimes and, for that purpose, it must hear and collect evidence, wherever it may be. That process cannot and should not be prevented.
>
> So there is no reason in fact why evidence should not be sought and heard, even in Eastern Bloc countries. There is no reason of policy why this evidence should be automatically excluded. There is no support in jurisprudence why this effort should be stopped *a priori*. Thus the law, the facts and the jurisprudence point to the advisability of the Commission pursuing its efforts, even on foreign soil.
>
> The Commission is of the opinion that it is both legal and advisable for it to hear and collect evidence available in foreign countries, whichever these may be."

No collection of evidence, he added, would take place unless six safeguards were observed: protection of reputations through confidentiality, independent interpreters, access to original documents, access to witnesses' previous statements, freedom to examine witnesses in accordance with Canadian rules of evidence and videotaping of all examinations. Mr. Justice Deschênes also provided that the testimony should be obtained not by himself, but by authorized deputy-Commissioners. The government deputized Commission counsel Michael Meighen and Yves Fortier to carry out the task.

The Commissioner added one final proviso, "that time constraints do not defeat the Commission's plans". In the end, the clock won out. No one went to the Soviet Union.

On November 26, 1985, the Deschênes Commission wrote to Moscow, asking the authorities to locate some seventy witnesses and to provide information on any other witnesses who might testify about fifteen persons under suspicion in Canada. By this time, however, the mandate of the inquiry was about to expire. At the time of its creation, the Commission had been allotted almost one year in which to deliberate and that period was to end on December 30, 1985. Early in December, at the request of Deschênes, the government agreed to extend the deadline another six months, until June 30, 1986.

The Soviet reply did not come until May 1, 1986. Moscow advised that it would be prepared to receive the Commission's delegates after June 10 for the examination of thirty-four witnesses who had been located to testify about two of the suspects. In the meantime, the Soviets were continuing to track down witnesses and documents concerning the alleged war criminals. Four days after that letter arrived, the Commission held its last public hearings on May 5 and 6, in Hull, Quebec. Surprisingly, neither the Commissioner himself nor Commission lawyers Michael Meighen and Yves Fortier made any mention of the correspondence.

On May 7, 1986, Meighen and Fortier wrote back to the Soviets and requested the names of the witnesses, the language in which they would testify and the place where they would testify. They also asked for assurances that the Commission's safeguards would be respected. By way of reply, Alexeie Makarov, the Soviet chargé d'affaires in Ottawa, wrote a letter on May 26 indicating that within the framework of the legislation of criminal procedure of the Ukrainian Soviet Socialist Republic, Canadian lawyers would be given the opportunity to clarify from witnesses all questions of interest to them. Videotaping and independent interpreters would also be permitted.

Noting that no specific reference had been made to two of the safeguards, access to original documents and previous statements of witnesses, the Commission counsel sent another letter on May 29, 1986. This letter was very negative in tone. Meighen and Fortier complained that Moscow had breached confidentiality by revealing the names of the two suspects to certain Canadian journalists. Finally, they stated, it was their view that the Soviets had rejected the safeguard concerning the use of Canadian rules of evidence. Because it appeared that no agreement as to the conditions had been reached, the lawyers said that the Commission would not travel to the Soviet Union to examine witnesses. They would, however, reconsider their decision, should the Soviet position change. My own reading of the Soviet letter did not disclose any rejection of the guidelines. At worst, Moscow had been ambiguous and a clarification was undoubtedly in order. But to state, as Meighen and Fortier did, that "you have not agreed," revealed an eagerness to seek a disagreement that simply did not exist, as subsequent events would make clear.

Shortly after that communication, the Commission deadline was again extended, this time until September 30, 1986.

In a letter dated June 9, 1986, the Soviets confirmed that all conditions had been accepted, underlining that they would provide documents and witnesses "in accordance with the procedural regulations laid down in the decision of the Commission." To this, Commission counsel replied on June 11 that, while the conditions had been met, they would not be travelling abroad after all due to the lengthy delay from the time of their initial correspondence. The Commission, said the letter, had already examined a good deal of evidence in Canada and one month abroad to collect evidence about two people would not be the best use of the Commission's time.

On September 30, Cabinet approved yet another extension of the Commission's mandate until November 30, 1986, and later, the deadline was postponed one last time, until the end of the year.

Given this chronology of events, the decision by the Commission was extremely troubling in several ways. The timing, for one, seems odd. Why was Deschênes initially prepared to go to the Eastern Bloc to examine seventy witnesses back in November 1985 when its original term was about to expire in five weeks? And again in May 1986, why did the inquiry appear willing to make the trip to see thirty-four witnesses, even though its deadline was only one month away? Yet, on June 11, when three and a half months remained before its deadline, the Commission felt it no longer had enough time. Since lawyers Meighen and Fortier had been deputized to make the journey, the Commissioner had no reason to worry about taking up his own time in the examinations overseas. If the Commission lawyers themselves were too busy, someone else could have been authorized. Surely the Commission could have found a qualified replacement to find some time within the next three and a half months to gather this potentially worthwhile evidence. What had changed by June 11, 1985?

The Commission could just as easily have notified the Soviets of this change of heart in the letters of May 7 or May 29. Any objection to the time involved should have been raised at the first possible opportunity. Obviously, if the Commissioner felt on June 11 that he was pressed, he must have been of the same view on May 29, and could have said as much. In retrospect, the whole exchange of correspondence with Moscow was a charade.

Strangely, the impression left by the turn of events was that one month was too brief to see thirty-four people. Had there been fewer witnesses, it appeared, the Commission might have been willing to conduct the investigation. One would expect the reverse to be true—the more probative evidence available, the more inclined Mr. Justice Deschênes should have been to travel to the Soviet Union. This inflexibility on the part of the Commission was astounding. It treated the opportunity to make the journey as all or nothing. Since it could not find the time to examine all witnesses being offered, it would meet with none. Had they been determined, surely Meighen and Fortier could have chosen to interview a smaller number of people.

While I am confident that the inquiry had reviewed masses of information here in Canada about its suspects, interviewing the witnesses in the U.S.S.R. was a golden opportunity to assess their credibility and the accuracy of the charges. Talking to each witness in person, judging his demeanour (the steadiness of his gaze, whether he fidgeted when giving answers to probing questions), would have added a dimension to the testimony that simply could not come out of reading typewritten documents in Canada.

Moreover, the stormy controversy surrounding the many dangers of Soviet-supplied evidence called for a firsthand assessment of the situation. It would have been invaluable for the Commission to report on its direct findings as a guide for future action by the government. To undermine this opportunity by focussing on Moscow's delay in responding to the Commission's letters is implausible. True, the Deschênes inquiry had been working fast and furiously. But Canada, as a country has waited over forty years to begin taking action, and after such a protracted delay by our government, it seemed ridiculous for a government-appointed body to complain of a five-month delay by the U.S.S.R. Cancellation of the proposed trip defied the urgency of the circumstances. The witnesses were people who could talk about the events they had seen decades ago. Most are elderly and some may have since died. A chance to meet with these Eastern Europeans who lived through the Holocaust may never come up again.

This unilateral retraction by the Deschênes Commission was all the more objectionable following, as it did, three days of legal argument and the firm decision that it was both legal and advisable to make the fact-finding mission. In reversing its own conclusion, without a second hearing, the Commission made a mockery of its own proceedings. Not only was the reversal unfair to everyone who took part in the original hearings, but it made the entire process seem nothing more than a sham. Certainly, all of our expectations had been dashed. We had read a well-reasoned judgment setting out why it was appropriate for the Commission to travel to the Eastern Bloc so long as certain conditions were met, and we had every ground to expect that decision to be carried out. It was tantamount to an undertaking, and by reneging, Mr. Justice Deschênes breached that undertaking. In the interests of good government, an administrative body should implement the decisions it makes. It is also in the interests of justice that legal undertakings are fulfilled.

With all of the lobbying by Ukrainian and Baltic activists to halt the Commission's efforts, when it was announced that the Commission would not travel to Eastern Europe, many Canadians were stunned by what appeared to be political interference. I do not believe that the government issued an ultimatum to the Deschênes inquiry. Nor do I believe that the Commissioner was motivated by the turbulent wrangling that went on endlessly. More likely, the Commission's real reasons for not going were the ones it gave. But they were weak reasons, all the same. There is a time-honoured maxim that justice must not only be done—it must also be seen to be done. In this context, it meant justice must not only be free from political meddling, but must be seen to be free from outside influences. Having reversed a highly sensitive decision in an unfair manner for reasons which do not stand up to scrutiny, the inquiry could barely avoid the semblance of external pressures. While I do not share that view, the Commission must shoulder the responsibility for the widespread public belief that political interference was a key factor.

Despite this misstep, I remained a supporter of the Commission's work, but I felt that its action tainted its credibility and would undermine the impact of the Deschênes report. The portion of the report which named suspects was submitted in private to Cabinet, so we will never know whether the two individuals against whom thirty-four Soviet witnesses were prepared to testify were mentioned, or whether they were left out for lack of evidence. We can only speculate on the thoroughness of the inquiry; the failure to investigate evidence in Soviet-controlled territory can only leave lingering doubts. Certainly, the League for Human Rights was beginning to wonder, and was gravely disappointed by the move. Harry Bick, president of B'nai Brith Canada released a statement expressing deep regret that the Commission had backtracked on its decision and urged Deschênes to reconsider. I formally suggested that the Commission revert to its earlier decision, or to interview as many witnesses as it could, and that alternate deputies be sent to the Soviet Union if time constraints prevented Michael Meighen and Yves Fortier from travelling. At the very least, I said, a full hearing should be held to permit all parties to air the issue in public before the Commission came to its final conclusion on whether to uphold its reversal. Somehow, this might have lifted the shadow from the process.

Mr. Justice Deschênes rejected these urgings. In a letter dated July 25, 1986, he wrote to me, "It is unjust to speak of a reversal of decision. It was solely circumstances independent of the Commission which prevent it from following through on its intention clearly expressed November 14, 1985. A trip, and perhaps more than one, lasting several weeks, followed by the necessary deliberations: that can no longer fit in, six months later, with the deadline within which the Commission must submit its report. The Commissioner, besides, foresaw that difficulty: in the very last line of its decision of November 14, 1985, the Commissioner had underlined that the conclusion was subject to three conditions, one of which was that time constraints do not defeat the plans of the Commission." (translated from the French by the author)

In all, twenty-nine cases were identified by the Commission where the seriousness of the allegations and the availability of evidence in foreign countries warranted the collection of evidence abroad. Besides the U.S.S.R. and Poland, Austria, Czechoslovakia, France, Hungary, Israel, the Netherlands, Romania, the United Kingdom and the U.S.A. were in the possession of highly valuable information concerning the investigations of these cases. The inquiry also pointed to ninety-seven additional files where incriminating evidence might well be found abroad, and left it to Parliament to decide whether, as a matter of policy, it would pursue these leads.

There are, I think, lessons for the Canadian government in this affair. It demonstrated that the investigative work on Nazi war criminals cannot end with the Deschênes Commission. Evidence from Eastern Europe and any other nation left unprobed by the inquiry must be collected by the federal authorities. A continuing process, far beyond the Commission's mandate, will be crucial if we are to obtain all relevant evidence against those suspected of Nazi war crimes. And, as Mr. Justice Deschênes said in his report, "Assuming a governmental decision to go ahead, it is clear that another monumental effort will be required to forge ahead with speed, organize work, assess the results and counsel the government as each case ripens."

Chapter Twelve

The Government's Response

At a tense gathering in Ottawa on the morning of March 12, 1987, spokesmen for the Ukrainian and Jewish communities became the first members of the Canadian public to set eyes on Part 1 of the Deschênes report. The complete report, over one thousand pages in length, was submitted to the federal government on December 30, 1986. Earlier, the Commission had notified suspects that would be named in the confidential second part that they were under serious investigation. After three months of detailed scrutiny, Minister of Justice Ramon Hnatyshyn and his staff were ready to release Deschênes' findings and the government's response.

Needless to say, the waiting period was not an easy one—as speculation mounted about the Commission's recommendations, so did everyone's hopes and fears. With each new press leak, the cross-fire between lobby groups intensified. This strained interval set the tone for the March meeting held by the Minister of Justice in the Langevin block of the Parliament Buildings. In an unusual move, Mr. Hnatyshyn summoned the key players in the war crimes debate to a special lock-up session to review the thrust of the report. His intention was to provide Jewish and Ukrainian leaders with the opportunity for an informed reaction to the report, which was to be released publicly in the House of Commons later that day.

The report made it clear that Canada was still a haven for Nazi war criminals, recommended immediate action against twenty suspects and advised the government to carry out investigations on 218 others. Altogether 698 allegations were dismissed because the accused persons never came to Canada, had already died here, or simply could not be found. At the same time, the Commission reported that the Galicia Division should not be indicted as a group because no conclusive proof could be found that its members committed war crimes. Although Mr. Justice Deschênes noted that Canadian policy on war crimes "was not worse than that of several Western countries which displayed an equal lack of interest," he charged that "the matter of war crimes officially lay dormant in Canada for a third of a century." To redress the situation, he approved of a wide range of legal remedies to bring alleged war criminals to justice and urged the government to act quickly and decisively.

Deschênes suggested that the government consider extraditing Nazi war criminals to countries with which it has operative extradition treaties, including Czechoslovakia, Romania, Yugoslavia and Hungary. He also recommended extradition to the U.S.S.R. and Poland pursuant to the Geneva Conventions. He strongly urged amendments to the Canada-Israel treaty to remove the 1967 cut-off date and to allow for extraterritorial jurisdiction so that Israel could request extradition for war crimes committed in Second World War Europe. In the words of Mr. Justice Deschênes, lifting the time restriction on this extradition treaty "should be the first task of those who are interested in bringing war criminals to justice."

Of the various proposals for prosecution in Canada, several were adopted by the Commission. Deschênes advised the federal government to amend the Criminal Code to permit all suspected war criminals, not only Nazis, to be brought to trial in Canadian courts. He asserted that the retroactive nature of the legislation was not in violation of the Charter of Rights and Freedoms, explaining that "article 11(g) of the Canadian Charter, far from being an empty shell, carries a fateful meaning for war criminals. When it adopted the article, Canada was acting in harmony with its international commitments. The time has now come for Canada to realize the concrete implications of the lofty ideals which were given expression by its elected representatives whilst the Canadian Charter of Rights and Freedoms was in gestation." His proposal was a new section in the Criminal Code adding war crimes and crimes against humanity as punishable offences under our law.

The report of the Commission rejected the possibility of private citizens launching their own prosecutions for war crimes under the Criminal Code, preferring to leave such matters in the hands of the federal attorney-general. Deschênes had no qualms that this requirement might allow politics to get in the way of proceedings, stating that with the enactment of new Criminal Code provisions, the attorney-general "would become morally and politically bound to give them effect." He continued, "No private prosecution should be authorized. The experience of this Inquiry has shown how high emotions do run and how barely skin-deep feelings are buried. In the matter of war crimes, no private citizen should be allowed to put the wheels of justice in motion on his own initiative."

As for other avenues of prosecution, the Deschênes inquiry took the position that no trials could be successfully launched under the War Crimes Act as it now stands. The procedures under that statute, which he viewed as an outdated piece of legislation, contravened the legal guarantees in the Charter of Rights and Freedoms. "It is a matter for parliamentary wisdom to decide that military justice should be meted out on the basis of less exacting rules of evidence than civil justice. What we are now searching for, however, is not another form of military justice. The regular justice system of the land should apply itself to the task of trying war criminals. These are entitled to the same quality of justice as any other person against whom criminal charges are preferred: however heinous the offences alleged, we must not be swayed in our faith in the rule of law nor must we let the rule be bent to accommodate some particular evidentiary difficulties. Experience shows that, if the need arises, Canadian prosecutors will be more than competent to overcome those obstacles. In the opinion of the Commission, the matter should be governed by the standard rules of evidence: no more, but no less."

Mr. Justice Deschênes also rejected the possibility of proceeding against suspected war criminals under the Geneva Conventions Act. He considered the Geneva Conventions Act to be substantive in nature—endowing jurisdiction on Canadian courts for offences not recognized at the time they were committed. Because the statute did not explicitly give itself retroactive application, the Commissioner found that it could not be applied to crimes committed during World War II.

Mr. Deschênes, although of the view that war crimes were not crimes as such at international law, did come to the conclusion that they were criminal according to the general principles of law recognized by the community of nations. It would, as a result, be possible to prosecute these as domestic common law offences even without the enactment of criminal legislation, but simply by relying on the Charter of Rights and Freedoms. He stated, "Canada could not have more clearly acknowledged its respect for international law; it could not have bowed more reverently to the universal belief in a basic law common to all mankind; it could not have more eloquently adopted that law into its own legal system. It follows that war crimes can now form the basis of a criminal prosecution in Canada, notwith-standing the lack of any domestic law, or even any domestic law to the contrary. Before any superior court of criminal jurisdic-tion in this country, a prosecution can therefore be launched against a war criminal on the basis of a violation of 'the general principles of law recognized by the community of nations.'"

A special office of investigations, based on the American model, was discarded by the Commission. In spite of many indications that he favoured this approach, Mr. Justice De-schênes, apparently influenced by forceful opposition from Eastern European groups, declined to appoint a unit with com-bined investigatory and prosecutorial powers on the grounds it would create ethnic tensions. Instead, he proposed a two-stage mechanism involving both the RCMP and Justice Department lawyers. RCMP officers would handle all investigations and submit their reports to the government prosecutors, who would decide whether or not charges should be laid.

Denaturalization and deportation, while at the bottom of the Commission's list of preferences, did offer certain scope for taking action against war criminals, according to the report. De-schênes accepted, in principle, that all applicants for immigra-tion and citizenship have a duty to disclose all facts and circum-stances that are material to their applications. But he was not sure that a court would agree that such a duty exists. If a court did not agree, he concluded, the routine destruction of immigration forms that could have been used in proceedings for the revoca-tion of citizenship meant that fraud on entry could simply not be proven in many cases. Without these documents, Deschênes was of the view that proceeding on this ground would bear little fruit. He did approve of an amendment to the Citizenship Act to prevent the granting of citizenship and allow for the revocation of citizenship of any person who committed, was involved in or associated with a war crime or crime against humanity. With this amendment, it would no longer be necessary to prove fraud on entry.

As for deportation, Mr. Justice Deschênes wanted to ensure that the government have more control over the country where a suspected Nazi war criminal might be sent. The choice between an Eastern Bloc country and an acknowledged haven for Nazis, he felt, was too draconian. So, he proposed an amendment to the Immigration Act giving the minister "full and sole discretion to select the country" to which a war criminal would be removed. He also recommended a change to immigration laws to enable Canada to keep out and deport anybody who has committed, been involved in or associated with a war crime or crime against humanity.

He also advised the government to make it crystal clear that war criminals could never claim refugee status in this country by adding into the definition of "refugee" under the Immigration Act a specific exclusion for any person who has committed, been actively involved in or associated with a war crime or crime against humanity.

Finally, the Commission of Inquiry on War Criminals proposed that the procedures leading to the revocation of citizenship and deportation be streamlined and consolidated. As Mr. Justice Deschênes explained, "The deportation hearing should be elevated to the level of the judicial process, as in denaturalization; the two hearings should then be joined before the same authority." He went on to suggest that the denaturalization phase proceed first and that the findings of facts in the first phase be conclusive in the deportation stage. He recommended that judicial appeals be denied, or limited to a single appeal against both denaturalization and deportation orders together.

This comprehensive package of changes was presented by Deschênes in order to provide the government with an arsenal of weapons against Nazi war criminals in this country. If extradition was not appropriate in a given case, then prosecution in Canada could be used. If neither of those remedies was suitable, then the denaturalization/deportation route might provide a solution. Anything less than full implementation of these measures, he indicated, might leave the government inadequately equipped to tackle the problem.

The response of the federal Cabinet, which Justice Minister Hnatyshyn outlined to those of us gathered in Ottawa and at a later press conference, was favourable—but selective. The government chose only one of the recommended legal options: prosecution under an amended Criminal Code. In rejecting extradition and deportation, Hnatyshyn explained that the government was guided by the principle that the issue of war crimes "should be dealt with here in Canada and every case must be resolved in a manner consistent with Canadian standards of law and evidence." This "made in Canada" solution, stressed the minister, reflected the government's political will to deal with the problem at home, rather than export a Canadian responsibility to other countries. While left unstated, political pressure from Eastern European communities was likely a major influence on the government's decision to steer clear of any remedy that might result in sending an individual to the Soviet Union. Consistent with this concern, the government also adopted the Deschênes suggestion that no special war crimes office be set up. Instead, Hnatyshyn promised that the resources of the RCMP and Justice Department would be beefed up with additional personnel and resources for the pursuit of war criminals. He also indicated that evidence from the Soviet Union might be considered, if appropriate, but only if it met Canadian standards of evidence.

Prosecution under only the Criminal Code was adopted. The government chose not to embark on prosecutions under the general principles of law recognized by the community of nations or to proceed under the War Crimes Act or Geneva Conventions Act. It also agreed with the Deschênes Commission's recommendation against allowing private prosecution. Although Cabinet decided not to opt for changes in the law permitting denaturalization of any Nazi war criminal who is already a Canadian citizen, it did go along with legislative amendments to prevent citizenship from being granted in future to those who were convicted, accused or under investigation for war crimes in other countries. In the same vein, the government refused to change the law to deport war criminals who are already here, but promised to introduce legislation to exclude war criminals who attempt to enter in the future. The federal Cabinet also rejected any consolidation of denaturalization and deportation proceedings. Hnatyshynindicated the government's intention to make the Immigration Act refugee definition expressly inapplicable to war criminals. As indicated in an earlier chapter, an amendment to that effect was introduced by the government on May 5, 1987.

Reaction from the Jewish and Ukrainian communities was, by and large, positive. Ukrainian leaders were pleased that the government had decided to pursue war criminals and criminals against humanity of every kind and not just Nazi perpetrators. They also expressed relief that no office of special investigations would be established, that there would be no extradition or deportation to the Soviet Union and that the Galicia Division had been exonerated as a group. The Jewish community was gratified to hear Hnatyshyn reiterate that the "government must be concerned if even one individual guilty of war crimes has sought refuge from justice in Canada." Jewish leadership, while disappointed with some of the restrictions imposed on the choice of remedies, commended the federal government on its unprecedented interest in the issue and urged immediate action.

The minister of Justice promised to introduce legislative reform before the end of the parliamentary session in early summer. His department went to work immediately drafting an omnibus bill incorporating every measure adopted by Cabinet. In the meantime, however, no other concrete steps were taken under existing laws. With time running out, it seemed that at the very least, the authorities might have gone to work on some of the pending extradition files or even deportation cases that had been put on hold throughout the duration of the inquiry. There was, for these cases, no reason to wait for new legislation—the law was already in place. Fears were expressed in some circles that suspects were being given ample opportunity to escape justice. Said former Solicitor General Robert Kaplan, "I would be very surprised if some of the people on the hit list have not already taken steps to protect themselves."

On June 23, Jewish and Ukrainian leaders were again summoned to Ottawa by the minister of Justice. He was about to introduce in the House of Commons what he called "historic legislation" encompassing amendments to the Criminal Code, Citizenship Act and Immigration Act. The community leaders were given an advance opportunity to question government officials responsible for drafting the legislation and to make their concerns known to the minister of Justice. Later that day, after tabling the amendments (contained in Bill 71) in Parliament, a jubilant Hnatyshyn announced that he hoped to see the legislation passed within the week—before the summer recess of the House of Commons. Both opposition parties lent their support to speedy passage of the bill and, to that end, agreed to waive the usual legislative committee process and a protracted debate.

The substance of Bill 71 reflected the government's response during the spring. Hnatyshyn referred to it as "a generic war crimes law," dealing with "war crimes wherever they were committed without reference to any particular set of events." The bill would make war crimes and crimes against humanity punishable offences in Canada, prohibit the future entry of persons who are reasonably believed to be war criminals or criminals against humanity and deny citizenship to persons convicted, accused or under investigation for such crimes.

While the overall effect of the bill accomplished what the government had promised to do, its wording left some areas grey and uncertain. The Criminal Code amendment, for example, might not cover a Romanian Iron Guard member who committed war crimes and crimes against humanity before Romania entered the war on the side of Nazi Germany in 1941. A second type of individual that might escape the sanctions of the legislation is an "enthusiastic volunteer"—a collaborator who was not formally working for the Nazi SS—whose victim was a citizen of an Axis country. These ambiguities stem from the fact that the bill was more restrictive than necessary. It would assert jurisdiction for Canadian courts only where the accused war criminal, when he committed his crimes, was a Canadian citizen or was in the employ of a wartime Canadian enemy country, or where the victim was a citizen of a country allied to Canada in war. The Romanian Iron Guard, who were not in the employ of enemies of Canada before 1941, and enthusiastic volunteers with victims from countries such as Germany and Italy fit none of these categories.

Another "catch-all" category in the bill purported to cover these situations by giving Canada the jurisdiction it would have had at the time under international law. In other words, if international law gave Canada the power to prosecute the Iron Guard member for crimes in 1940 or the Nazi collaborator in 1942, a Canadian court could prosecute today. Unfortunately, what was international law at the time is strictly a matter of opinion. In my own view, international law did give Canada jurisdiction. But, it is the opinion of Justice Department lawyers that counts, not mine. Moreover, the bill provided that only the federal attorney-general could launch a prosecution. If the lawyers from the Department of Justice were to determine that Canada had no jurisdiction under international law for crimes such as these, that would end the matter. The cases would not go to court and no judge would have an opportunity to make a legal ruling on the issue. It would be resolved internally, within the bowels of the bureaucracy.

By creating a potential loophole, persons who have committed war crimes and crimes against humanity might go free, on a technical jurisdictional issue. Whether this theoretical escape hatch becomes a real one, we may never know. The federal government did not state its position on the question of jurisdiction under international law—only that it would make a case by case determination about whether to bring suspects to trial. Where the attorney-general decides against going to court, the public will never know what the facts were or why the decision was taken.

The justification for the loophole was what the government called a cautious approach. "We want to get prosecutions where prosecutions are possible," explained Mr. Hnatyshyn. In their attempt to guard against retroactivity, though, the drafters of the bill were overly zealous. Rightly so, the bill prohibited the prosecution of anyone for an offence that was not considered an offence at international law at the time it was committed. But the bill went too far. It also prohibited the assumption of jurisdiction by Canadian courts today if no jurisdiction could have been assumed at the time the offence was committed. The need to prevent retroactive laws does not require this sort of prohibition. The Canadian Charter of Rights and Freedoms expressly forbids the creation of retroactive crimes, but it does not prohibit the retroactive assumption of jurisdiction over crimes. At Nuremberg, the Tribunal applied the international law of war crimes and crimes against humanity as they were when the crimes were committed. The Tribunal did not need to prove, in 1946, that it would have had jurisdiction over the crimes when they were committed in say, 1942 or 1943. In the same way, Bill 71 could simply have asserted jurisdiction in the present, rather than send us on a search into the past to find out what the international law of jurisdiction was historically. So long as the acts in question were crimes then, that should suffice.

Deschênes himself did not advise this sweeping restriction. He acknowledged that there is a universal jurisdiction over war crimes and crimes against humanity. So long as the accused person is in this country, Canada has the authority to put him on trial. Every other international law offence in the Criminal Code gives Canadian courts jurisdiction simply on the basis that the alleged offender is in Canada—hijacking, theft of nuclear materials, attacks on diplomatic personnel, torture, and hostage taking. There is no reason why war crimes and crimes against humanity should not be in line with these other universal crimes.

This excess of caution also created another loophole, which left Ukrainian spokesmen very concerned. Perpetrators of the 1930s forced famine in the Ukraine might also escape prosecution under the proposed legislation. Those who inflicted the starvation on millions of people were neither employees of any country at war with Canada nor were their victims citizens of a Canadian ally. Clearly, both Ukrainian and Jewish communities have reasons for wanting this loophole closed.

The government's self-imposed legal constraints did not reflect obstructionism. The draughtsmen of Bill 71 were not using the law to perpetuate Canada's history of negativism. But in their efforts to avoid any unfairness in the legislation, they imposed a standard so high that it can find no support in the Canadian Charter of Rights and Freedoms, in international law or in common sense. With this unwarranted yardstick of fairness, heinous criminals could go free. The principle against retroactivity protects individuals from being punished for acts that were innocent and lawful when committed, because it would be most unfair to change the rules of the game at a later stage. The same cannot be said for jurisdiction. There is nothing unfair about Canadian courts now assuming authority to prosecute someone who committed acts which were criminal at the time, no matter where they took place. In a situation where Canada did not have jurisdiction when the crime was committed, a war criminal might have thought that he could flee to this country to escape justice elsewhere. By changing the law, we deprive the criminal of the safe haven he has enjoyed for so many years. Can this be called an injustice? On the contrary—it would be unjust to maintain his undeserved immunity. What the principle against jurisdictional retroactivity really amounts to, then, is once a safe haven, always a safe haven. Seen in this light, the government's approach is truly nonsensical.

A second restriction in the bill limited prosecutorial power to the federal government. Unlike any other offence in the Criminal Code, for this offence provincial attorneys-general would not be permitted to launch prosecutions under the proposed legislation. In opting for this unusual feature, the government acted on Deschênes' advice that war crimes proceedings require specialization and should not be spread out among eleven different jurisdictions. He also argued that exclusive federal prosecution would ensure uniformity in application of the law. Finally, he reasoned, the federal government would be in the best position to handle aspects of the cases which would impinge on Canada's relations with other countries, such as gathering evidence abroad. But all of these objectives could have been accomplished without granting exclusive power to the federal attorney-general. Giving provincial authorities a concurrent jurisdiction to launch prosecutions would have added a safeguard to the process. If, for any reason, the federal government chose not to proceed in a given case, the provinces could take on the prosecution. This extra recourse to justice could be important, especially with a reluctant federal administration.

Bill 71 raised another type of uncertainty. The wording of the legislation left doubt as to whether its sanctions applied to persons who perpetrated crimes against humanity on only one victim. Crimes against humanity were defined as crimes against "any civilian population or any identifiable group of persons." A single victim is neither a population nor a group. Under international law, a crime against humanity can indeed be committed where there is only one victim. In France, Klaus Barbie was convicted and sentenced to life imprisonment for crimes against humanity in July of 1987. French law allows representatives of victims to have standing in court, as "parties civiles." In the Barbie case, the court granted "partie civile" status to a Madame Gompel, on behalf of her father, a Jewish Resistance fighter. Her father had been murdered, allegedly by Barbie, by reason of his membership in an identifiable group. As such, his death was a crime against humanity, and Madame Gompel was permitted standing at Barbie's trial, even though she represented only one victim. The Canadian bill should define a crime against humanity as an act perpetrated on any individual member of an identifiable group. That would allow for prosecution even where the victimization of only one person could be proved.

The immigration and citizenship components of Bill 71 contained one welcome change to the law. By giving authorities the power to bar any person from Canada who is reasonably believed to have committed war crimes or crimes against humanity, officials might be able to prevent someone like Kurt Waldheim from entering the country.

Other facets of the Immigration Act and Citizenship Act amendments were more troublesome. Under the existing statute, a Nazi war criminal who acquired Canadian domicile between the years 1953 and 1971 could not lose that domicile and therefore could not be deported for gaining admission to Canada under false pretenses by hiding his Nazi criminal past. Deschênes recommended that the law be changed to prevent the retention of domicile by anyone who is later found to have committed war crimes or crimes against humanity. Bill 71 did not incorporate that measure because of the government's general reluctance to develop deportation as a remedy. Canadian authorities did not want to create a situation in which suspects might have to be sent to the Soviet Union, Europe or Israel. The citizenship provisions of the bill were even more timid. War criminals and criminals against humanity who have already managed to become Canadian citizens—or who go undetected and obtain Canadian citizenship in the future—can never be de-naturalized, according to the amendment. All the bill does is deny the grant of citizenship to persons who are under investigation, accused or convicted of these crimes.

In spite of the defects in Bill 71, war crimes justice advocates wanted the legislation to be passed without delay. They believed that the details could be addressed at a later date and that future amendments could be passed by Parliament. Although the flaws in the bill might let some suspects off the hook, without the new law in place, every war criminal in the country would escape justice. With each day that passes, valuable investigation time is lost. The RCMP has refused to undertake certain aspects of the investigations on the twenty and possibly more suspects who might be prosecuted until they have the statutory authority of this enactment. Given the context of a forty-two year holdup and the urgency of the situation, Canada simply cannot afford the luxury of months of debate about an ideal piece of legislation. Besides, for two years, the Deschênes Commission had gone through all that. It was for this reason that lobby groups and politicians alike were prepared to forgo drawn-out parliamentary committee hearings and permit Bill 71 to be passed before the House of Commons, or "in committee of the whole."

Certainly this had been the intention of Mr. Hnatyshyn on June 30, 1987, the last day before Parliament rose for the summer. To do this, the government required the consent of every single member of Parliament. In the preceding days, it became clear that two Conservative backbenchers were preparing to block the unanimous consent needed to pass the bill without debate or amendment. Dr. Alex Kindy, MP for Calgary East, and Andrew Witer, MP for Toronto Parkdale High Park, both of whom represent significant Eastern European communities, were determined to delay passage of the bill by forcing it to go through the committee stage for study during the summer or fall. In spite of repeated appeals throughout the day by fellow members of Parliament and Cabinet, Kindy refused to change his mind.

Witer indicated that he might allow the bill to pass, provided the government was prepared to accept five amendments he had drawn up. He proposed that all suspected war criminals in the country be prosecuted, and not just those employed by countries "in armed conflict" against Canada. Next, the power of the deputy attorney-general to authorize prosecutions should be removed, leaving that power solely to the federal attorney-general. Third, a publication ban should be imposed on the reporting of war crimes trials, with information release only if an accused was convicted. Fourth, deportation should be allowed only to countries with which Canada has an extradition treaty. Last, the Immigration Act should be relaxed by barring entry only to persons proved to be war criminals rather than all those against whom "reasonable grounds" exist on which to believe they might be war criminals.

The League for Human Rights of B'nai Brith Canada, the Canadian Jewish Congress and Canadian Jewish Students Network, all anxious to get the legislation through, decided not to insist on delay even if the government accepted the Witer amendments, although they disagreed with all but the first of his proposals. They found the publication ban particularly offensive. One value of war crimes trials and of any criminal proceedings for that matter, is public education. War criminal trials not only can have a deterrent effect, but can teach the lessons of history. While a guilty verdict may eventually be reported, it cannot have the same effect as the daily reporting of the entire testimony. Certain types of cases do call for confidentiality, such as litigation over trade secrets or sexual assault cases, where publicity could harm the victim. But mere embarrassment to the accused war criminal or his family is no justification for a publication ban. Secrecy, in such circumstances, would be an attack on Canadian constitutional freedoms. Publicity ensures adequate checks on the judicial process and prevents injustices. "Publicity," in the words of British philosopher Jeremy Bentham, "is the very soul of justice."

In spite of these criticisms, the Jewish organizations would have preferred the government to have presented the War Crimes Bill to the House of Commons rather than delay any longer. After a full day of heated negotiations between Witer, Hnatyshyn and Jewish community representatives, the Justice minister advised Mr. Witer that his entire package was unacceptable. Justice Department lawyers had advised that the publication ban and the extended definition of war criminal could run afoul of the Charter of Rights and Freedoms. Once it became clear that no agreement could be reached, the government decided, in any event, to put the original bill forward for second reading that day. Having passed that stage, at least a legislative committee could go to work immediately on amendments.

In the end, not even a second reading was achieved on June 30. The government was defeated by an overloaded House of Commons agenda and competition from other ministers with different legislative priorities. The clock simply ran out. By the time Mr. Hnatyshyn presented the bill, only five minutes remained until the 8 p.m. adjournment deadline. The unanimous consent needed to permit an extension of the parliamentary day could not be mustered. Deflated, the minister of Justice promised to complete second reading in the fall. "It's still a priority for me," he told reporters later, "and I will bring it back as soon as the next sitting of the House."

Naturally, war crimes justice advocates were sorely disappointed by the whole turn of events. Alex Kindy had been destructive. He not only refused unanimous consent to Bill 71, but to several other pieces of legislation that day. Andrew Witer had been exorbitant in his demands. He asked for far too much, and insisted that it all be accepted. It should have been enough for him to have his concerns put on record in the House of Commons. He was unrealistic to expect that he would get everything he asked for. Hnatyshyn was intransigent in his refusal to consider any of Witer's proposals. The opposition had other priorities. NDP Member of Parliament John Rodrigues consumed the end of the parliamentary day debating the business of moving hamburger buns between provinces. Another politician refused to consent to an extension of the adjournment deadline unless the House agreed to pass another bill that would have increased his annual salary.

The government has to be commended for appointing the Deschênes Commission and for committing itself to bring about some of the recommended legislative reforms. Its genuine attempt to have the Parliament pass the War Crimes Bill speedily also deserves praise. But the failure to achieve that goal was disconcerting. Despite everything the government has accomplished over the last two-and-a-half years, and it is a substantial amount, the process of bringing Nazi war criminals to justice in this country has yet to begin. The government is not just the people who hold the reins of power today—it is an institution with historical continuity. And as an institution, the government, over the course of the past forty-two years, has acted with inexcusable delay. Prompt action at this late date cannot alter that fact, but it can provide some small hope for redress against the remaining Nazi war criminals before time runs out.

• • •

In choosing a course of action, it is quite interesting that Canada has opted for different legal mechanisms to deal with war criminals than those put into effect in the United States. There are three notable distinctions—in choice of legal remedy, the scope of legislation to be passed, and the investigative and prosecutorial framework. Of course, the Canadian response has come long after that of the Americans, who amended their laws in 1978 to allow deportation and denaturalization and set up the OSI the following year. But the government's choice not to follow the U.S. model cannot be viewed as an implied criticism of the American response. Later does not mean better. Canada has not taken a different path because of any faults in the U.S. system. And those who have led the exaggerated campaign in that country to derail all efforts to bring Nazi war criminals to justice should not, in principle, find any comfort in the distinct Canadian approach.

In terms of remedies, the choice of prosecution over deportation can be explained by the technical differences between the constitutions of the two countries. The U.S. constitution of 1787 prohibited the passage of *ex post facto*, or retroactive laws. American courts have interpreted that to forbid any criminal legislation that imposes or increases penalties for conduct that was lawful before its enactment. Deportation, a civil procedure, falls outside the prohibition. Although the "Holtzman amendment" was retroactive in nature, it was not a violation of the American constitution because it did not deal with criminal law. At the trials of accused war criminals Andrija Artukovic and Conrad Schellong, both argued unsuccessfully that the Holtzman deportation legislation infringed the constitution.

Since immigration laws do not fall prey to the same retroactivity problems as criminal laws under the American constitution, it is not surprising that U.S. legislators chose the deportation route. The Canadian Charter of Rights and Freedoms of 1982, while also forbidding retroactive criminal legislation, contains an important exception. It permits retroactive law that makes an act criminal domestically that was, at the time it was committed, already criminal at international law or according to the general principles of law recognized by the community of nations. Any retroactive criminal legislation passed today to penalize war crimes and crimes against humanity committed during World War II is explicitly sanctioned by our constitution. The exception was inserted into the Charter for that very purpose after vigorous lobbying by war crimes justice advocates. It was taken from the International Covenant on Civil and Political Rights, which Canada has both signed and ratified. The Covenant, in turn, drew its inspiration from Nuremberg.

The Canadian Charter provisions are therefore historically linked to the judgment at Nuremberg. While the Americans have signed the International Covenant on Civil and Political Rights, they have not ratified it. Their signature might be enough to permit a successful argument in favour of valid retroactive criminal laws to cover World War II crimes, but the point is debatable. In Canada, there is no room for argument—prosecution is an undisputable remedy. It also has the advantage of leading to punishment of war criminals, which is not guaranteed by deportation. It is for all of these reasons that the Canadian authorities favoured this legal avenue.

Canada also departed from the U.S. approach in committing itself to the passage of general legislation to deal with all war criminals, and not only Nazis. This difference may be more theoretical than real, since it is a matter of pure speculation whether other war criminals are here. The Deschênes Commission mandate was limited to the investigation of Nazi criminals. In the United States, as mentioned earlier, Elizabeth Holtzman had tried to have general legislation passed. Along with her bill to deport the perpetrators of Nazi activities, she introduced a second proposal to deport anyone engaged in persecution. The House of Representatives Sub-Committee on Immigration approved the second broadly-based bill, but it did not get past the floor of the House. Opponents feared it would be used to block the entry of friends and allies of the U.S. government who have been involved in the persecution of others. Its scope was narrowed to cover only Nazi persecution. The grounds for restricting the scope of the legislation were hardly worthy, since, after the war, some top government officials numbered Nazis among the friends and allies of the United States because of their virulent anti-Communism. In any event, the presence of non-Nazi war criminals in that country is uncertain. I have little doubt that any well-founded allegations against perpetrators from other regimes would lead to a drive for more general American legislation.

Last, the Canadian government opted against an agency modelled on the U.S. Office of Special Investigations, a choice which reflects badly not on that agency, but on Canada because of the superficial, purely political grounds on which it was rejected. In his report, Deschênes expressed his approval of the OSI model. "This formula," he wrote, "presents undeniable advantages: acquisition of experience, centralization of decisions, streamlining of the whole process from denunciation to conviction." But, instead, he dismissed the approach because "serious difficulties have arisen which tend to outweigh those advantages; and they are growing out of the very fabric of the matter of Nazi war criminals. Without insisting more than necessary, the Commission only wishes to recall the noisy clashes between Jewish organizations and Eastern European groups as well as the never-ending debates over the reception of Soviet-supplied evidence and the alleged co-operation between the OSI and the KGB. The Commission has seen by itself that the same ingredients of dissention are at work in this country." Mr. Justice Deschênes appeared to be pandering to the objections raised within Ukrainian and Baltic communities and the kind of vitriolic attacks on the OSI in ads like "Protect the Innocent," that were, quite frankly, without substance. One would have expected a high court judge such as Deschênes to carefully assess the merits of those objections. Only if he concluded, after careful analysis, that they were well-founded should he have upheld them. But the Commissioner did not so much as identify any specific ground of opposition. His only justification was that "internal peace between the various ethnic groups which form now such an important part of the population of Canada is more important."

Given the manner in which it was done, the Canadian failure to establish a specialized agency does not undercut the viability of the American OSI. Rather, it leaves Canadians wondering. Penalizing mass murderers should not be a matter of politics, nor should the investigation and prosecution techniques employed. They should be matters of principles.

Canada and the United States are now going down different paths to bring Nazi war criminals to justice. Perhaps more important than the divergence in their methods is the similarity of the goal. Finally, forty-two years after the fact, Canada has joined the U.S. in making a serious effort to root out those who killed innocent people during the Second World War.

Chapter Thirteen

After the Commission of Inquiry

Given the ethnic dimension of the debates surrounding the Deschênes Commission, the relations between Jews and Ukrainians in Canada have been significantly altered by the two-year process. On one level, it is wrong and even offensive to speak of the Nazi war criminal issue as an ethnic question. Bringing mass murderers to justice is a matter of human rights, not minority group politics. Although many have labelled this a Jewish-Ukrainian problem, that is a misnomer. Even if not one Jew or Ukrainian lived in this country, Canada should still, in principle, redress the injustice of harbouring known or suspected killers.

True, the Jewish community has been pushing the Canadian government through the years to take legal action against Nazi war criminals. These urgings, though, do not stem primarily from any self-interest on the part of Canadian Jewry. Punishing the perpetrators of the Holocaust would not bring back a single victim or alter the irreparably shattered lives of the survivors. Rather, Jews have been motivated by a sense of what they believe is right and just. The perpetual refusal by those in power to act because they did not view the Jewish lobby as politically influential—or on the contrary, government action designed to placate the community—miscasts the nature of the issue. What is not ethnic becomes ethnicized. A question of principle is perverted into one of cultural politics.

The same can be said of the Ukrainian community. It also approached the issue of war criminals from the perspective of principle. Ukrainians had their own feelings about what was right and wrong, what should or should not be done. For the government to accede to their positions, simply because they emanated from a particular ethnic group and without assessing their merits, is demeaning to the Ukrainian community and its views. Both Jewish and Eastern European groups have hoped their objectives would be realized, but for the right reasons—because government accepted the logic and the values behind them.

From the vantage of principle, then, the ethnic dimension is really illusory. What both communities wanted from the Deschênes Commission was a report on principle, and from the government, an ethical response. Yet at the practical level, the question of war criminals has been very much an ethnic debate. One would have to be blind to reality not to observe the intensity with which Ukrainians and Jews embraced the subject. The Deschênes Commission did not so much prompt their involvement by granting legal status to their representative organizations, as it reflected the special interest of the two communities. Throughout the tenure of the inquiry, each community took stands, lobbied, advocated, argued and publicized their positions. On specific issues the two groups were in disaccord. Sometimes the conflict deflected attention from the real concern of bringing Nazi war criminals to justice. People across the country deplored the ethnic disharmony, suggesting that it was harmful to Canadian unity, that it was tearing apart the multicultural fabric of our society. In his report, Mr. Justice Deschênes himself fell prey to the fixation on "internal peace between the various ethnic groups" and fears about the infliction of "serious and incurable wounds".

In fact, the involvement of Ukrainians and Jews in the inquiry process probably led to an enhanced report, as well as a more appropriate government response than we might have seen otherwise. The result not only benefits the two communities, but Canada as a whole. The debate that developed along ethnic lines should not be deplored, but commended. Canada is better off both multiculturally and legally. Each community learned more about the other, and the country gained insight into both. Moreover, the issue brought Jews and Ukrainians into contact with one another in a more meaningful way than ever before. Multiculturalism is more than folklore. It is more than perogies and blintzes, than colourful costumes and dancing and artisan work. But, by and large, multiculturalism policy in this country has never moved beyond this very superficial level. As Canadians, we can truly appreciate our ethnic diversity only if we probe deeper into the concerns, the history and the politics of each culture that makes up our population. The war crimes debate has enabled at least two communities to get past the surface. Jews and Ukrainians are now aware of not just what the other group eats, but what it thinks.

From the legal standpoint, the two-way discussion enriched the study of the various options, particularly regarding the prosecution of war criminals, the application of penal legislation to all war criminals and the consideration of evidence from Eastern Europe.

Prior to the establishment of the inquiry, government policy had always been that absolutely no remedies were available. Under the Clark administration in 1979, his Justice minister, Senator Jacques Flynn held the view that the law permitted no action and that the government should not change the law. Jean Chretien, minister of Justice in the ensuing Liberal government stuck to that position. In the eyes of that government, any amendment to the law to deal with Nazi war criminals was offensive to Canadian standards. At most, they were willing to concede that extradition requests from a Western democratic country sharing a treaty with Canada would be accepted. Of course, none were forthcoming (the Rauca case came later), so the situation festered and the growing number of allegations remained unresolved. Chretien's successor, Mark MacGuigan, went one step further. Although he never reversed the negative opinion prevailing in the Justice department, he did show a readiness to have the courts rule on the legality of deportation and denaturalization, and instructed his officials to prepare a few suitable cases for trial. When the Mulroney Conservative government took power in 1985, the new minister of Justice, John Crosbie, seemed willing to pursue the test cases that MacGuigan had started on. Once the Deschênes inquiry was appointed, this initiative ground to a halt and all files were put on hold. Despite the government's assurances that it would pursue the pending cases against suspected war criminals, no further action took place until the Commission made its report and recommendations.

Both the League for Human Rights and the Canadian Jewish Congress have always maintained that *something* should be done. Whatever the ultimate choice of remedy, anything was preferable to inaction. Jewish lobbyists, while they viewed certain avenues as more fruitful, were not going to assault one legal route on the ground that another might be preferable. They were not prepared to make "better" an enemy of "good". All the same, the Jewish organizations did present their suggestions to the government in descending order of preference.

At the top of the list came extradition to a country with an operative treaty, because of the availability of evidence and the foreign nation's close connection with the crime. But this, it was recognized, was impracticable. Canada has no treaties with the Soviet Union or Poland, where the bulk of requests would originate, nor would they have proposed that Canada enter such treaties. Prosecution in Canada became the second choice, offering the possibility of actual punishment of a convicted Nazi war criminal. Deportation, a civil procedure leading only to the displacement of a criminal, might result in little or no real penalty.

When the Deschênes Commission was appointed, my own assessment was that denaturalization and deportation would be the recommended approach. The government had already shown an interest in launching several test cases. Moreover, the United States had been going this route for a number of years, and there is an inevitable tendency for Canadians to imitate Americans, which I thought would manifest itself in this case. But Ukrainian involvement changed the whole configuration of the debate. If the Jewish organizations were worried that Nazi war criminals might simply be shipped of to a tourist resort, the Ukrainian Canadian Committee feared that deportation for failing to disclose past Nazi activities would result in far worse consequences. In their view, a suspected criminal would be sent to the U.S.S.R. without any determination of his innocence or guilt by a Canadian court, and subjected to a biased Soviet trial on trumped-up Nazi war crimes charges.

Deschênes himself seemed to agree with the ranking of remedies proposed by the Jewish intervenors—extradition, then prosecution in Canada, and finally deportation—with one significant difference. He felt that the law did permit extradition to the U.S.S.R. by means of the Geneva Conventions, multilateral treaties which both Canada and the Soviet Union have signed. In his view, a separate extradition treaty was not necessary.

The government, I feel, responded to the concerns of the Ukrainian community by shifting its earlier preference for deportation to the "made in Canada" solution of prosecution in our own courts. The change was welcome, not only to East European groups, but to Jewish advocates as well and resulted in Canada's commitment to a much more effective remedy. I attribute this improvement to Ukrainian participation in the process.

Another result was the government's decision to go after all war criminals, not only Nazis. Jewish advocates have always supported the principle that all war crimes are abhorrent and deserve punishment. The slogan "Never Again" has often been associated with the Holocaust. It means never again a Nazi genocide destined to eliminate the Jews. Moreover, it signifies that we must never again see a Holocaust directed at any group. Granted, the Holocaust was a unique event. But it ought not be isolated and set aside from the rest of human experience. If the tragedy is to have any impact, we must learn from it and take steps to prevent its recurrence. That calls for prosecution of every war criminal. In a sense, the entire international human rights movement has its roots in the experience of the Holocaust. The very important expressions of worldwide concern for human rights—the provisions of the UN Charter, the Universal Declaration of Human Rights, the Genocide Convention and the Refugee Convention—all bear a direct linkage to the atrocities of Nazi Germany. Making all war crimes and crimes against humanity punishable under the Canadian Criminal Code demonstrates how the lessons of the Holocaust have been absorbed.

Before the advent of the Commission and the involvement of the Ukrainian community, there seemed little likelihood that a generalized approach would carry the day. The government's previous commitment under Justice Ministers MacGuigan and Crosbie had been limited to the deportation of Nazi war criminals and no others. In the United States, an attempt by Congresswoman Elizabeth Holtzman to bring in general deportation legislation to cover all war crimes and crimes against humanity, and not just Nazi war crimes, was fiercely opposed and defeated. Again, it appeared Canada would follow suit. Ukrainian concerns changed all that. Fearing the selective prosecution of Nazis, while Soviet war criminals with Ukrainian victims remained at large, they urged a general policy. Both Deschênes and the government accepted their position.

A final area of law that gained from the debate was the consideration of evidence from Eastern Europe. Jewish advocates believe that the trail of evidence should be followed wherever it might lead. Nevertheless, distrust of Soviet motives has created a cloud of suspicion over any information emanating from the U.S.S.R., even though none has been proven false in any war crimes trials. Ukrainian opposition to Soviet-supplied evidence led to a full airing of the issue in the public hearings of the Deschênes Commission, and to the imposition of safeguards in the gathering of archival materials and oral testimony from Eastern Bloc countries. These precautions will help clear away the overriding doubts about the reliability of the evidence and eliminate the situation that has sometimes arisen in the United States where even possibly truthful evidence was rejected out of hand. By grappling with the issue here and establishing safeguards, we are assured of having war crimes trials in which all the evidence, whatever its source, will be given fair consideration.

These are the successes of the Ukrainian-Jewish give and take. There are, however, also two failures, which can be attributed to an unhealthy fixation on the ethnic dimension as opposed to the substance of the issues.

One was the rejection by Mr. Justice Deschênes of an Office of Special Investigation without giving any reason other than a fear of discord between the two communities. Instead, he recommended that specialized war crimes work be carried on within the Department of Justice and the RCMP. In reality, the difference between a special office and special units within existing departments may only be a matter of semantics. The recommendation is no less disturbing, though, because of its failure to analyze the basis of Ukrainian objections to the OSI. Deschênes did us all a disservice in refusing to articulate good, sound reasons. Not only were we deprived of a potentially valuable structure to prosecute and investigate war criminals, but also of any guidance the Commission might have provided on how to avoid the pitfalls of the debate centering around the American OSI.

The second failure was Deschênes' refusal to forward the names of certain war crimes suspects to the Eastern Bloc for follow-up investigation. The Commissioner divided his list of alleged war criminals in Canada into two groups. One consisted of people against whom allegations had previously been made by Eastern European governments. In the other group were people who had not been specifically identified by Communist states. Mr. Justice Deschênes did forward the first group of names, but refused to release the second. The reasons he gave were his fear that the identities of suspects would not be kept confidential and that their relatives in those countries might be victimized. While in theory these are legitimate concerns, there was absolutely no indication in the Deschênes report that there was any real threat of a breach of confidentiality. Indeed, it appears to have been no more than a suspicion. In the United States, the OSI has never faced any violations of secrecy by Eastern Bloc states. Was the danger to relatives real? That too seems to be only a hunch. Once again, Mr. Justice Deschênes made his decision on very superficial grounds and failed to substantiate his findings. More than this, the decision to withhold these names appears inconsistent with the commission's willingness to collect evidence in the Soviet Union. Deschênes, in that case, accepted a Soviet undertaking to keep all matters under investigation confidential. Why, then, did he not seek a similar promise of secrecy for the purposes of referring the additional names?

These criticisms of the Deschênes report do not undercut its overall worth. It was a good report leading to positive results. Many findings are commendable. The flaws themselves are instructive, highlighting areas where fear and suspicion took over from principle. What we see is a desire to avoid ethnic confrontation. John Stuart Mill, in his essay "On Liberty," wrote that truth has to be made "through the rough process of a struggle between combatants fighting under hostile banners." The Ukrainian and Jewish communities are not hostile, but on some issues they are combatants. This struggle is not something to be feared. Diversity of opinion is the lifeblood of democracy. Different points of view, when confronted and resolved, lead to the right conclusions. They should not be avoided in attempting to side-step ethnic conflict.

These conflicts may now be behind us with the Commission's report and the government's positive response. What is not behind us is the need for war crimes justice advocates to press the government into enacting the promised legislation and launching cases. While the report of the Commission of Inquiry on War Criminals has totally and irrevocably changed the nature of the war crimes debate in this country, the need to fight for government action has not diminished in the slightest. However, the nature and strategy of advocacy must be modified.

Before Deschênes, war crimes justice activists put forward every possible remedy Canadian law had to offer in order to counter the negativism running rampant through both the Parliament and the civil service. For every option proposed, government raised objections. When advocates shot down those objections or presented new solutions, a whole new set of barriers was erected by an unwilling government. The point of this interminable battle back and forth, for advocates, was to reveal that the true basis of government inaction was political. Legal difficulties were merely a convenient cover. In large measure this strategy, although time-consuming, labourious and extremely technical, was successful. Eventually, the grounds for bureaucratic opposition wore so thin that they no longer camouflaged the real motives of government.

The Commission of Inquiry on War Criminals was appointed to put an end to this game of legal volleyball. Mr. Justice Deschênes, as one would have expected, did not exercise his ingenuity only to discover more reasons why nothing could be done. Instead, the Commissioner examined all the sides of every argument fairly and judiciously, and found options for action, as he should have done. On balance, from an advocate's perspective, the report was positive, even though Deschênes did not endorse every course of action urged. In terms of remedies, our order of preference was extradition, then prosecution, and last deportation. A similar ranking was adopted by the Commission, with variations in the way each might be achieved. One significant difference, though, was Deschênes' selectivity over the choice of remedies. War crimes justice activists have urged all remedies to be used in concert, even though some may be better than others. Deschênes was much more strict, recommending deportation only as a "last resort," if no other option is available, and prosecution, only if extradition does "not afford a workable remedy."

As could be expected, the government did not go beyond Deschênes. It accepted some, but not all of Deschênes' recommendations, and did not adopt any remedy rejected by the Commission. Where does all this leave war crimes justice advocates? Well, for one thing, it is pointless now to continue urging options that have been disposed of by both the inquiry and the government, even if they are valid. Any attempt to change the government position would be a waste of scarce advocacy resources.

Cabinet did promise the passage of new prosecution legislation, although this has yet to materialize. Pressure must now be exerted to ensure that the Criminal Code amendments are enacted with the utmost speed so that cases can be launched as soon as possible. The government also conceded that it could extradite, denaturalize and deport under existing laws. Proponents of justice for war criminals should be urging that suitable cases already on file be brought to court immediately. With each day that slips by, the opportunity to see that justice is done dwindles.

Some of the legal avenues available are mutually exclusive. Canada cannot, for example, both prosecute an accused war criminal and then extradite him or her for trial in another country. That would amount to double jeopardy, a violation of the Canadian Charter of Rights and Freedoms. No person can be tried, convicted and punished twice for the same offence.

On the other hand, extradition and deportation proceedings can be mounted concurrently. In the United States, John Demjanjuk was both ordered deported from that country and then, at the request of Israel, extradited there for trial. Because of the outstanding deportation order, Demjanjuk would be unable to return to the U.S. upon his release from an Israeli prison, if he is convicted. The process was completed by the American authorities. In the case of Helmut Rauca, Canada extradited him, but never ordered him to be denaturalized or deported. He died in a West German prison, before his trial. Had he survived and been convicted, Rauca could conceivably have returned to Canada after serving his sentence. Upon his return, Canada would be faced with having to initiate proceedings to revoke his citizenship and deport him.

Prosecution and deportation are compatible remedies. In Canada, the two are commonly linked. Quite often, landed immigrants are prosecuted for an offence, and then deported because of their criminal record. Canadian immigration policy is, in fact, to deport any landed immigrant who has committed a serious criminal offence.

Advocates of action on war crimes, therefore, will continue to urge using deportation together with either prosecution or extradition, depending on which is the most appropriate in any given case. There can be no valid reason for Canadian authorities to hold off on launching any pending extradition or deportation cases while it awaits passage of the Criminal Code amendments. Such a delay would, in effect, render these viable alternatives useless. As with any new legislation, Royal assent may take some time. Denaturalization, deportation and extradition can begin immediately. Twenty cases have been identified as urgent and ready for action. Let them begin without further ado. More than two hundred others require further investigations. Suspects have been on notice since before December 1986. Who knows how many have already fled the jurisdiction to escape justice?

Another fruitful area for war crimes justice proponents is to ask for action on some Commission recommendations to which the government made no response. One of these concerns amendments to the Old Age Security Act. The Department of Health and Welfare refused to provide Mr. Justice Deschênes with information from old age pension files that might assist in tracking down a suspected Nazi war criminal. The Commission urged changes in the legislation to put an end to this obstruction, which the authorities have failed to address. It is up to advocates to urge action in this area.

Following these efforts, activists must seek a response to some concerns that neither the Deschênes Commission nor the government have dealt with, such as cross-checking war criminal lists with various rosters held by government agencies and departments. Deschênes did not deal with this issue, and so advocates will have to undertake this responsibility. In addition, they must urge the government to seek evidence abroad on the suspects whose names Deschênes refused to forward to Eastern Bloc countries for investigation. To date, the only response has been the vague comment that "any gathering of evidence abroad will be restricted to those cases where, in the opinion of Canadian authorities, there are specific, credible and serious allegations of war crimes requiring further investigation." It is urgent that information from every source be collected, provided safeguards are in place to protect the integrity of the evidence.

Last on the list of priorities for advocates, and the most difficult task of all, is to get the government to reconsider its negative stance on several of the Commission's recommendations. In particular, a rewording of the Canada-Israel treaty to permit the extradition of war criminals to Israel for trial and changes to the Immigration and Citizenship Acts simplifying the grounds for denaturalization and deportation would greatly enhance Canada's scope for action. While it may be an uphill battle to change the mind of those in power, it is a job that activists must attempt.

After forty-two years of indifference, the voice of commitment coming from the government is a welcome change. That should not, however, lull anyone into complacency. The process of bringing Nazi war criminals in Canada to justice has not ended. We are just beginning the final phase. It is up to the government to ensure that its expressions of concern were not mere rhetoric. But it is up to advocates to push until the process is complete. The price of justice, which is really part of the price of liberty, is eternal vigilance.

And so, war crimes justice advocates cannot slacken their efforts in the slightest—not until every last war criminal has been dealt with. But the ethnic communities involved in the war crimes debate can now approach the issue with an enlightened understanding of one another's priorities and concerns.

Chapter Fourteen

Freedom of Information and War Criminals

The battle to bring Nazi war criminals to justice has been, on one front, a battle to remove the cover of secrecy that has for so long sheltered government from taking action. Freedom of information is important so that the public can know exactly what the government is doing, judge its actions and participate in the policy debate about what ought to be done. Secrecy gives scope for corruption, favouritism and arbitrariness. Canada's practice of doing virtually nothing to prevent Nazi criminals from entering Canada and its "hands-off" policy once they arrived could not long survive the cold glare of publicity. Exposing government apathy became a crucial step in mobilizing rigour and activity.

On another front, secrecy has impeded efforts to locate and prosecute suspects. The hunt for Helmut Rauca was in part stymied for so many years by confidentiality rules which prevented the civil service from sharing valuable information with the RCMP—files relating to old-age pension benefit payments, passport renewals, and other crucial facts and figures which might have led them to his door far sooner. In the United States, the process of cross-checking war criminal lists with the registers kept by a whole range of government departments has enabled the OSI to track down and prosecute war criminals who would otherwise have lived out their quiet lives in North America undetected.

Access to records is critical to any effort by Canada to locate war criminals. Co-operation by the bureaucracy in disclosing relevant information can mean the difference between bringing Nazi fugitives to justice and permitting them to remain at large. As the Deschênes inquiry also proved, secret correspondence and confidential files buried deep in departmental archives often hold the key to past mistakes of government and help develop better guidelines for the future.

The Commission, if it served no other purpose, did shed light on just how Nazi war criminals came into Canada and how their presence was tolerated for forty years. By means of the many witnesses called to testify before it, the inquiry exposed defective immigration policies and practices, an RCMP code of non-action, and a one-sided legal memorandum, the Low report, which argued that the leaders of this country ought to keep their hands off war criminals.

Through requests made under Canada's Access to Information Act, the government agreed to the release of a shocking batch of files relating to the 1962 Mengele incident—revealing for the first time a series of embarrassing inter-departmental memos that sometimes reeked of bigotry. Although Mengele's name was blacked out from the documents, it was clear that he was the person referred to by officials who warned against the evils of "Jewish revenge."

But not every appeal for information was granted. Department of Justice lawyers were, at times, over-zealous in protecting the secrecy of federal records and needed coaxing by Commission counsel. Outside of the Commission, one request to the solicitor-general for related records by journalist David Vienneau was repeatedly refused, in spite of a finding by Canada's Freedom of Information Commissioner Inger Hanson that the record in question should be made public. Prepared to take the solicitor-general to court on the matter, the information commissioner was thwarted by a Federal Court of Canada ruling in the case of another government agency. The court refused to interfere with the decision of the Canadian Radio and Telecommunications Commission to withhold information under certain exemptions to the freedom of information legislation. As a result of this decision, important documentation pertaining to Nazi war criminals remained undisclosed, in spite of a statute intended to promote public access to this type of information. The Access to Information Act went through a parliamentary review and in 1987 a House of Commons committee recommended that the Federal Court be entitled to step in and release classified materials where it believes government officials are being overly restrictive.

In its report, the Deschênes Commission expressed dismay at being turned down by the Department of Health and Welfare when it requested old age pension information on several suspects. "Clearly", wrote Mr. Justice Deschênes, "the knowledge that an individual alleged to be a war criminal resident in Canada receives such a pension or that he ceased to receive it on a certain date would have been of great assistance to the Commission in attempting to locate the individual or ascertain that he had died. In addition, it would have been, in almost all cases, more recent information than landing records and citizenship or passport applications." The government refused to supply the information on the basis of a provision in the Old Age Security Act which precludes the disclosure of information about people applying for old age pensions or recipients. Deschênes filed a complaint with the Privacy Commission, which was dismissed. As a result, Deschênes recommended changes to the statute so that addresses of old age pensioners could be made available to the RCMP. The government has yet to respond.

By and large, the Deschênes Commission itself was forthcoming in relation to intervenors with data in its possession that did not threaten to reveal the names of suspected war criminals. In one instance, however, a major controversy did arise. Mr. Justice Deschênes hired eight legal scholars on contract to research the law in depth and provide opinions on the various issues of law facing the inquiry. A press release dated June 25, 1985 announced the formation of a working group of professors and practitioners from across Canada—Professor Jacques Bellemare (Montreal), Mr. Donald P. Bryk (Winnipeg), Mr. Gowan T. Guest (Vancouver), Mr. John I. Laskin (Toronto), Mr. E. Neil McKelvey (St. John, N.B.), Professor J. George Neuspiel (Ottawa), Mr. Michel Proulx (Montreal), and Professor Sharon A. Williams (Toronto).

Given the way the Low report had been suppressed for five years, it seemed only logical that these opinions should be made available to the intervenors at the inquiry for analysis and comment. As someone who had been a war crimes justice advocate for quite some time, I had no desire to repeat the futile experience of shadowboxing with government legal opinion. Only a direct opportunity to respond to these latest opinions could be constructive.

At a sitting of the Commission in July, 1985, I asked the Commissioner to release these opinions. He said only, "We will see. I will not commit myself in advance either way." I made the same proposal again on September 23, 1985. In support of my request, I drew an analogy between the material under consideration by the Commission and the Low memorandum, which had influenced the government's decision to do nothing on the issue of war criminals in the intervening years. This time the Commissioner was more negative, stating, "I do not feel inclined to agree to your request. I think a line has to be drawn somewhere where the debate must be closed. I am just wondering whether it is advisable that these opinions that I am in the process of obtaining in turn be submitted to outside analysis and in turn be the object of comments either by yourself or by others who have already had the opportunity of filing very substantial briefs before the Commission. In all fairness, then, to the authors of those opinions, I suppose that I would have to return to them and tell them, 'Here is the criticism that you have been submitted to' and give them an opportunity to answer that. There would be no end to it, especially when one knows the talent of counsel and academics to rebut whatever argument may be put against the opinions that they have been putting forward. I feel that I have received enough advice in legal fields to be able to use up much of my time between now and the target date that has been given to this Commission. I think I have all the material I need." The Commissioner did say, however, "I may change my mind."

In October, 1985, I tried once more. On that occasion I raised the issue of fairness. As a party with legal standing before the inquiry, the League for Human Rights had a specific interest in the outcome of the Commission to see that steps are taken against Nazi war criminals. It was an interest that was entitled to be treated in accordance with the judicial requirements of procedural fairness. All parties with standing before the Commission, including counsel for the federal government, supported the request for the release of the papers. "What I fear," said Department of Justice lawyer Ivan Whitehall to the Commissioner, "is that if there is a non-disclosure of the legal material on which you are to write your report, then we are going to be running into the very opposition, the very criticism that we heard about the Low report and the other reports. Even though the final opinion may be written by an eminent jurist such as yourself, in my respectful submission, the very credibility of this Commission can be adversely affected by non-disclosure of these reports, because of the very suggestion that there is a fifth column operating behind the scene. Mr. Matas, used the expression "shadowboxing." So as to remove any suggestion of shadowboxing, so that this issue be resolved once and for all, it would be my recommendation, sir, that indeed the legal opinions, once they crystalize to the point of being a firm legal opinion or advice to you, they be made available not by way of argument but simply for the purposes of written reply should any party wish to respond to any of those opinions."

Commission counsel Yves Fortier did not join in the otherwise unanimous request, rejecting the notion that a shadow would be cast over the report of the Commission: "In due course, I anticipate, when you do submit your report, that these opinions will be appended and will be there for all to see." By then, of course, it would be too late for any rebuttal.

On this occasion, Mr. Justice Deschênes replied with irony, stating, "The only problem with you gentlemen, if I may say so—and I am saying it without any intention of disparaging anybody—is that you are a group of too able lawyers. You, of course, have clients to represent, for whom the issues in this Commission are highly emotional. I am sure that in dealing with this matter you are capable and prepared to argue your cases until doomsday. Unfortunately, I do not have that kind of a delay to work with." After reading through the long list of submissions he had received to date, the Commissioner concluded, "I have the legal advice that I need, and that additional debates on this matter would not really throw any additional useful light once I have been able to go through this whole material."

With this firm refusal, there was little choice but to proceed to the Federal Court of Canada, Trial Division, to ask the court to order the release of the legal opinions by the Commission. The motion, argued before Mr. Justice Cullen on November 21, 1985, was based on the legal principle that a public inquiry must be arranged in such a way as to provide members of the public with a reasonable opportunity to know the subject matter under investigation. The law contemplates a meaningful inquiry, one which enables the Commission to reach a conclusion that adequately reflects public interest—not merely one where citizens are given a chance to blow off steam.

This obligation to be fair, known in law as the "duty of fairness," applies to agencies that conduct investigations and make recommendations that are preliminary steps to legal action by government. Clearly, the Commission of Inquiry on War Criminals was the lead up to possible legal reforms to bring Nazi war criminals in Canada to justice. The recommendations of Deschênes would influence and might be decisive in the government's subsequent plan of action. Once the Commission granted standing to the League for Human Rights and other intervenors, it undertook a duty to be fair to those parties, a duty owed to anyone with a special or direct interest in the proceedings. As a result, the Commission was required to disclose documents which would affect the outcome of the inquiry, even if the disclosure of reports might lengthen the proceedings. Any added work for the Commission would be justified by increased fairness. It would be unfair for the Commission to consider opinions while depriving interested parties of their right to refute them.

In the Federal Court of Canada proceedings, Commission counsel Yves Fortier conceded that the Commissioner have a duty to be fair, but argued that consideration of secret reports was not unfair. It lay within the discretion of the Commission, he submitted, to decide whether and how to solicit opinions on legal matters under investigation. The Commission had afforded the intervenors ample opportunity to submit opinions of law and had enjoyed the benefit of those views on numerous occasions. Whether to allow parties to rebut the legal opinions solicited was also up to the Commission's discretion and it had exercised its prerogative in a fair manner.

The Federal Court agreed and denied the motion. In refusing to order the release of the legal opinions, the judge said, "Mr. Justice Deschênes has accepted his responsibilities, has indicated the voluminous material he had to consider and the complexities of the issues. Time is a very important factor he must consider and indeed says so in his reasons for not acceding to the League's request. We are told the reports will be made public. To suggest, as the League does, that this is really their last chance to comment is hardly accurate. Whether the

Commission concludes nothing can be done or that five or ten options are open to the Government, the League and others will have several opportunities to present their comments on the report of the experts, albeit in different fora [forums]."

We appealed the decision to the Federal Court of Appeal in February, 1986, on the ground that Mr. Justice Cullen had erred in holding that the League for Human Rights would have other opportunities to comment on the experts' reports. The Commission was a unique forum. A public forum had never before been created to deal with these issues and would likely never be again. No other institution could perform the functions of the Commission. Its legal duty to comply with its mandate meant the Commission could not refuse disclosure on the basis that other arenas could do the work it had been asked to do.

This time, the court agreed with our arguments and ordered the Commission to release the legal opinions. In its reasons, the Court of Appeal wrote, "In the particular circumstances of this Commission, the reports of the working group will not play the peripheral or incidental role which legal opinions usually play in the result of an inquiry. Instead, they are directed precisely to matters which the Commission is expressly required to address in its report. They are in the nature of expert evidence and to be dealt with accordingly. One would ordinarily expect the advice to a commission of any independent expert chosen by it to carry significant weight. The degree of an expert's interest, if any, in the outcome of the proceeding is always a criterion against which the validity of his opinion is to be measured. We do not, of course, know what the reports have concluded. They may, in greater or lesser measure, support the views already presented by the League or by some other party granted status. What is clear is that, to the extent they favour the position of one, they will militate against that of another. While there is, of course, no *lis* [dispute] between the Commission and any of the parties granted standing before it, it is pure sophistry to suggest that the opinions of its working group are not certain to be a significant part of the case against the interests of one or more of the League and others granted standing. It cannot be said that the opportunity afforded the League and other interested parties to present their own views and comment on the views of others fulfils the duty of fairness absent the opportunity to comment on the opinions of the independent experts."

The legal opinions, long since written and reviewed by the Commission, were finally released for comment. The effort had taken five attempts—three before the Commission and two in court. Of the seven opinions (one of the experts did not file a report), only one, by Jacques Bellemare, was uniformly negative. Three needed no comment and the remaining three were essentially positive, with certain reservations. Having an opportunity to refute the Bellemare paper alone made the long process of obtaining these documents worthwhile. His position was hauntingly like that of the inter-departmental committee headed by Martin Low—a rejection of every available remedy. In my rebuttal I disagreed with twenty-one separate arguments he raised. Lawyers for both the Canadian Jewish Congress and the Canadian Jewish Students Network also filed extensive responses to the experts' reports.

At the conclusion of the Deschênes Commission, the question of secrecy arose once more, when the government decided to suppress the report prepared by Alti Rodal. A thorough examination of how Nazi war criminals entered Canada and an integral part of the Deschênes report, the 560-page study was a chilling confirmation of all suspicions that the authorities were not doing what they could to keep Holocaust perpetrators out of the country. Mr. Justice Deschênes called it an "outstanding contribution", and submitted it to the government along with his report in December, 1986. The Deschênes report itself was withheld for more than two months before being made public in March, 1987, but the Rodal paper was kept hidden for a full seven months, until August, 1987. What is more, the study was not released willingly, but by force of law under the Access to Information Act at the request of a journalist. One cannot help but wonder whether, without the assistance of the statute, the study would ever have been released at all.

When it finally did appear, the study was slashed with major deletions which left whole portions of the document blacked out. Deschênes himself had consented to cuts made to his own report to exclude any reference to named individuals, but they were minor in comparison to the wholesale alteration of the Rodal study. In one section, for example, Rodal refers to an alleged Nazi war criminal from Yugoslavia who was deliberately allowed into Canada by a joint effort of U.S. and Canadian intelligence services. Five pages of information concerning the individual were blacked out by the government without so much as consulting the author of the study.

The government's justification for censorship was that the study contained information that had been obtained in confidence, that it touched on international affairs, defence, law enforcement and investigations, that it disclosed Cabinet secrets and personal information, and that it was necessary to protect solicitor-client privilege. Under the guise of solicitor-client privilege, deletions to the report encompassed communications between Martin Low, the inter-departmental committee he headed and Prime Minister Trudeau, expressing opposition to any action on Nazi war criminals. This was a needless move. Although solicitor-client privilege is a recognized exception under the Access to Information Act, it does not apply in a situation such as this. That privilege does not cover everything a lawyer tells his client or that a client discloses to his lawyer. It is confined to circumstances connected with intended or expected lawsuits, or ones that have already begun. In 1981, when the Low memorandum was prepared, no lawsuits against Nazi war criminals had been commenced, nor were any in the works. In fact, that was the whole point of the communications—to discuss why a policy of inaction should be continued. Exchanges of this sort do not fall within the protection of solicitor-client privilege. It was on this very ground that the Federal Court of Canada ordered Deschênes to release the legal opinions prepared for the Commission.

Of course, the government's refusal to release these important exchanges between Prime Minister Trudeau and his legal advisors can be appealed. But, as we already know what the positions of Trudeau and the Justice Department were at the time, there may be little point to launching a protracted court case to have these deletions reversed. The views of Martin Low and his committee have all been discussed earlier on in this book at length, but a few words about Trudeau may be appropriate at this point. Rodal describes his attitude as reflecting the notion that "people coming to Canada should leave the baggage of wounds and problems in the old country behind them," and that, at least during his tenure, the fabric of Canadian society was "too fragile to sustain the kind of tension resulting from seeking out war criminals." In hindsight, the Deschênes Commission proved that the fabric of Canadian society was sufficiently strong, and that with the widespread agreement on the government's response, Canada became a more united country.

It is ironic that Pierre Trudeau, who was so audacious in asserting minority language rights in this country to strengthen Canadian unity, would have feared that raising ethnic concerns could be harmful. The assertion of francophone rights outside Quebec and anglophone rights in that province have played a role in fortifying Canadian unity. Surely the assertion of the right to life and the necessity of bringing mass murderers to justice can only do the same. On this issue, Trudeau, like every other government leader for the past four decades, suffered from a blind spot. Referring to the Nazi extermination of six million Jews as "baggage" from "the old country" ignores the universality of the crimes and bespeaks insularity. Admittedly, immigrants to Canada should leave behind their foreign political squabbles, which have no relevance in a Canadian context. But the moral and legal duty to bring Nazi war criminals to justice has no borders.

With the release of the Rodal study, two conclusions can be drawn. First, government negativism on Nazi war criminals had a life of its own. Official inactivity went far beyond even the flimsiest excuses. Inaction by the authorities was pervasive and perpetual. Whatever the initial reasons for doing nothing— inertia, rationalization and self-justification all compounded the problem. Continuing inaction became necessary to justify past inaction. The government wanted to avoid embarrassment, and carrying on doing nothing seemed the easiest way. A reversal of the policy of inaction would have been an implied criticism that the government was not prepared to inflict on itself. It took an independent commission of inquiry to tell the government the obvious: that the crime of mass murder should not go unpunished. The desire to avoid embarrassment continues even today. This, more than solicitor-client privilege, led to many of the deletions in the Rodal study. The government blacked out exchanges between the Justice Department and the Prime Minister's Office because it was ashamed to have this negativity form part of the public record.

Secondly, the revelations in the Rodal study underline the need for legislation, not only to provide the legal mechanism necessary to bring war criminals to justice, but in order to establish clear, unequivocal principles to ensure that the government will act. With its obligations set out in black and white, the government can no longer hide behind feeble excuses in secret files to justify further inaction.

On an international level, freedom of information and complete access to documentation is a critical element in the long-awaited efforts of several Western countries to hunt war criminals in a systematic fashion. Australia, the U.S., and with the conviction of Klaus Barbie, France are all part of a world-wide move to expose and punish Nazi mass murderers before time runs out. For them, the 38,000 United Nations war crimes files compiled after the war are of utmost importance. The fact that they remain hidden away in the UN archives has grave implications for all nations, including Canada, involved in the pursuit of war criminals. These valuable dossiers were accumulated after the war by the United Nations War Crimes Commission's seventeen member nations (of which Canada was one) for the purpose of bringing suspects to trial. When the War Crimes Commission abruptly halted its work, the files were transferred to the UN. Today, Javier Perez de Cuellar, the UN secretary general has refused to make them public. He has ruled that only governments may request the files and has imposed an oath of secrecy on any nation that is granted access to them. Israel, which has requested them all, is forbidden to disclose their contents.

This ruling, ostensibly for the purpose of protecting the reputations of individuals identified in the dossiers, makes little sense. Although the detailed information in them remains confidential, the 38,000 names—and the charges and degree of involvement in war crimes—are all on the public record. Among them is Kurt Waldheim, listed in the category of major suspects against whom a clear-cut case has been made out.

Perez de Cuellar has indicated that he will release the files only if the nations which formed the UN War Crimes Commission give their consent. Australia has agreed to their publication and the U.S. government has shown its support for broader access to the files. But this will not satisfy de Cuellar. The Canadian government has gone along with a call for broader access after some delay in making up its mind.

These records should be opened up—and soon—not only to allow researchers to fill significant gaps in the history of the Western world, but also to enable the unencumbered pursuit of war criminals who are still in hiding. Keeping the files under wraps cannot protect anybody's privacy, when we already know every one of the thousands of names and the allegations against them. Further, these files do not contain just rumours and ill-founded allegations, all of which might legitimately be kept locked away. The eminent jurists who sat on the UN War Crimes Commission excluded from the dossiers they put together any allegations that could not be authoritatively documented. So a self-imposed veil of secrecy, in these circumstances, appears to be merely one more device to put roadblocks in the way of bringing Nazi mass murderers to justice. The consensus sought by the UN secretary general is unreasonable. Merely giving governments access to the files, without enabling them to make meaningful use of them in investigations, can only defeat the efforts of countries interested in seeing that justice is done.

Chapter Fifteen

Kurt Waldheim and Canada

At the site of Vienna's Parliament, Kurt Waldheim was sworn in as President of Austria on July 8, 1986, with all the pomp and ceremony befitting a head of state. Three hundred yards away, at the Hofburg, the site of the presidential offices, three Americans and three Austrians held up a sign saying: "No to the war criminal president." In a nearby square, Nazi hunter Beate Klarsfeld, instrumental in tracking down Klaus Barbie, took part in a silent candlelight vigil to protest Waldheim's election and Austria's resistance to facing its past. Simultaneously, other demonstrators throughout the country and around the world cried out in disgust as the former Nazi officer joined the distinguished ranks of national leaders.

In the bitter election campaign leading up to his six-year term of office, Waldheim's opponents contended that he was involved in war crimes as a German army officer in the Balkans, and that he knew Jews were being deported to death camps but lied about it for forty years. Earlier allegations by the World Jewish Congress, since corroborated by the United States Justice Department, revealed that Kurt Waldheim had participated in "activities amounting to persecution of Jews and other innocent victims in Greece and Yugoslavia during World War II." Waldheim served with Hitler's high command following the surrender of Italy, as the Nazis seized 100,000 Italian soldiers and deported them to German camps in 1943. Waldheim remained with the high command in Greece, when 48,000 Jews from Salonika and Corfu were rounded up in 1944 and sent to their deaths in Auschwitz and Bergen-Belsen. He also worked for the Nazi high command in Yugoslavia that massacred thousands of partisans and their families the same year. His immediate superior, General Alexander Lohr was executed in 1947 after being tried and convicted as a war criminal.

The Yugoslav State Commission on War Crimes, after a review of documentary evidence and the testimony of witnesses concluded that Waldheim was a "WAR CRIMINAL" (emphasis in original), and asked that he be surrendered to stand trial. A copy of the Yugoslav file was transmitted to the United Nations War Crimes Commission, and after an independent appraisal and evaluation of its contents, the UN Commission assigned Waldheim its highest suspect classification, known as Category "A", and reserved for clear-cut cases meriting immediate attention. He was also placed on the Central Registry of War Criminals and Security Suspects (CROWCASS), designated as a "War Criminal" wanted for "murder." These listings have been in circulation since the war.

Kurt Waldheim has continually fabricated stories to cover up the sordid details of his past. In a 1977 biography, he wrote of a leg wound that earned him a discharge from the German forces in 1941. Even when confronted with the irrefutable links to his former life—his army record, a membership card in the Nazi student union, his identity card for the cavalry unit of the Nazi storm troopers and even his own photograph—Waldheim persisted in upholding the deception. "No, not me, not true," he lied. He later acknowledged serving in reprisals against civilians, but has adamantly disclaimed any personal wrongdoing.

These outrageous denials led the Austrian chancellor, Fred Sinowatz, to step down in protest upon Waldheim's election. In leaving office he said with biting irony, "Waldheim was never a member of the Nazi storm troopers, but his horse was." The theme was picked up by protestors, and during Waldheim's inauguration, angry demonstrators unveiled a wooden Trojan horse sporting a swastika and the brown cap of the Nazi's dreaded Brownshirts in Vienna's main square. The horse bore the slogan, "A Horse Trusted by the World," a parody of Waldheim's election slogan, "An Austrian Trusted by the World."

And Waldheim had been trusted by the world. He held the highly esteemed post of secretary general of the United Nations for two successive terms, from 1972 until 1982. Had it not been for a Chinese veto in 1982, that position would still be his today.

Although it was not widely known, Canada bears no small measure of responsibility for Kurt Waldheim's rise to power. As early as 1948, Canada was a member of the United Nations War Crimes Commission, joining in the UN decision which placed Waldheim in the "A" category of most serious war criminal suspects. On the basis of very good authority, then, the Canadian government has been aware of the *prima facie* case against Waldheim since 1948. (Later that year, the UN War Crimes Commission disbanded prematurely for political reasons—before it ever got around to dealing with Waldheim and many others. The same year, Canada was acceding to Britain's request to terminate all Nazi war crimes trials.)

Canada's connection to the current "Waldheim Affair" became direct when he came to this country as a representative of Austria in 1956. The government passively stood by as Waldheim was installed in Ottawa as Austrian minister plenipotentiary from 1956 to 1958, and later as ambassador from 1958 to 1960. Incredibly, Canada accepted Waldheim's credentials as ambassador, though it was under no obligation to do so. Had the country's leaders rebuffed him at that time, Waldheim would never have been able to attain the rank of UN secretary general or president of Austria. Canada likes to pride itself in its role at the United Nations and in contributing to the establishment of other international bodies. Lester Pearson, who was secretary of state for External Affairs when Waldheim arrived in Ottawa, had done much for the world community. But by welcoming an accused Nazi into the diplomatic circle, thereby enabling him to be foisted on the United Nations later, he undercut much of Canada's efforts to strengthen that international body. Waldheim's term of office in the UN has besmirched the name of a highly respected institution, and our country carries at least some of the blame.

It is all too easy for today's leaders to plead ignorance of his ugly record. But Canada had the CROWCASS list with Waldheim's name on it, and a simple glance over the war crimes rosters that were gathering dust in Canadian Archives would have exposed him as a wanted man. One suspects that even had officials from the Department of External Affairs checked, they would have kept silent. Canada, as the chronicles show, had other priorities during that era. (The Mengele incident, two years after Waldheim's departure, revealed that Canada's international relations were a far weightier concern than the pursuit of war criminals in this country. Top policy advisers were warning the Cabinet of the day against any efforts to get to the bottom of allegations that the "Angel of Death" might have found sanctuary here, for fear of antagonizing West Germany.)

Times have changed. With the 1985 creation of an inquiry on war criminals, a new era of Canadian responsibility began. Or so we thought. But when, in the wake of the newly uncovered charges, I requested Mr. Justice Deschênes to look into Waldheim's five-year stint in Ottawa and his ready acceptance by Canada, the Commissioner refused. Kurt Waldheim, he said, did not fall within the mandate of the inquiry, because he had not yet been convicted of any crimes. This illogic astounded me. None of the suspects under investigation by the Commission have been tried and found guilty. They are all "alleged" war criminals. Joseph Mengele was never convicted, nor was Helmut Rauca. So I wrote to Secretary of State for External Affairs Joe Clark in May 1986, asking for a complete investigation into the Waldheim matter and requesting that the government bar his entry to Canada. On June 20, a few weeks before the inauguration in Vienna, the issue was again raised in the House of Commons by Member of Parliament Pauline Jewett. She asked Prime Minister Mulroney what actions the government intended to take. He referred to the government's initiatives in appointing the Deschênes Commission, but what he failed to note is that Mr. Justice Deschênes had already decided such an investigation was outside its terms of reference.

Canada has every reason to probe the very grave allegations against Waldheim, to get to the truth about his Nazi activities. Other governments have been mobilized. The American Justice department has looked seriously into the recently uncovered allegations and Attorney-General Edwin Meese III issued orders not to permit him into the U.S. on the basis of his participation in Nazi persecution. The Israeli minister of Justice stated that Waldheim could be put on trial as an accessory to war crimes. Canada should follow the lead of these nations in barring Waldheim from this country.

The ramifications of the "Waldheim Affair" go far beyond an incident involving a single head of state. This predicament represents a breakdown of the Canadian system for accrediting diplomats. Canada needs to articulate a policy and set up a screening procedure to ensure that it will never again accept the credentials of a suspected war criminal—especially when the evidence against him is crystal clear. By the same token, the United Nations cannot afford to choose another chief who has actually joined forces with regimes that repudiate its most basic principles of peace and respect for human rights. The UN is in dire need of a method for scrutinizing the background of anyone who aspires to its high offices.

War criminals, criminals against humanity and their cohorts proliferate in the corridors of power. Their grisly deeds are committed for and on behalf of governments. They exploit position and standing as refuges from retribution, as vehicles for exoneration. If Canada is going to maintain one ounce of credibility as a promoter of human rights, it has no choice but to renounce the violators and their henchmen. Unless we reject them—as diplomats, as world leaders, as representatives of foreign nations—we have acquiesced.

In light of these arguments, Prime Minister Mulroney's decision to recognize Waldheim's 1986 election into office was distressing. Canada's Jewish community protested the victory and urged the government to do the same. In a telex on behalf of the League for Human Rights, I asked External Affairs Minister Clark to boycott the inauguration. It would have been, at the very least, a small gesture of disapproval. Over these objections, the government forwarded a congratulatory telegram, and Canada's Ambassador to Austria, Michael Shenstone, attended the ceremony. Several countries, including the United States and Israel, kept their official representatives away. Canada ought to have followed suit.

Still, in replying to my original letter, the Right Honorable Joe Clark seemed genuinely concerned:

> "We have carefully reviewed the files relating to the accreditation of Mr. Waldheim as Minister Plenipotentiary and later, as Ambassador of Austria. These files contain no reference to any allegation of wrongdoing on the part of Mr. Waldheim nor to the issue of war criminals generally. On the basis of Mr. Waldheim's credentials, experience, and favourable reports of diplomats who had dealt with him overseas, *agrement* [acceptance] was granted. In short, there was no appar-

ent reason to question Mr. Waldheim's credentials and he was accredited in accordance with normal practice.

I share your view that proper procedures should be in place to screen proposed diplomatic appointments. Thus, whenever a foreign state seeks to accredit a proposed head of mission, the Government of Canada examines the request very carefully. If there is some irregularity, *agrement* would probably be withheld. I am satisfied that the present procedures are appropriate. In the event that an error is made in accepting a diplomat, it is always open to us, in accordance with the Vienna Convention on Diplomatic Relations, to revoke *agrement* or declare him *persona non grata.* [italics added]

Finally, with respect to your suggestion that the Government undertake an investigation of Mr. Waldheim to determine whether or not he should be barred entry to Canada, I can confirm that there are at present no plans to invite him to Canada, nor has he expressed a desire to visit this country. However, as serious allegations have been made against Mr. Waldheim, we consider that it is important to ascertain the facts relating to this matter in order to decide what action might be appropriate. Accordingly, we are continuing our examination of the relevant files covering the period in question. We wish to ensure that we have as much factual information as possible, including all relevant documentation held by the United Nations. I have asked the Permanent Mission in New York to follow up with the UN Secretariat in this regard. In addition to considering all available information, we will pay particular attention to any measure taken or proposal made by those countries most directly connected with the allegations."

That letter was, in itself, a positive response. I continued to press the matter by writing to Joe Clark urging that his staff undertake their own research before coming to any premature conclusions about Waldheim. Since he has never been brought to trial, much of the key evidence against him has never been examined, and his culpability or innocence cannot be assessed only on the basis of currently available material. A great deal of new information has been turned up by the researchers of the

World Jewish Congress. As a volunteer organization with limited resources, though, its findings are by no means exhaustive. A thorough probe would be a mammoth task. Only by ferreting out Nazi archives around the world—in the U.S., Israel and Europe—could investigators develop a complete picture of Waldheim's wartime activities. Preferably, Canada could take part in an international tribunal, which would be better equipped to accumulate the resources and expertise necessary to complete the job.

Chapter Sixteen

Justice Delayed

Why is it morally imperative that Nazi war criminals be brought to justice this late in the day? To people unfamiliar with the issue, a typical first reaction is that these people are old, their crimes took place decades ago on another continent, and they pose no danger to society. They have been model citizens in Canada. What's past is past.

True, all war criminals should have been exposed, tried and punished immediately following the war. But justice is governed by no time limitations. The crime of murder always calls out for punishment. Canada's shameful forty-year delay cannot provide an excuse for the denial of justice now. This country has no statute of limitations for murder and there is no justification for Canada imposing one upon itself. And while it is true that the accused are now old, old age is no defence. To leave them be would be to forgive and forget their vicious crimes.

That it took this long to mount sufficient pressure to force the government into action may in part be explained by the very horrors committed by the Nazi regime. That it was millions who lost their lives has, hitherto, stunned many into silence. The size of these numbers and the depravity of the crimes defies the mind's understanding and numbs the heart's feelings. Indeed, the Nazis counted on the psychological barriers of attempting to assimilate mass murder to ensure their "final solution."

The crime of murder calls for punishment, not for retribution but as a means of deterrence. As grotesque and unimaginable as the Nazi Holocaust was, by no means was it an isolated crime in our history. The genocide perpetrated by Turkey on Armenian citizens during the First World War preceded it. Since, we have seen the killing fields of Kampuchea, the mass killings in Uganda under Idi Amin, and the wholesale disappearances, or the *desperacidos* in Argentina. The need to deter mass murder continues. We cannot take for granted that it will never happen again—it has yet to cease.

We have a distinct obligation to the victims who perished in the Holocaust and to future generations of survivors to ensure that there will never be a recurrence of the Holocaust. The victims cannot testify that the Holocaust took place, but the survivors can. Although it may be difficult and painful to go over again and again the events of the Second World War, it is necessary so that those who perished will not be forgotten. To forget the murderers is to cast the victims into oblivion. We cannot bring the dead back to life, but by asserting justice, we can give some semblance of meaning to their death. By ignoring justice we make their death meaningless, which is a posthumous cruelty. The memory of the victims should be hallowed. Doing nothing desecrates their memory and victimizes them a second time.

The Holocaust is just one point in a long continuum. Today we face the threat of a nuclear Holocaust and the obliteration not just of one people but the entire human race. Jonathan Schell, in his book *The Fate of the Earth,*[1] wrote that Hitler's attempt to exterminate the Jews is the closest historical precursor to the ultimate extinction of the species. By remembering our own capacity for insanity, we can learn that crimes like the Holocaust are not prevented from happening just because they are unthinkable. On the contrary, they may be all the more possible for that very reason. Only by recalling the "gaping unmendable holes in the fabric of the world" left by these crimes—in this case the entire *shtetl* culture of Europe was wiped out—can we hope to respond to the threat of nuclear Holocaust before it is realized. Forgetting or overlooking the Nazi Holocaust is much like pretending that nuclear extinction is an impossibility. If we do that, we court disaster. This world cannot face squarely the dangers that threaten it by forgetting the disasters it has suffered.

Application of the law, then, is not only concerned with punishment, but also with education. Although the actual crimes were the work of a relative handful of individuals, they were facilitated by the passivity of whole populations. We must undertake the task of ensuring that never again will the citizenry of any country stand by in the face of mass murders organized by a few. The prosecution of war criminals teaches society in an immediate way that war crimes are not permissible. Failure to act can only leave the impression that such deeds will be tolerated among nations.

The anti-Semitism that prompted the attempted annihilation of a people has in recent years taken the form of "Holocaust denial"—disputing that the mass murders ever took place. Hate propaganda in Canada is becoming more common, more pervasive, more bold. The seeds of future hatred are sown by indifference to the consequences of past hatred. Neo-Nazism itself represents a danger to Canadian society. While not a popular phenomenon, it represents an ongoing latent threat. The activities of people such as Jim Keegstra, Ernst Zundel, John Ross Taylor, Donald Clarke Andrews, Robert Wayne Smith and Malcolm Ross are the harvest of Canadian inaction over Nazi war criminals. In failing to prosecute war criminals, the government ignores the Holocaust and gives tacit approval to those who deny it. The strongest rebuttal to this strain of anti-Semitism is the active pursuit of Holocaust perpetrators. Criminal trials lift the burden of establishing the historical record from the shoulders of the victim. Facts proved in court beyond a reasonable doubt carry a status far greater than those left simply as assertions of survivors. Prosecuting those who killed under Hitler's banner is an effective way of combatting the peril of Neo-Nazism. The way to dispose of the past is by dealing with it—not by turning a blind eye toward it.

The urgent need to deal with Nazi war criminals living in Canada today is by no means a question of revenge. Revenge is personal, inflicted on select targets by relatives or friends of victims. Justice is impartial, imposed by the state even-handedly. Justice provides a sentence—a punishment—only after proof of guilt beyond a reasonable doubt at a fair trial and with an appellate process to challenge every verdict. Nor is dealing with Nazi criminals strictly a "Jewish problem." The bringing to justice of Nazi war criminals in Canada has, it is obvious, its unique Jewish dimension. Nazism was and is a demonology blaming all the world's evils on the Jewish people. The Nazi Holocaust was an attempt to exterminate the whole Jewish people and culminated in the actual murder of six million Jews. Its victims were ordinary people—the same breed as their relatives in Canada who could do nothing to sponsor them for admission as immigrants or refugees. It is more than a tragic irony that the Jews who lived through the Nazi horror and survived death camps, tortures and starvation inconceivable to the imagination were denied refuge to Canada by virtue of a racist immigration policy which made it possible for their very oppressors to enter.

But the issue is, to repeat, not a narrow Jewish concern. It is a fundamental human rights issue. In 1982, the Canadian Charter of Rights and Freedoms came into effect, representing a new era and a deepening respect for human rights in Canada. Punishment of the worst violators of human rights is consistent with our heightened consciousness. As one of the world's leading democracies, Canada has a particular responsibility to fight racism in every form. The Holocaust was the culmination of racism. By playing host to the perpetrators of the Holocaust, Canada can only undermine the rational, lawful, non-racist foundations of democratic life. Our government cannot credibly combat racial discrimination but ignore racially motivated mass murders. Respect for human rights involves prosecuting for genocide. In so doing, Canada can only strengthen the rationality and lawfulness upon which democracy depends.

As a member of the international community, Canada not only has obligations under international laws, but also a duty to set examples of lawfulness within its borders to ensure mutual respect among nations. A respect for law and compassion for victims of oppression should motivate Canada to strive for justice. If we as a country accept that murder is unjust, then murderers must be brought to justice under the rule of law. The scene of the crimes is irrelevant. Canada has habitually insulated itself from the events of the Holocaust as being a foreign phenomenon. But Canadians are not a world apart. We should be concerned about murder, wherever it happened.

Ideally, the offenders ought to be tried and punished in the countries where they committed their wrongdoing. But gaps in current extradition treaties, and the unfairness of the Soviet justice system make that impossible for the vast majority of Nazi war criminals in Canada today. Deportation, another alternative, is no guarantee that a criminal will ever be prosecuted. Trial in Canada is the best assurance that perpetrators of Nazi crimes will be not only be forced to face the charges against them, but also that they will receive fair treatment. This will require legislative change to make the Canadian justice system responsive to World War II crimes. Amendments to our criminal law, though, do not violate any principle of retroactivity. There is nothing unfair about setting up machinery to penalize deeds that were always criminal.

Unfortunately, the punishment of government-orchestrated mass murder inevitably falls prey to political complications. When the crimes are committed, the perpetrators are in power and power becomes a refuge from which they must be dislodged. However, the fact of the matter is that most governments that sanction genocide do not survive for long. Any regime that kills huge numbers of its population is unlikely to sustain the support even of the minority necessary to keep it in power. Prosecuting the perpetrators of the Nazi genocide is no different than bringing any criminal to trial—wrongdoers cannot be punished unless they are apprehended.

When Canada brings Nazi war criminals to justice, it does so not only in memory of the victims, but for the accused as well. These trials are not simply "victor's justice." They must be fair. If we hold fair and open trials, history will never have to ask, "What could these accused have said in their favour?" Whatever could possibly be said, the defendants will have an opportunity to say. We give them the full benefit of the law, even though none of them were so generous with their victims. The imposition of justice does not mean that the law will be unfairly applied or that the principle of mercy will be side-stepped. Even for men and women who showed not the slightest compassion for the targets of their perversity, the law requires mercy. But clemency is a valid consideration in sentencing only—it has no place in the determination of an individual's innocence or guilt. Forgiveness, yes, but never forgetfulness. It is appropriate where a person admits his crime and shows remorse. None of the accused war criminals suffered any such anguish. Klaus Barbie, torturer of Jean Moulin, killer of children, remained defiantly unrepentant even as he was sentenced to life imprisonment by a court in Lyon. He complained that his detention in France was illegal and called his trial unfair. Other convicted war criminals have reacted with the same self-righteousness. Clemency has no application when a perpetrator feels no regret, justifying his crime, denying it, claiming forgetfulness, asserting mistaken identity, or charging that the evidence was forged. Mercy does not require us to allow a mass murderer to go free.

Tracking down Nazi murderers does not mean generating ethnic disharmony. The concerns raised by various communities have focussed on the ways and means rather than the overall objective of justice. No group has maintained that Nazi war criminals should go free. Putting criminals on trial is an affirmation of individual responsibility. Nazis persecuted and killed their victims because of the group to which they belonged. Convicting the people who gave the death orders and those who carried them out is a negation of collective guilt—it serves to blame the guilty and exonerate the innocent.

Above all, prosecuting war criminals benefits humanity and Canadians. Our government's inactivity and the indifference of our citizenry have tainted our integrity as a nation. Ultimately, failure to bring Nazi war criminals in this country to trial is a Canadian failure—a blight on our justice system. What we do about mass murderers in our midst reveals much of ourselves. We define the limits of our responsibility. Until now, the clear message Canada has sent out is one of tolerance for vicious killers. Do we want this country to be remembered in history as a Nazi haven? I believe that we would rather have it said that Canada did not stand idly by, that we respected the right to life and cared about all humanity.

It must never be forgotten that Canada fought World War II to oppose Nazism and to defeat Hitler. The war was not just about territory in Europe. It was a battle against the racism and totalitarianism for which Nazi Germany stood. Canadian soldiers gave their lives so that those values would not triumph. Permitting war criminals to remain at large is an insult to the entire war effort. As Canadian philosopher Emil Fackenheimhas observed: "By not bringing anyone to justice we, in a sense, give Hitler a posthumous victory." Punishment, on the other hand, is an assertion that this country chose correctly in fighting alongside the Allies.

How are we to deal with the horror of mass murder? We can either confront it or turn our eyes away. Only confrontation permits us to assimilate the experience. Refusal to face this reality is a denial of history and of suffering, an escape from the human condition. The legal system is one way to confront genocide, providing an expression for the abhorrence we feel. At the level of punishment, of course, no amount of justice could match the crime of mass murder. A killer of one thousand innocents can only be tried once, and he can receive but one life sentence. At the level of values, though, justice can be commensurate with the crimes of the Holocaust, for it asserts the values the Nazis denied. These criminals destroyed forever the peace and tranquility of millions. They rounded up, hunted down and shipped off Jews to the death camps of Auschwitz, Belzec, Chelmo, Majdanek, Sobibor and Treblinka. For too long, Canada has given rest to the wicked. Now the time has finally come for the hunters to be hunted.

Justice delayed is justice denied. Time swallows up huge chunks of evidence needed to convict the guilty parties: witnesses die, recollections blur and the ravages of old age alter appearances drastically. We have now allowed four decades to slip away. Justice will not be denied to the accused who stand trial at this late date, although it was withheld from the victims. The best one can hope for is some small gesture to counter the gross injustice of the past.

For too long, Canada has been an accessory after the fact to mass murder. Our Criminal Code makes it an offence for anyone who, knowing that a person has committed an offence, receives, comforts or assists him for the purpose of facilitating his escape. If a person takes a murderer into his home, offers him shelter, protects him from the authorities because he does not want the murderer brought to trial, he is guilty of a criminal offence. Canada's government has known about the presence in this country of at least some Nazi mass murderers. Canadian society has taken them in, providing them with food, clothing, homes and employment. Until the Deschênes report, civil servants have convinced successive governments that these suspects should not be prosecuted here.

Canada has also committed another offence: the obstruction of justice. The Criminal Code penalizes those who willfully attempt in any manner to obstruct, prevent or deflect the course of justice. A person may be punished for this offence if he endeavours to dissuade another from reporting an incident to the authorities.[2] How different is this from Canada's actions in relation to Nazi war criminals? For years, the RCMP refused even to take reports or investigate allegations. Complainants were fobbed off to the External Affairs Department under the guise of pursuing extradition requests which never came. This history of obstructing justice makes any argument against action that is based on the lapse of time particularly offensive. The delay in bringing Nazi war criminals to justice did not just happen. It was the result of willful government policy and should not now be invoked as a justification for doing nothing now. That would be an affront to justice.

Because of the dimensions of the Nazi Holocaust, unprecedented in its techniques and its horrors, the wheels of justice should have been spinning faster and faster to keep apace with the enormity of the crime. Canada, far from making the extra effort required, has managed, through inattention and indifference, to grind justice to a halt for over four decades. And now the problem is urgent, since it has been left to fester for so long. We owe it to future generations of Canadians to be able to say that—before it was too late—we invoked some measure of justice. Even in advance of any war crimes trials in Canada or denaturalizations, deportations and extraditions, we have a trial taking place in this country. It is the trial of the Canadian justice system. Unless the government moves at once against war criminals in our midst, the verdict of history will stand. Canada will remain guilty, as charged, on every count—as an accessory after the fact of murder, of obstructing justice, and of providing sanctuary to cold-blooded killers. Against this verdict there will be no appeal.

Canada's inaction over Nazi war criminals cannot be divorced from its harsh treatment of Jews fleeing the Holocaust. This country must share in the guilt of Hitler's genocide because of its anti-Semitic immigration policy which virtually excluded Jewish refugees. Of all the countries in the Western world that could have offered succor, Canada's record was the worst. Yet while Jews were turned away at our borders, Nazis came in with relative ease.

Had the exclusion of war criminals been a priority, there are a number of steps Canada could have taken. First, the government might have prohibited their admission altogether. Next, immigration authorities could have set up decent security machinery at overseas posts and made sure every applicant to Canada went through the screening process. Immigration and RCMP personnel would have been well-trained in detection, conducting interviews with every relevant witness and going through all the background documents. The Department of External Affairs would have circulated CROWCASS and UN War

Crimes Commissions lists of war criminals to every single immigration post throughout Europe. Prospective immigrants could have been asked, point blank, whether or not they had committed crimes. Any person who failed security screening might have been turned away. Admission records could have been retained to enable Canadian authorities to investigate undesirable individuals who managed to slip through the system. Once the evidence showed that war criminals had made their way into Canada, they could have been expelled. Not one of these steps was taken. I do not believe the government deliberately devised a scheme to admit Nazi war criminals and keep them here, but had it wanted to, there is little it would have had to do differently. Virtually every common sense precaution was omitted, replaced by slipshod procedures that practically guaranteed their arrival. In what numbers, we can never know.

Canada's dismal record of keeping out victims while letting in their oppressors calls for some degree of atonement. Bringing war criminals to justice is one way to overcome this country's participation in events that made the Holocaust possible. It is an acknowledgement that Canada's refusal to grant refuge was wrong. Permitting the last of the Nazis' cohorts to go free puts an unrepentant face on this country. In the context of restrictions inflicted upon Jewish refugees, failure to act now will make a bad record even worse. Moreover, action or inaction about Nazi war criminals is not just something we say about ourselves, it is something we do to ourselves. In attempting to redress mass inhumanity, we make ourselves more just, more human. Our failure to do so makes us prone to injustice and new forms of inhumanity. It becomes harder to combat new horrors if we do nothing about those committed in

Simple respect for the rule of law suggests that crime must be punished. The rule of law is a standard by which the laws of all nations are measured. It requires even-handedness in applying the principles which govern us and provides that no one is above the law. Every person, no matter what his status, religion, or race is subject to the same protections—and penalties. The Nazi system abandoned the rule of law, sanctioning murder, so long as it was perpetrated on Jews. In allowing Nazi war criminals to go unpunished while invoking justice against all other criminals, Canada is in serious violation of the rule of law. It is this facet of the issue that has engaged the interests of the

Jewish community, who stand to gain nothing either economically or politically from war crimes trials. Canadian Jewry does, however, have cause for concern when a democratic legal system provides that all killings are punishable except the killing of Jews. This discrimination has never been expressed as the motive for inaction, but it was the inevitable effect.

Our Charter of Rights and Freedoms states that Canada is founded upon principles that recognize the supremacy of God and the rule of law. By disregarding the rule of law we not only undermine the rudiments of justice, but the very structure on which this country is built. Canada is coming up against a deadline. Soon the last of the perpetrators, survivors and witnesses will have died of old age. The final opportunity to see justice done will have been lost. Canada can never claim to have done everything that should have been done—forty years of inaction cannot be erased. What remains is one last chance to remedy a historical wrong. If Canada is not to have a permanent stain on its justice system, if we are not to rip the foundations of justice from beneath future generations, we, as a country, must waste no more time in bringing the remaining Nazi war criminals in Canada to justice.

FOOTNOTES

Chapter One

[1] Joseph Weschberg, ed., *The Murderers Among Us: The Wiesenthal Memoirs* (McGraw Hill, 1967), pp. 194-195

Chapter Two

[1] From the transcript of the public hearings of the Commission of Inquiry on War Criminals before the Honourable Justice Jules Deschênes, Winnipeg session, May 22, 1985. Unless otherwise indicated, all references or quotes in this book are from the *Report of the Deschênes Commission, Part 1: Public,* and from submissions, testimony or documents entered as evidence and exhibits before the Deschênes Commission in public hearings from April 10, 1985 until May 6, 1986, including the Low memorandum entitled *Alleged War Criminals in Canada,* and the report prepared by Alti Rodal entitled *The Nazi War Criminals in Canada: The Historical and Political Setting from the 1940s to the Present.* Specific references are available on request to the publisher.

[2] Theodore S. Hamerow, "The Hidden Holocaust", *Commentary,* March 1985, p. 33

[3] Allan A. Ryan, Jr., *Quiet Neighbors: Prosecuting Nazi War Criminals in America* (New York: Harcourt Brace Jovanovich, 1984), pp. 9-12

[4] Hamerow, op. cit., p. 33

[5] Irving Abella & Harold Troper, *None is Too Many* (Toronto: Lester & Orpen Dennys, 1983), pp. 105-124

[6] Lucy Davidowicz, *The War Against the Jews, 1933-1945* (New York: Bantam Books, 1976), p. 544

[7] Ibid.

[8] Ryan, op. cit., p. 8

[9] Ibid., pp. 13-14

[10] Abella & Troper, op. cit., p. 198

[11] The minutes of Security Panel meetings were entered as exhibits before the Deschênes Commission and are referred to throughout this chapter.

[12] Abella & Troper, op. cit., p. 279

[13] Tom Bower, *The Pledge Betrayed* (Garden City: Doubleday, 1981), p. 115

[14] Ryan, op. cit., p. 20

[15] Abella & Troper, op. cit., pp. 254-255

16   Ibid., p. 254

17   Ryan, op. cit., p. 23

18   David Vienneau, "U.S. lies let Nazis settle in Canada, report says", *Toronto Star*, August 7, 1987

19   David Vienneau, "U.S., Britain helped Nazi supporters get into Canada, secret report says", *Toronto Star*, March 14, 1987

20   From a radio interview on CBC radio's *As It Happens*, August 7, 1987

21   *Trial of the Major War Criminals Before the International Military Tribune*, v. XXII, August 27, 1946-October 1, 1946, p. 517

22   Sol Littman, *War Criminal on Trial: The Rauca Case* (Markham: PaperJacks Ltd., 1984), pp. 174-175;

23   "Hnatyshyn says he'll release 'sensitive' report on Nazis," *Globe & Mail*, March 18, 1987

24   Ibid.; Irwin Cotler, *Submissions and Recommendations of the Canadian Jewish Congress to the Deschênes Commission of Inquiry on War Criminals*, July 10, 1985, p. 14

25   For a thorough treatment of this topic, the reader is referred to Abella & Troper, op. cit.

Chapter Three

1   Richard Cleroux, "Hnatyshyn says he'll release 'sensitive' report on Nazis", *Globe & Mail*, March 18, 1987

2   "Canada altered its rules for scientists, study says", *Toronto Star*, March 14, 1987; also, see *Report of the Commission of Inquiry on War Criminals, Part 1: Public*, pp. 273-274, pp. 776-827

3   David Vienneau, "Pius XII pressured St. Laurent into taking collaborator in '49", *Toronto Star*, August 7, 1987

4   Lorne Slotnick, "A war hero, Barbie aide was the darling of Quebec's conservatives", *Globe & Mail*, February 11, 1983; Other valuable insights into De Bernonville and the Vichyites are contained in the *House of Commons Debates*, December 9, 1949, pp. 3033-3042 and February 22, 1949, pp. 791-797

5   *House of Commons Debates*, op. cit., December 9, 1949, p. 3034, as quoted by CCF member of Parliament Alistair Stewart

6   Ibid., February 22, 1949, pp. 796-797, as quoted by Alistair Stewart

7   Slotnick, op. cit.

8   "Story of war crimes buried in hidden study, Kaplan says", *Globe & Mail*, March 17, 1987

9   Slotnick, op. cit.

10   David Vienneau, "St. Laurent, aides 'personally' linked to suspected Nazis", *Toronto Star*, August 7, 1987

11   *House of Commons Debates*, op. cit., February 22, 1949, p. 795

12   Ibid., p. 795, as quoted by Alistair Stewart

13   *As It Happens*, August 7, 1987

Chapter Four
1   Irving Abella, "Time running out for Canada on war criminals", *Globe & Mail*, May 26, 1987

2   Bower, op. cit., p. 220

3   F. B. Czarnomski, ed., *The Eloquence of Winston Churchill* (New York: Signet Key ed., 1957), p. 65

4   *Deschênes Report*, op. cit., Chapter I-6, "The Mengele Affair" provides a detailed account of this incident

5   Public Archives file No. 102-DLP-40; *Toronto Star*, November 1, 1985

6   Harold Troper, speech delivered to the Learned Society, MacMaster University, May, 25, 1987

7   The Canadian Jewish Congress had, in fact, been granted standing in the Rauca case for the limited purpose of arguing the issue of constitutionality of the extradition remedy. The judge refused to allow us to present the arguments set out in our brief dealing with the legal options for dealing with Nazi war criminals. We did not wish to appear to be circumventing the judicial process by publicizing our study outside of court while the Rauca matter was still being determined. As a result, we did not submit our work to the government until some time later.

8   *As It Happens*, August 7, 1987

Chapter Five
1   Quincy Wright, "The Law of the Nuremberg Trial", (1947) 41 American Journal of International Law 38, at pp. 45, 46

2   Honourable Jules Deschênes, *The Sword and the Scales* (Toronto: Butterworths, 1979), p. 187

3   Francis Biddle, "The Nuremberg Trial", 1947 Virginia Law Review 679, at pp. 680-681

4   Robert H. Jackson, "Nuremberg in Retrospect", 1949 Canadian Bar Review 761, at p. 771

5   (1947) 41 American Journal of International Law at p. 305

Chapter Six
1   A more specifically legal treatment of the remedies available can be found in a monograph I wrote entitled "Bringing to Justice Nazi War Criminals in Canada" published by the League for Human Rights of B'nai Brith Canada in 1985. The legal sources for the arguments in this chapter can be found in that monograph.

2   I, personally, have taken the position that *prima facie* proof of wrongdoing is necessary. However, the position of the government in cases unrelated to war crimes has been that foreclosure of inquiries is enough.

3   Hugo Grotius, De Jure Belli Ac Pacis (Oxford: Clarendon Press, 1925), v. II, book I, p. 18

Chapter Seven
1   *Record of the Proceedings*, Public Archives, Record Groups 25 F 3 (d), Volume 2609, p. 14

2   *Trial of Heinrich Gerike and Seven Others*, edited by George Brand (William Hodge, 1950), p. xi

3   Ibid.

4   Ibid., p. xv

5   *Hadamar Trial*, 1 Law Reports of the Trial of War Crimes 46, at p. 53

6   (1947) 41 American Journal of International Law 17, at p. 216

7   (19476-7) 60 Harvard Law Review 857, at p. 886

8   As quoted by Irwin Cotler, op. cit., p. 69

9   Justice Robert H. Jackson, Chief American Prosecutor, *Trial of the Major Nazi War Criminals before the International Military Tribunal*, Nuremberg, 1944

10   The rebuttal prepared by Irwin Cotler in *Submission and Reply by the Canadian Jewish Congress to the Commission of Inquiry on War Criminals*, December 4, 1985, makes this point rather well.

11   Canada-Federal Republic of Germany Treaty, 1979, *Canada Gazette*, Part l, p. 6777, Article I (1), Article I (2); *Criminal Code*, Section 6 (2)

12   (1962–3) Tulane Law Review 641, at pp. 657–658

13   (1980) 2 Supreme Court Reports 320

14   See (1954) 32 Canadian Bar Review 624, at pp. 630-632, 637

15   Regulations 6 (1) and 5

16   *Maxwell on Interpretation of Statutes*, 12th edition by P. St. J. Langan
(London: Sweet and Maxwell, 1969), p. 222

17   Paragraph 17

18   *Rex v. Jawala Singh*, [1938] 3 Western Weekly Reports 241; *Michelidakis v. Regimbald*, (1917) 23 Revue de Jurisprudence 375

19   1970 *Revised Statutes of Canada*, Chapter I-2, Section 4 (6)

20   *Hulkes v. Day*, (1840) 59 English Reports 527, at p. 530; *Western Minerals v. Gaumont*, (1953) 1 Supreme Court Reports 345, at p. 368

21   Memorandum from Christopher A. Amerasinghe to Mr. D. H. Christie,
Q.C., Assistant Deputy Attorney- General, May 27, 1983, filed before the Deschênes Commission as Exhibit P-101

22   6254 Statutes 1009, Section 2, incorporating the definition of displaced
persons defined in Annex I to the Constitution of the International Refugee Organization

23   8 United States Code 1451 (a)

24   *Federenko v. U.S.*, 66 Lawyers Edition (2nd) 686, at p. 706 (1981, U.S.S.C.)

25   *Schtraks v. Israel*, 1964 Appeal Cases 556 (House of Lords), at p. 593

26   *Attorney General for Canada v. Canadian National*, (1983) 2 Supreme
Court Reports 206; *Regina v. Wetmore*, (1983) 2 Supreme Court Reports 284

27   Article 15, Covenant; Section 11 (g), Charter

28   Regulation 4 (1)

29   *Johannessen v. U.S.*, 225 U.S. 227

30   Charles Gordon and Harry Rosenfield, *Immigration Law and Procedure*,
(New York: Matthew Bender, 1986), Volume 3, *Immigration Law and Nationality*,
Chapter 20, "Loss of American Citizenship or Nationality", pp. 17, 18

31   728 Federal 2d 1314 (1984)

32   Article 8 (2) (b)

Chapter Eight

[1]   Ryan, op. cit., p. 46

[2]   Ibid., p. 47-48

[3]   Konnilyn G. Feig, *Hitler's Death Camp--The Sanity of Madness* (New York: Homes & Meirer, 1979), pp. 330-332

[4]   *Maikovskis v. Immigration & Naturalization Service*, 773 F2d 435 (1985); Littman, op. cit., p. 174-175

[5]   Commission of Inquiry Concerning Certain Activities of the Royal Canadian Mounted Police, Second Report, *Freedom and Security Under the Law*, Volume I, p. 632

[6]   I. A. Shearer, *Extradition in International Law*, (New York: Oceana Publications, 1971), p. 21

Chapter Nine

[1]   *Student, Canada's Newspaper for Ukrainian Students*, November/December 1985

[2]   For example, the *Winnipeg Sun*, October, 1985

[3]   Interview on June 18, 1987, with Brian Derrah, former Executive Assistant to John Crosbie

[4]   John Braxton, in a letter to the *Winnipeg Sun*, dated December 20, 1985

[5]   *New York Daily News*, May 16, 1986

Chapter Ten

[1]   Murray Campbell, "War crimes probe raises community, racial tensions", *Globe & Mail*, March 1, 1986

[2]   "Karl Linnas dies in Soviet hospital", *Canadian Jewish News*, July 9, 1987

[3]   "No Nazi hunt, they say", editorial in the *Globe and Mail*, February 4, 1987

Chapter Eleven

[1]   Anti-Defamation League of B'nai Brith, U.S., Special report, *The Campaign Against The U.S. Justice Department's Prosecution of Suspected Nazi War Criminals*, New York, N.Y., June, 1985

Chapter Sixteen

[1]   (New York: Avon Books, 1982), p. 145-147

[2]   *Regina v. Whelan*, (1974) Canadian Criminal Cases (2d) 217

INDEX